Land Registry Ad

H Crosby

Land Registry Adjudication

Dominic Crossley
Barrister, Chancery House Chambers, Leeds

Bloomsbury Professional

The author gratefully acknowledges the assistance of his colleague in Chambers, Anna Stubley, who substantially wrote Chapter 7, and Andrew Etheridge, who gave invaluable assistance with Chapters 2 and 9.

Bloomsbury Professional Limited, Maxwelton House, 41–43 Boltro Road, Haywards Heath, West Sussex, RH16 1BJ

© Bloomsbury Professional Ltd 2013

Bloomsbury Professional, an imprint of Bloomsbury Publishing Plc

A CIP Catalogue record for this book is available from the British Library.

ISBN: 978 1 84766 946 9

Typeset by Phoenix Photosetting, Chatham, Kent
Printed and bound by CPI Group (UK) Ltd, Croydon, CR0 4Y

Contents

Contents

Table of Cases

Table of Statutes

[References are to paragraph number]

Table of Statutes

Table of Statutory Instruments

Chapter 1

Introduction

1.01 The Adjudicator to Her Majesty's Land Registry came into being as a result of the Land Registration Act 2002 ('LRA 2002').[1] The term 'Adjudicator' can refer to the individual who holds the specific office of Adjudicator to HM Land Registry, to the corporate name of the judicial body over which he presides, and also (informally) to any of the individuals who sit on that judicial body and determine matters referred to it. Curiously, as a result of LRA 2002, Her Majesty's Land Registry was rebranded as 'Land Registry' for most practical purposes,[2] whilst the new office created contained reference to the traditional name. For the sake of clarity, in this chapter the office is referred to as 'AHMLR' and the office holder is referred to as the 'Adjudicator'.

1.02 AHMLR is distinct, and independent, from the Land Registry itself. In relation to AHMLR's powers of determining references from the Land Registry (essentially certain categories of dispute concerning registered land), AHMLR has inherited the previous functions of the Solicitor to HM Land Registry, although, so far as users of the previous regime were concerned, disputes were to all intents and purposes determined by HM Land Registry. The creation of AHMLR was thus intended, at least in part, to address any perception that the previous regime was less than independent.

1.03 AHMLR was previously administered as part of the former Tribunals Service, whose name appeared on the heading of AHMLR paperwork. Despite this, AHMLR has never strictly speaking been a tribunal but rather a specific judicial office. Following the 2010 merger, AHMLR has, since 1 April 2011, been administered by the new HM Courts and Tribunals Service. AHMLR should not be confused with other judicial entities dealing with property matters such as the former Lands Tribunal (now the Lands Chamber of the Upper Tribunal[3]), which determines such matters as the level of compensation following a compulsory purchase order or Leasehold Valuation Tribunals.

1.04 AHMLR has the very specific statutory powers covered in Chapter 2 of this book, which it exercises in respect of registered land. Although, as stated above, entirely independent of the Land Registry, users of AHMLR should have an idea of how registered land works and why the Land Registry exists.

1.05 The predecessor of the present Land Registry was created in 1862 as a result of the Land Registry Act 1862. From the very start the process of land registration had as its objects simplicity and certainty in the transfer and ownership of land,[4] objects very much at the heart of parliament's

---

1   LRA 2002, s 107, in force 28 April 2003.
2   It seems that the original title is preserved for some official purposes.
3   Following the Tribunals, Courts and Enforcement Act 2007.
4   See the preamble to the Land Registry Act 1862.

intention in enacting LRA 2002. The system, and the Land Registry itself, were subsequently overhauled by the Land Transfer Act 1875 and the Land Transfer Act 1897. The most fundamental change, introduced by the latter piece of legislation, was the idea that land registration should no longer be an entirely voluntary process left to the whims of landowners, as had been the case since 1862. However, even under the Land Transfer Act 1897 control of land registration was essentially left to local authorities and it was not until the Land Registration Act 1925, one of that important group of Acts which re-shaped English real property law, and the subsequent Land Registration Acts that followed, that what would now be termed a 'rolling programme' of compulsory registration of land area by area commenced. The final areas of England and Wales were incorporated into the registered land scheme on 1 December 1990.

1.06   Registration has always depended upon the occurrence of a 'trigger' event. For much of the history of land registration, the only trigger event was sale of the property. However, the Land Registration Act 1997 introduced a number of new categories: conveyance by gift, first legal mortgage, assent, and assignment, or grant by way of a gift, of a lease with more than 21 years left to run. The length[5] of compulsorily registrable leases has been gradually reduced from not less than 40 years to more than 21 years (by the Land Registration Act 1986), and finally to more than 7 years (by LRA 2002) with provision for this figure to be reduced further in the future.

1.07   The Land Register is now an entirely electronic database which is maintained by the Chief Land Registrar. Each piece of land which is registered, whether freehold or leasehold, is given a unique Title Number. The principal manifestation of the database as far as landowners are concerned is in the form of an individual Title Register of which an Official Copy[6] together with the associated filed plan can be obtained by any member of the public who either knows the relevant Title Number or has undertaken an index map search at the Land Registry. Electronic copies of entries on the Register can now be ordered efficiently online at www.landregistry.gov.uk although these are not strictly speaking admissible in evidence in court proceedings to the same extent as an Official Copy, nor does an error on an electronic copy engage the Land Registry's indemnity policy. An example of an electronic copy of a Register entry is shown at Figure 1.1.

---

5   Ie the period remaining of the term of the lease from the date of delivery of the grant or the assignment.
6   Formerly known as an 'Office Copy'.

Figure 1.1 Electronic copy of a Land Register entry

This is a copy of the register of the title number set out immediately below, showing the entries in the register on 26 AUG 2012 at 22:02:32. This copy does not take account of any application made after that time even if still pending in the Land Registry when this copy was issued.

This copy is not an 'Official Copy' of the register. An official copy of the register is admissible in evidence in a court to the same extent as the original. A person is entitled to be indemnified by the registrar if he suffers loss by reason of a mistake in an official copy. If you want to obtain an official copy, the Land Registry web site explains how to do this.

A: Property Register

This register describes the land and estate comprised in the title.

WEST YORKSHIRE : BRADFORD

1   (22.09.1983) The Freehold land shown edged with red on the plan of the above Title filed at the Registry and being 52 Windhill Old Road, Thackley.

2   The land has the benefit of the following rights granted by a Deed of Grant dated 26 August 1983 made between (1) William George Green (Grantor) and (2) Kevin John Wood and Gillian Sandra Wood (Grantees):-

"The Grantor as Beneficial Owner hereby grants unto the Grantees FULL right and liberty on foot only but with or without wheelbarrows and other gardening equipment to pass and repass over and along so much of the red land as is necessary to afford access to the rear garden of the green land SUBJECT to the Grantees or other the persons for the time being exercising such right paying to the Grantor or other the owner or owners for the time being of the red land a fair and proper proportion (according to user) of all costs reasonably incurred by the Grantor or his successors in maintaining and repairing the area of land over which the said right is exercised AND ALSO full right and liberty from time to time and upon giving reasonable noice to the Grantor or his successors to enter upon so much of the red land as may be necessary with or without tools equipment and other appliances for the purpose of (a) inspecting maintaining repairing and cleansing the north easterly gable end of the green land and all fall pipes spouts gutters gullies and flues attached thereto and (b) repairing the south easterly boundary wall or fence of the green land SUBJECT to the Grantees or other the person for the time being exercising such right making good forthwith any damage occasioned by the exercise of such right."

NOTE :-The red land referred to is Number 38 and the Green land referred to is Number 52 Windhill Old Road.

B: Proprietorship Register

This register specifies the class of title and identifies the owner. It contains any entries that affect the right of disposal.

Title absolute

1   (11.10.1993) Proprietor: KEVIN JOHN WOOD of 52 Windhill Old Road, Thackley, Bradford, W Yorkshire BD10 0SN.

C: Charges Register

This register contains any charges and other matters that affect the land.

1   The land tinted pink on the filed plan is subject as mentioned in a conveyance thereof dated 30 March 1968 made between (1) S. B. Building Company Limited and (2) Gladys Emmie Clissold in the following terms:-

"SUBJECT to all existing rights of way light drainage and other easements so far as the same relate to or affect the said property."

2   The garden hut erected on the north east side of the garden is subject to rights of user in favour of 38 Windhill Old Road.

End of register

3

1.08   The Title Register comprises three parts:

- the Property Register, which describes the extent of the property together with details of any rights (eg easements) that the property enjoys over neighbouring properties;
- the Proprietorship Register, which sets out who legally owns the property and gives details of any restrictions on how the property can be dealt with – it does not however include details of beneficial ownership of property, which the Land Registry is unable to register;
- the Charges Register, which gives details of restrictions to which the property is subject, most often financial charges (such as mortgages) and the burden of easements.

The Title Register may refer to additional documents, which have been filed with the Land Registry and (if so) copies can be obtained on payment of a fee.

1.09   In order to register a property for the first time, record a change of ownership (eg on sale), or record particulars of an easement or charge to which the property is subject, the usual process is to submit an application to the Land Registry on the appropriate practice form stating the nature of the change to the Register that is required. Disputes over the effect of such applications form the most important of AHMLR's roles, namely references from the Land Registry. On the resolution of a reference from the Land Registry – generally by an oral hearing – the Adjudicator will usually direct the Land Registry either to allow the application made, or to allow the objection to the application, and as a result some amendment to the Title Register may be necessary.

1.10   Procedure before the Adjudicator is dealt with substantially in Chapter 3 of this book.[7] The Adjudicator himself, as stated above, is a statutory office holder, and he is assisted by a number of full-time deputy adjudicators as well as part-time adjudicators who are typically practising barristers or solicitors. All these individuals carry out the judicial functions of AHMLR, acting both at the procedural stages and determining the outcome of final hearings should these be necessary.

1.11   A major difference between AHMLR and most tribunals (in the broad sense of the word) is that the majority of litigants before AHMLR will not have commenced proceedings before AHMLR or even intended that their cases should go to AHMLR. As set out in Chapter 3, where an application to the Land Registry is disputed and cannot be resolved, the reference to AHMLR will be automatic and does not require the parties' approval (though they are warned in advance of the procedure)). After the reference has been made, the applicant will have a specified number of days in which to put together a statement of case. This differs from most civil proceedings where the only formal time constraint is likely to be the expiry of a limitation period.

1.12   The other roles of AHMLR are the rectification or setting aside of certain categories of document, which is the only original jurisdiction that AHMLR possesses (ie applications can be made directly to AHMLR), and an appellant jurisdiction concerning decisions of the Land Registry on Network Access Agreements. At the present time, the former involves approximately 10 per cent of AHMLR's case load, and as Network Access Agreements have not yet come into being, the latter jurisdiction has not yet been exercised. The three jurisdictions are considered in more detail in Chapter 2.

---

7   In respect of the Adjudicator's jurisdiction in relation to references and rectification of documents, there have not yet been any actual cases of Network Access Appeals.

Chapter 2

The Adjudicator's Jurisdiction

SOURCE OF ADJUDICATOR'S JURISDICTION

2.01   The Adjudicator came into being as a result of the Land Registration Act 2002 (LRA 2002) and his jurisdiction is derived entirely from statute. The Adjudicator has three distinct powers, which are set out at LRA 2002, s 108:

'(1) The adjudicator has the following functions—
    (a) determining matters referred to him under section 73(7), and
    (b) determining appeals under paragraph 4 of Schedule 5.
(2) Also, the adjudicator may, on application, make any order which the High Court could make for the rectification or setting aside of a document which—
    (a) effects a qualifying disposition of a registered estate or charge,
    (b) is a contract to make such a disposition, or
    (c) effects a transfer of an interest which is the subject of a notice in the register.
(3) For the purposes of subsection (2)(a), a qualifying disposition is—
    (a) a registrable disposition, or
    (b) a disposition which creates an interest which may be the subject of a notice in the register.
(4) The general law about the effect of an order of the High Court for the rectification or setting aside of a document shall apply to an order under this section.'

Each of these powers will now be considered in turn.

References

2.02   By far the most common exercise of the Adjudicator's jurisdiction is in determining references from the Land Registry. The historical development and precursor of this process is discussed in the previous chapter. Put at its simplest, where one party makes an application to the Land Registry (usually with the object of amending the Register in some way) and another party objects, if the dispute cannot be resolved then the Land Registry must refer the matter to the Adjudicator.

2.03   The relationship between the Land Registry and the Adjudicator in respect of references is set out in LRA 2002, s 73 and the Land Registration (Referral to the Adjudicator to HM Land Registry) Rules 2003[1] (the 'Referral Rules') (see Appendix 3). Relevant procedure under the Referral Rules is covered in Chapter 3. Section 73 of the LRA 2002 provides:

'(1) Subject to subsections (2) and (3), anyone may object to an application to the registrar.

---

1   SI 2003/2114.

(2) In the case of an application under section 18, only the person who lodged the caution to which the application relates, or such other person as rules may provide, may object.

(3) In the case of an application under section 36, only the person shown in the register as the beneficiary of the notice to which the application relates, or such other person as rules may provide, may object.

(4) The right to object under this section is subject to rules.

(5) Where an objection is made under this section, the registrar—
   (a) must give notice of the objection to the applicant, and
   (b) may not determine the application until the objection has been disposed of.

(6) Subsection (5) does not apply if the objection is one which the registrar is satisfied is groundless.

(7) If it is not possible to dispose by agreement of an objection to which subsection (5) applies, the registrar must refer the matter to the adjudicator.

(8) Rules may make provision about references under subsection (7).'

Thus anyone may object to an application to the Registrar, save for the exceptions noted in LRA 2002, s 73, namely an application under LRA 2002, s 18 (for cancellation of a caution against first registration) or LRA 2002, s 36 (for cancellation of a unilateral notice). Subject to these exceptions, there is no apparent requirement for the objector to have a particular (or any) interest in the land affected although the extent to which the objector has such an interest may determine (i) whether he is notified of the application by the Land Registry and (ii) the weight of his objection.

2.04   References to the Adjudicator by the Land Registry are an increasingly common means by which property disputes (relating to, for example, easements, adverse possession, or existence/size of beneficial interests in property) are determined. Such disputes would previously have been decided by the court or, on some occasions, by the Land Registry. There are some important distinctions between adjudication proceedings and court proceedings:

- parties cannot apply to the Adjudicator directly;
- a reference is made by the Land Registry automatically if an objection to an application cannot be resolved, although the parties are notified in advance;
- the Adjudicator has no power to award costs prior to the Reference, although in some circumstances the Land Registry can do so;
- the Adjudicator's powers are limited to resolving the dispute and making an appropriate order in relation to the Land Registry Application (usually allowing it or cancelling it in whole or in part) which is binding on the Registrar, and a costs order which is binding on the parties;
- the Adjudicator cannot award injunctive relief, damages, or make an order for sale under the Trusts of Land and Appointment of Trustees Act 1996: only the court can do this although in some circumstances, the Adjudicator may direct the parties to issue court proceedings (see further Chapter 3).

Network Access Agreement Appeals

2.05   A major policy initiative behind the new land registration regime introduced by LRA 2002 was the facilitating of electronic conveyancing.

The eventual idea is for electronic conveyancing to replace paper-based conveyancing entirely although this is still many years in the future and appears to have been delayed indefinitely by the recession.

2.06   As part of the electronic conveyancing regime, the Land Registry operates an electronic conveyancing network. In order for electronic conveyancing to progress, it will be necessary for other parties involved in the conveyancing process (eg solicitors) to have access to the network in some form. The LRA 2002 makes provisions for this and for the regulation of the process by rules, which presently take the form of the Network Access Appeal Rules 2008,[2] as amended in 2011 (the 'Network Access Rules').

2.07   Paragraph 4 of Sch 5 to LRA 2002 provides as follows.

'(1) A person who is aggrieved by a decision of the registrar with respect to entry into, or termination of, a network access agreement may appeal against the decision to the adjudicator.

(2) On determining an appeal under this paragraph, the adjudicator may give such directions as he considers appropriate to give effect to his determination.

(3) Rules may make provision about appeals under this paragraph.'

2.08   This power of the Adjudicator is thus an appellant jurisdiction, by which a party appeals from a decision of the Registrar. That decision may relate to the terms on which a party is permitted access to the network, a refusal of access to the network, or the termination of a party's access to the network. The Network Access Rules provide specified criteria which a party must fulfil to be permitted access, and specified grounds of termination.

2.09   As yet, no cases under this jurisdiction of the Adjudicator have been heard. The procedure that will be followed is set out in the 'Network Access Rules (see Appendix 5).

Rectification of Documents

2.10   The Adjudicator's third power is that under LRA 2002, s 108(2), which affords the Adjudicator concurrent jurisdiction with the High Court for rectification or setting aside of a document falling within that subsection. Unlike the Adjudicator's other powers, this is an original jurisdiction and proceedings are commenced by completion of the relevant form. This power should not be ignored, especially with a view to the probable cost savings inherent in bringing the matter before the Adjudicator rather than the High Court.

2.11   Examples of documents that can potentially be rectified, or set aside, within the meaning of s 108 are as follows (LRA 2002, s 27(2)):

- A transfer of land (eg TR1 document), including a transfer by operation of law, other than a transfer on the death or bankruptcy of an individual proprietor, or a transfer on the dissolution of a corporate proprietor.
- Grant of a lease of a term of more than seven years; however, it is anticipated that in due course, leases granted for a term of more than three years will be made registrable dispositions, as there is a power for the Lord Chancellor to substitute a different term.

---

2   SI 2008/1730.

- Grant of a lease which is to take effect in possession after the end of the period of three months beginning with the date of the grant.
- Grant of lease under which the right to possession is discontinuous (eg possession during office hours only) – this is registrable as there may not be any physical evidence of the occupation.
- Grant of a lease in pursuance of Part 5 of the Housing Act 1985 (the right to buy).
- Grant of a lease of any duration and in circumstances where s 171A of the Housing Act 1985 applies (disposal by landlord which leads to a person no longer being a secure tenant).
- Where the registered estate is a franchise or manor, the grant of a lease.
- Express grant or reservation of an interest of a kind falling within s 1(2) (a) of the Law of Property Act 1925, other than one which is capable of being registered under Part 1 of the Commons Act 2006.
- The express grant or reservation of a rentcharge issuing out of or charged on land, that is either perpetual or for a term of years absolute, or a legal right of entry annexed for any purpose to a legal rentcharge. The circumstances in which rentcharges can be created is limited due to the Rentcharges Act 1977. Rights of entry in a legal lease are not required to be registered.
- The grant of a legal charge. The creation of a legal charge does not have to be registered when it is created, namely where the charge arises by operation of law under statutory powers and is registrable as a local land charge. In these circumstances, the charge takes effect as an unregistered interest that may override a registered disposition and will therefore bind any successor who acquires the land.
- A contract to effect any of the above.
- A document which effects a transfer of an interest which is subject of a notice in the register (eg a Deed of Variation of an easement where the dominant and servient owners agree to vary the terms of an easement or a transfer of the burden of a personal covenant under an authorised guarantee agreement under the Landlord and Tenant (Covenants) Act 1995).

2.12   Rectification proceedings before the Adjudicator are commenced by completing the relevant form, which is available on the Adjudicator's website, and is reproduced at **Figure 2.1**.

Figure 2.1 Rectification application to the Adjudicator to rectify or set aside documents

The Adjudicator to HM Land Registry

RECTIFICATION APPLICATION TO THE ADJUDICATOR TO RECTIFY OR SET ASIDE DOCUMENTS

Part 1   Details of Applicant

Please fill in the contact details of the person making the application.

Name	
Address	
Post Code	
Telephone (work)	
Telephone (home)	
Telephone (mobile)	
Fax	
Email	

ALRForm.dot

9

(Figure 2.1 cont)

Part 2   Details of Applicant's Solicitor or Other Representative

If applicable, please fill in the details of the applicant's solicitor.

Name	
Address	
Post Code	
Telephone	
Fax	
Email	

In the case of a lay representative (i.e. someone who is not a qualified solicitor or barrister), the Applicant's signature is required below to authorise the lay representative to act on their behalf.

Signature: Date:

ALRForm.dot

(Figure 2.1 cont)

Part 3   Details of Person(s) Against Whom an Order is Sought

Please enter the contact details of the person(s) against whom you are seeking an order.

Name	
Address	
Post Code	
Telephone (work)	
Telephone (home)	
Telephone (mobile)	
Fax	
Email	

Part 4   Details of Application

Please enter the details of the application, including the Land Registry Title Number.

Description/Address	
Title Number	
Remedy Sought	
Grounds on which Application is Based	

[Please continue on a separate sheet if necessary]

ALRForm.dot

(Figure 2.1 cont)

Part 5   **List of Documents**

Please list the documents in your possession or control which –
- are central to your case, or
- the Adjudicator or any other party to the proceedings will require in order properly to understand the rectification application.

Description	Original/ Copy	Date of Document	Parties	Document Number

[Please continue on a separate sheet if necessary]

Part 6   **List of Witnesses**

Please list any witnesses that you intend to call to give evidence to support your application.

[Please continue on a separate sheet if necessary]

ALRForm.dot

(Figure 2.1 cont)

Part 7   Copy Documents to Include With Your Application

Pursuant to rule 16(1) of The Adjudicator to HM Land Registry (Practice and Procedure) Rules 2003 (as amended), which is reproduced overleaf, you are required to include the following with your application:

- **A copy of each of the documents you have listed in Part 5**
- **A copy of the document to which this application relates**

Part 8   Statement of Truth

The application must be verified by a statement of truth before it can be accepted.

I believe/the Applicant believes that the facts stated in this application are true.

Signed: Date:

I am the Applicant / Applicant's Representative   (delete as applicable)
and my relationship to the Applicant is ....

Part 9   Where to Send This Form

Please return the completed form and copy documents to:

     The Adjudicator to HM Land Registry
     7th Floor, Victory House
     30-34 Kingsway
     London WC2B 6EX

     Telephone: 020 3077 5800
     DX: 141420 Bloomsbury 7

August 2008

ALRForm.dot

(Figure 2.1 cont)

The Adjudicator to H M Land Registry (Practice and Procedure) (Amendment) Rules 2008 set out a series of amendments to the Adjudicator to H M Land Registry (Practice and Procedure) Rules 2003.

The text below is intended to set out the relevant 2003 Rules incorporating the amendments effected by the 2008 Rules. This is not an official document. It has been prepared by the Adjudicator's office and is intended only for the guidance of parties to proceedings before the Adjudicator. It should not be used for any other purpose.

Please note that, while every care has been taken to ensure that the text is accurate, no liability is accepted for any errors which remain. In the case of any conflict between this text and the 2003 and/or 2008 Rules, the Rules will prevail.

The amended rules only apply to cases where either the reference from the Land Registry or the application for rectification is received by the Adjudicator on or after 25 August 2008. They may also apply to cases received on or after 25 July but before 25 August, but only if the Adjudicator specifically directs that they shall apply.

Form and contents of a rectification application

16. - (1) A rectification application must —
    (a)   be made in writing;
    (b)   be dated and verified by a statement of truth;
    (c)   be addressed to the adjudicator;
    (d)   include the following information—
        (i)   the name and address of the person or persons against whom the order is sought;
        (ii) details of the remedy being sought;
        (iii) the grounds on which the rectification application is based;
        (iv) a list of witnesses that the party intends to call to give evidence in support of the rectification application; and
        (v) the applicant's name and address for service;
    (e)   include the following copies—

        (i) copies of any documents in the applicant's possession or control which—

           (aa) are central to the applicant's case; or

           (bb) the adjudicator or any other party to the proceedings will require in order properly to understand the rectification application; and

        (ii) a copy of the document to which the rectification application relates, or if a copy is not available, details of the document, which must include available, its nature, its date, the parties to it and any version number or other similar identification number or code that it has; and
    (f)   be served on the adjudicator.
    (2)   Following receipt by the adjudicator of a rectification application, the adjudicator must enter the particulars of the rectification application in the record of matters.
    (3)   If, having considered the rectification application and made any enquiries he thinks necessary, the adjudicator is satisfied that it is groundless, he must reject the rectification application.

ALRForm.dot

(Figure 2.1 cont)

Disclosure and inspection of documents

27. - (1) Any document supplied to the adjudicator or to a party under this rule or under rule 28 may only be used for the purpose of the proceedings in which it was disclosed.

(2) Within 28 days after service of the respondent's statement of case under rule 13 or the lodging of an objection under rule 18, each party must—

    (a) serve on the adjudicator and each of the other parties a list, which complies with rule 47, of all documents in that party's possession or control which—

        (i)   that party intends to rely upon in the proceedings;

        (ii)   adversely affect that party's own case;

        (iii)   adversely affect another party's case; or

        (iv)   support another party's case; and

    (b) send to the adjudicator copies of all documents in the list served under sub-paragraph (a).

(3) Paragraph (4) applies to documents--

    (a) referred to in a party's –

        (i)   statement of case;

        (ii)   rectification application under rule 16(1); or

        (iii)   written statement under rule 18(a)(i); or

    (b) appearing on a list served by a party under paragraph (2).

(4) In addition to any other requirement in these rules to disclose or provide copies of documents, in relation to any document referred to in paragraph (3) each party must--

    (a) permit any other party to inspect and take copies on reasonable notice and at a reasonable time and place; and

    (b) provide a copy if requested by another party on payment by such other party of reasonable copying costs.

(5) Paragraphs (2), (3) and (4) are subject to any direction of the adjudicator to the contrary

(6) The adjudicator may at any time give directions requiring a party to state whether that party has any particular document, or class of documents, in its possession or control and, if so, to comply with the requirements of paragraphs (2), (3) and (4) in relation to such documents as if one of the categories at paragraph (2)(a) applied to them.

ALRForm.dot

(Figure 2.1 cont)

ADJUDICATOR TO HER MAJESTY'S LAND REGISTRY

PRACTICE DIRECTION

RECTIFICATION APPLICATIONS UNDER S108(2) LAND REGISTRATION ACT
2002 AND OBJECTIONS THERETO

The Adjudicator to HM Land Registry makes the following practice direction:

Rule 27 (Disclosure and Inspection of Documents) of the Adjudicator to Her Majesty's Land Registry (Practice and Procedure) Rules 2003 as amended by the Adjudicator to Her Majesty's Land Registry (Practice and Procedure) (Amendment) Rules 2008

Paragraph (2) of rule 27 is to apply to any rectification application under Rule 16 and any objection under Rule 18 subject to the following modifications:

1) The list of documents required to be served by the applicant under that paragraph is to be included in the application and is to be limited to documents which are in his possession or control and which –

(a) are central to the applicant's case; or

(b) the adjudicator or any other party to the proceedings will require in order properly to understand the rectification application.

2) The list of documents required to be served by an objector to a rectification application is to be included in the objection and is to be limited to documents which are in his possession or control and which –

(a) are central to the objector's case; or

(b) the adjudicator or any other party to the proceedings will require in order properly to understand the party's written statement.

Dated this Thursday 21 August 2008

ALRForm.dot

2.13   Initial procedure on rectification applications is set out at rr 15–18 of the Adjudicator to Her Majesty's Land Registry (Practice and Procedure) Rules 2003[3] ('the Procedure Rules'), (see Appendix 4). These stipulate that the

---

3   SI 2003/2171.

person making the application must provide certain specified information. In particular, the applicant must provide:

- the name and address of the person or persons against whom the order is sought;
- details of the remedy being sought;
- the grounds on which the rectification application is based;
- a list of documents on which the party intends to rely in support of the rectification application;
- a list of witnesses that the party intends to call to give evidence in support of the rectification application; and
- the applicant's name and address for service.

2.14   The applicant must also provide copies of:

- each of the documents listed in the party's list of documents; and
- the document to which the rectification application relates, or if a copy is not available, details of the document, which must include if available, its nature, its date, the parties to it and any version number or other similar identification number or code that it has.

2.15   The applicant must serve the application on the Adjudicator who will enter the particulars in the record of matters, and, if he considers the application groundless, reject it.

2.16   If the application is not rejected by the Adjudicator at this early stage, he must serve written notice of the application together with a copy of it on the person against whom the order is sought and on anyone else who the Adjudicator considers should be a party. Any person receiving notice must lodge an objection within 28 days of service of the notice.

2.17   In order to lodge an objection, a party receiving notice of an application must within the specified time period serve on the Adjudicator and all other parties:

- a written statement addressed to the adjudicator and dated and signed by the person lodging the objection or his duly authorised representative setting out the grounds for the objection;
- a list of documents on which the party intends to rely to support his objection;
- a copy of each of the documents listed in the list of documents;
- a written list of witnesses that the party intends to call to give evidence in support of the objection; and
- written confirmation of his name and address for service;

2.18   An Objection to Rectification Application Form is available on the Adjudicator's website, and is reproduced at **Figure 2.2**.

Figure 2.2 Objection to rectification application form

The Adjudicator to HM Land Registry
OBJECTION TO A RECTIFICATION APPLICATION TO THE ADJUDICATOR

Part 1   Details of Objector
Please fill in the contact details of the person making the objection.

Name	
Address	
Post Code	
Telephone (work)	
Telephone (home)	
Telephone (mobile)	
Fax	
Email	

ALRObj.dot

(Figure 2.2 cont)

Part 2   **Details of Objector's Solicitor or Other Representative**

If applicable, please fill in the details of the objector's solicitor.

Name

Address

Post Code

Telephone

Fax

Email

In the case of a lay representative (i.e. someone who is not a qualified solicitor or barrister), the Objector's signature is required below to authorise the lay representative to act on their behalf.

Signature: Date:

ALRObj.dot

(Figure 2.2 cont)

Part 3   **Grounds for the Objection**

Please enter the Grounds for the objection.

**Grounds on which
Objection is Based**

[Please continue on a separate sheet if necessary]

ALRObj.dot

(Figure 2.2 cont)

Part 4　　　　List of Documents

Please list the documents in your possession or control which
- Are central to your case, or
- The Adjudicator or any other party to the proceedings will require in order properly to understand your statement setting out your grounds for objection

Description	Original/ Copy	Date of Document	Parties	Document Number

[Please continue on a separate sheet if necessary]

Part 5　　　　List of Witnesses

Please list any witnesses that you intend to call to give evidence to support your objection.

[Please continue on a separate sheet if necessary]

ALRObj.dot

(Figure 2.2 cont)

Part 6 Copy Documents and Service

Rule 18 of The Adjudicator to HM Land Registry (Practice and Procedure) Rules 2003 (as amended), which is reproduced overleaf, requires you to:

- **Include a copy of each of the documents you have listed in Part 4 of this form; and**
- **Serve on the other party a copy of all the information and documents served on the Adjudicator**

Part 7 Statement of Truth

The objection must be verified by a statement of truth before it can be accepted.

I believe/the Objector believes that the facts stated in this objection are true.

Signed: Date:

I am the Objector / Objector's Representative   (delete as applicable)
and my relationship to the Objector is ....

Part 8 Where to Send This Form

Please return the completed form and copy documents to:

> The Adjudicator to HM Land Registry
> 7th Floor, Victory House
> 34 Kingsway
> London WC2B 6EX
>
> Telephone: 020 3077 5800
> DX: 141420 Bloomsbury 7

August 2008

ALRObj.dot

(Figure 2.2 cont)

The Adjudicator to H M Land Registry (Practice and Procedure) (Amendment) Rules 2008 set out a series of amendments to the Adjudicator to H M Land Registry (Practice and Procedure) Rules 2003.

The text below is intended to set out the relevant 2003 Rules incorporating the amendments effected by the 2008 Rules. This is not an official document. It has been prepared by the Adjudicator's office and is intended only for the guidance of parties to proceedings before the Adjudicator. It should not be used for any other purpose.

Please note that, while every care has been taken to ensure that the text is accurate, no liability is accepted for any errors which remain. In the case of any conflict between this text and the 2003 and/or 2008 Rules, the Rules will prevail.

The amended rules only apply to cases where either the reference from the Land Registry or the application for rectification is received by the Adjudicator on or after 25 August 2008. They may also apply to cases received on or after 25 July but before 25 August, but only if the Adjudicator specifically directs that they shall apply.

Objection to a rectification application

18. A person lodges an objection under rule 17(3) if within 28 days of service of the notice under rule 17(2)(a) he serves –

    (a) on the adjudicator--

        (i) a written statement addressed to the adjudicator, dated and verified by a statement of truth, setting out the grounds for the objection;

        (ii) *Omitted*

        (iii) copies of any documents in the party's possession or control which--

            (aa) are central to the party's case; or

            (bb) the adjudicator or any other party to the proceedings will require in order properly to understand the party's written statement;

        (iv) a written list of witnesses that the party intends to call to give evidence in support of the objection; and

        (v) written confirmation of his name and address for service; and

    (b) on the other parties a copy of all the information and documents served on the adjudicator under sub-paragraph (a).

Disclosure and inspection of documents

27. - (1) Any document supplied to the adjudicator or to a party under this rule or under rule 28 may only be used for the purpose of the proceedings in which it was disclosed.

(2) Within 28 days after service of the respondent's statement of case under rule 13 or the lodging of an objection under rule 18, each party must—
    (a) serve on the adjudicator and each of the other parties a list, which complies with rule 47, of all documents in that party's possession or control which—
        (i) that party intends to rely upon in the proceedings;

ALRObj.dot

(Figure 2.2 cont)

        (ii)   adversely affect that party's own case;
        (iii)   adversely affect another party's case; or
        (iv)   support another party's case; and
  (b) send to the adjudicator copies of all documents in the list served under sub-paragraph (a).

  (3) Paragraph (4) applies to documents--
    (a) referred to in a party's –
        (i)   statement of case;
        (ii)   rectification application under rule 16(1); or
        (iii)   written statement under rule 18(a)(i); or
    (b) appearing on a list served by a party under paragraph (2).

  (4) In addition to any other requirement in these rules to disclose or provide copies of documents, in relation to any document referred to in paragraph (3) each party must--
    (a) permit any other party to inspect and take copies on reasonable notice and at a reasonable time and place; and
    (b) provide a copy if requested by another party on payment by such other party of reasonable copying costs.

  (5) Paragraphs (2), (3) and (4) are subject to any direction of the adjudicator to the contrary

  (6) The adjudicator may at any time give directions requiring a party to state whether that party has any particular document, or class of documents, in its possession or control and, if so, to comply with the requirements of paragraphs (2), (3) and (4) in relation to such documents as if one of the categories at paragraph (2)(a) applied to them.

(Figure 2.2 cont)

ADJUDICATOR TO HER MAJESTY'S LAND REGISTRY

PRACTICE DIRECTION

RECTIFICATION APPLICATIONS UNDER S108(2) LAND REGISTRATION ACT
2002 AND OBJECTIONS THERETO

The Adjudicator to HM Land Registry makes the following practice direction:

Rule 27 (Disclosure and Inspection of Documents) of the Adjudicator to Her Majesty's Land Registry (Practice and Procedure) Rules 2003 as amended by the Adjudicator to Her Majesty's Land Registry (Practice and Procedure) (Amendment) Rules 2008

Paragraph (2) of rule 27 is to apply to any rectification application under Rule 16 and any objection under Rule 18 subject to the following modifications:

1) The list of documents required to be served by the applicant under that paragraph is to be included in the application and is to be limited to documents which are in his possession or control and which –

   (a) are central to the applicant's case; or
   (b) the adjudicator or any other party to the proceedings will require in order properly to understand the rectification application.

2) The list of documents required to be served by an objector to a rectification application is to be included in the objection and is to be limited to documents which are in his possession or control and which –

   (a) are central to the objector's case; or
   (b) the adjudicator or any other party to the proceedings will require in order properly to understand the party's written statement.

BY ORDER OF THE ADJUDICATOR TO HM LAND REGISTRY

ALRObj.dot

2.19   Thereafter, procedure on rectification applications follows essentially the same procedure as references,[4] and this is examined in Chapter 3.

4   Rules 19 ff of the Procedure Rules.

Chapter 3

Procedure for references under LRA 2002, s 73(7)

3.01 Procedure before the Adjudicator is governed by the Adjudicator to Her Majesty's Land Registry (Practice and Procedure) Rules 2003 (as amended) (the 'Procedure Rules').[1] The original Procedure Rules were amended by the Adjudicator to Her Majesty's Land Registry (Practice and Procedure) (Amendment) Rules 2008,[2] which came into force on 25 July 2008. There was a transitional period between 25 July 2008 and 24 July 2009 when it was open to the Adjudicator, on receipt of a reference from the Land Registry or a rectification application, to specify whether or not the Procedure Rules would apply in their amended form. The Procedure Rules are set out in full at Appendix 3.

3.02 The Procedure Rules cover much of the same ground as the Civil Procedure Rules (CPR) in civil proceedings, but are simplified in line with the more specialised nature of proceedings before the Adjudicator. Unlike the CPR, there are no rules hidden away in practice directions, protocols, or court user guides. At the time of writing, there is no equivalent of the detailed practitioner commentaries available on the CPR.

3.03 The Procedure Rules contain their own 'overriding objective',[3] a concept familiar to all users of the civil courts, which applies to all types of proceedings before the Adjudicator. This reproduces CPR, r 1.1 almost word for word, the only material difference being that the requirement to deal with the matter proportionately to the amount of money involved (CPR) is replaced with a requirement to deal with the matter proportionately 'to the value of the land or other interests involved'.

3.04 This chapter covers the procedure for references pursuant to LRA 2002, s 73(7). Procedure for rectification applications and network access agreements is set out in the chapters dealing with those topics, although there is considerable overlap in the case of the former.

3.05 Section 73(7) of LRA 2002 provides that, where an objection has been made to an application to the Registrar, and it has been impossible to dispose of that objection by agreement, the Registrar must refer the matter to the Adjudicator.

3.06 A flowchart prepared by the Adjudicator's office which shows the first stages of the reference process appears at **Figure 3.1**.

---

1   SI 2003/2171.
2   SI 2008/1731.
3   Rule 3.

Figure 3.1 Statement of Case Procedure

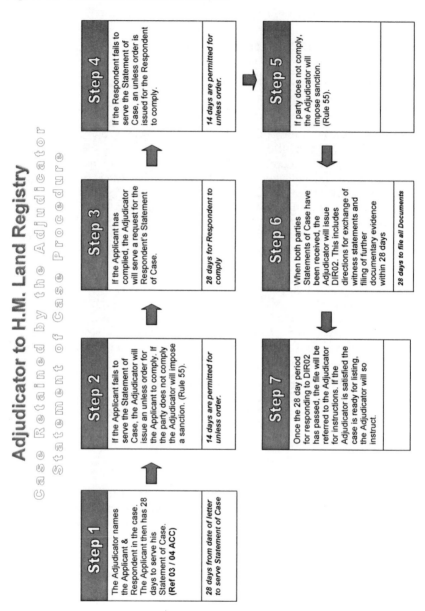

Adjudicator to H.M. Land Registry

Case Retained by the Adjudicator

Statement of Case Procedure

Step 1

The Adjudicator names the Applicant & Respondent in the case. The Applicant then has 28 days to serve his Statement of Case. **(Ref 03 / 04 ACC)**

28 days from date of letter to serve Statement of Case

Step 2

If the Applicant fails to serve the Statement of Case, the Adjudicator will issue an unless order for the Applicant to comply. If the party does not comply the Adjudicator will impose a sanction. (Rule 55).

14 days are permitted for unless order.

Step 3

If the Applicant has complied, the Adjudicator will serve a request for the Respondent's Statement of Case.

28 days for Respondent to comply

Step 4

If the Respondent fails to serve the Statement of Case, an unless order is issued for the Respondent to comply.

14 days are permitted for unless order.

Step 5

If party does not comply, the Adjudicator will impose sanction. (Rule 55).

Step 6

When both parties Statements of Case have been received, the Adjudicator will issue directions for exchange of witness statements and filing of further documentary evidence within 28 days

28 days to file all Documents

Step 7

Once the 28 day period for responding to DIR02 has passed, the file will be referred to the Adjudicator for instructions. If the Adjudicator is satisfied the case is ready for listing, the Adjudicator will so instruct.

CASE SUMMARY AND PRELIMINARY DOCUMENTS

3.07   Rules 3 and 5 of the Land Registration (Referral to the Adjudicator to HM Land Registry) Rules 2003[4] ('the Referral Rules') provide that the Registrar must send to the Adjudicator a written notice, accompanied by certain documents, informing him of the reference, and notify the parties that the matter has been referred. Chief among the documents to be provided by the registrar to the Adjudicator (and to the parties) is the 'case summary', prepared by the Land Registry, in which the Registrar summarises the nature both of the application and the dispute. The Registrar must give the parties an opportunity to make comments on the contents of the case summary within a specified time,[5] defined as not ending before 12 noon on the fifteenth business day after the date on which the Registrar sends a copy of the case summary to a particular party, or such earlier time as the parties may agree.[6] Following receipt of any such comments, the Registrar may (but is not obliged to) make appropriate amendments.[7]

3.08   The case summary is crucial to the Adjudication since, together with the original application to the Land Registry, it effectively defines the parameters of the Adjudicator's jurisdiction. As explained in the previous chapter, the Adjudicator does not have the wide powers that a court would normally have to make orders on his own initiative, or even to allow the parties to raise additional issues in the Adjudication proceedings that were not part of the reference by the Land Registry, however relevant those issues may be to the practical nature of the dispute between the parties. It is therefore very important for solicitors who are instructed in Adjudication proceedings to have sight of the case summary at an early stage and to provide this document to other professional advisers who are instructed in the case, especially counsel.

3.09   A specimen case summary is shown at **Figure 3.2**.

---

4   SI 2003/2114.
5   Rule 3(1)(c) of the Referral Rules.
6   Rule 6(1) of the Referral Rules.
7   Rule 3(3) of the Referral Rules.

Figure 3.2 Specimen Case Summary

HM LAND REGISTRY

Case Summary

This Case Summary accompanies a notice to the Adjudicator to HM Land Registry under rule 5 of the Land Registration (Referral to the Adjudicator to HM Land Registry) Rules 2003.

Title number:

Property:

Applicant:

Applicant's address:

Applicant's legal or other representative:

of:

DX:

Tel:

Fax:

Email:

Objector:

Objector's address:

Objector's legal or other representative:

of:

DX:

Tel:

Fax:

Email:

Ref:

Summary of core facts:

(a) The Objector is the sole registered proprietor of title number

(b) The Applicants are the joint registered proprietors of title number

(c) The Applicants have applied to register a right of way by prescription over the land in title number   for the benefit of title number

(d) The Applicants claim to have acquired a right of way and other rights over the land edged blue on the plans to statements of truth

(Figure 3.2 cont)

	(e) The Objectors accept that there may be a pedestrian right of access but deny that there has ever been a right of way with vehicles or a right to park, load or maintain vehicles, and any such use has been with their permission.
Details of application:	Date of Application Application for prescriptive easement made in Form AP1 dated
Details of objection:	Date of Objection Objection made by letter dated
Anything else that the registrar considers to be appropriate:	
Copy documents accompanying case summary:	1. Application in Form AP1 dated
	2. Official copy register entries and title plans for title number
	3. Form DL and documents 1-18 listed on it.
	4. Letter dated from the Objector.

Signed: *Patrick Timothy*

Patrick Timothy
Land Registrar
Durham Office
for and on behalf of the Chief Land Registrar.

Date

Specimen Case Summary

3.10   The case summary must contain the following information:[8]

- names of the parties
- addresses of the parties
- details of the legal or other representatives (if any)
- summary of the core facts
- details of the disputed application
- details of the objection to that application
- a list of any documents that will be copied to the Adjudicator
- anything else that the Registrar may consider to be appropriate.

3.11   The 'Summary of Core Facts', often in the form of numbered paragraphs, will normally include at least a description of the standing of the applicant and the objector with reference to their ownership of land germane to the dispute, a précis of the application made to the Land Registry and the basis on which it was made, and a précis of the objection and the basis on which it was made. The summary of core facts should set also out details of any matters that have been conceded or agreed at the Land Registry stage. It might be, for

---

8   Rule 3(2) of the Referral Rules.

example, that an application to the Land Registry which sought the registration of a number of easements resulted in agreement between the parties in relation to one of the easements, the remainder being disputed. In such a case, it would normally be unnecessary for the parties to expend any time in the adjudication on matters relating to the agreed or conceded point.

3.12   The case summary continues with details of the specific documents which set out and support both the application and the objection. The former are likely to be readily identifiable (for example, a Land Registry Form AP1 and accompanying Statutory Declaration) and will be the documents which caused the Land Registry to initiate the application. The latter will be the objector's response on receiving notification of the application from the Land Registry, and will very often be in the form of a letter prepared by the objector personally or by a director or employee of the objector (if a company). The objection document(s) may therefore be relatively unsophisticated insofar as it or they attempt(s) to state the objection in legal terms.

3.13   The Registrar then has the opportunity to include any further information that he decides may be appropriate. Attached to, and listed at the end of, the Case Summary are the core documents that the Registrar considers the Adjudicator needs to see at the commencement of the Adjudication process. As a minimum these will normally include copies of all the relevant titles, as well as the application and objection documents.

3.14   Receipt of a reference from the Land Registry requires the Adjudicator to take the following steps:[9]

- enter the particulars of the reference in the record of matters
- serve on the parties notice in writing of:
    - the fact that the reference has been received
    - the date when the reference was received
    - the matter number allocated to the reference
    - the name and any known address for service of the parties
    - which party is named as applicant and which as respondent.

3.15   Typically the parties who were applicant(s) and objector(s) before the Land Registry will be, respectively, the applicant(s) and respondent(s) in the proceedings before the Adjudicator. However, this may not always be the case. As in most judicial processes taking place under English law, the applicant (or equivalent) will be expected to discharge the burden of proof. It may be unfair or inappropriate to expect a party to bear this burden simply because that party made the initial application to the Land Registry. An obvious example would be where A applies for first registration of property and is met with an objection from B, a proprietor of an adjacent title who claims some kind of right over A's land. In that scenario, the substantive dispute on which the Adjudicator's decision is sought would be being advanced by B. Accordingly, the Adjudicator may decide that B should be listed as the applicant in the Adjudication proceedings, and bear the corresponding burden of proof.

Court proceedings

3.16   Section 110 of LRA 2002 allows the Adjudicator to direct a party to commence court proceedings within a specified time, instead of deciding the dispute himself. He may make this direction in relation to part of the dispute

---

9   Rule 5 of the Procedure Rules.

only. If this happens, the parties may make representations or objections to the Adjudicator limited to the following issues:[10]

- whether the Adjudicator should make such a direction
- which party should be directed to commence court proceedings
- the time within which court proceedings should commence
- the questions which the court should determine.

3.17 Rule 7(2) of the Procedure Rules provides that a party who has been directed to commence court proceedings must serve on the Adjudicator the following:

- within 14 days of the commencement of the court proceedings, a written notice stating:
  - that court proceedings have been issued in compliance with the Adjudicator's directions
  - the date of issue of the court proceedings
  - the names and any known addresses of the parties to the court proceedings
  - the name of the court at which the court proceedings will be heard
  - the case number allocated to the court proceedings
- within 14 days of the date of the court's decision on any application for an extension of time, a copy of that decision
- within 14 days of the date that the matter before the court is finally disposed of, a copy of the final court order.

3.18 The Procedure Rules[11] provide that the Adjudicator must adjourn proceedings before him on receipt of a notice that court proceedings have been issued. Once the court has decided the matter, the Adjudicator must close the proceedings before him without making any substantive decision, although he is able to make any order necessary to implement the decision of the court, for example an order directing the Registrar to make amendments to the Register, or any order that he could have made following a substantive decision in the adjudication, for example in relation to costs of the adjudication. These requirements apply equally where the Adjudicator has directed a court resolution of part of a dispute, in relation to that part only. Pending resolution of part of a matter by the court, the Adjudicator may adjourn any other part of the matter.

3.19 Where court proceedings have been issued otherwise than in accordance with a direction of the Adjudicator under LRA 2002, s 110 (for example, by one of the parties while the matter was still at the Land Registry stage), the situation is similar to above, with the following modifications:[12]

- the party who issues court proceedings has 14 days from commencement of the court proceedings to serve the required notice on the Adjudicator or (if later) seven days from the service on that party by the Adjudicator of the reference notice under Rule 5(b) of the Procedure Rules;
- in addition to the matters listed above, the notice served on the Adjudicator must contain details of the way and the extent to which the court proceedings concern or relate to the matter before the Adjudicator;
- the Adjudicator *may* adjourn the proceedings before him (in whole or in part) pending a decision by the court.

---

10 Rule 6 of the Procedure Rules.
11 Rules 8 and 9 of the Procedure Rules.
12 Rules 10 and 11 of the Procedure Rules.

Initial directions

3.20–21 When the Adjudicator serves notice of the reference on the parties under r 5 of the Procedure Rules, he will usually also give preliminary directions to the parties to the dispute.

3.22 The first and most important direction is typically for all parties to serve[13] statements of case on the Adjudicator and all other parties. These documents will set out the parties' cases in the same way as statements of case (eg particulars of claim, defence, and reply) in proceedings before the civil courts. The contents of these documents are discussed below. The direction will usually require the applicant to serve its statement of case within a relatively short time period following receipt of the reference notice and case summary, normally 28 days, with the respondent being required to serve its statement of case 28 days thereafter. There is no requirement for the respondent to acknowledge service, as in the equivalent process under the CPR. Presumably this is regarded as a superfluous step as the respondent should already be aware of the proceedings by virtue of having entered an objection at the Land Registry stage.

3.23 Thus the applicant may find itself in the position of being thrust immediately into Adjudication proceedings where, in a comparable claim before the civil courts, it would have had the luxury of months or even years in which to consider whether to issue proceedings. Whilst the Land Registry do notify parties, in advance of a reference to the Adjudicator, that this will be the inevitable result in the event that the parties are unable to resolve their dispute, it is suggested that many parties are unaware of the consequences of the reference taking place, in particular the tight timescales which follow. This situation may be especially acute where parties have been unrepresented before the Land Registry and are suddenly faced with the necessity of drafting a legal document within a specified time frame. The Adjudicator's website contains specimen examples of statements of case, and many parties will choose to draft and submit this document on their own, only taking legal advice later in the proceedings. However, the statements of case are vital documents which repay careful drafting and it is always advisable for the parties both to have the statements of case drafted by a legal professional, and to take preliminary legal advice on the strength of their case at this early stage.

3.24 In fact, it is not strictly necessary for the Adjudicator to make directions requiring service of the statements of case since the default position under the Procedure Rules[14] is that, unless the Adjudicator orders otherwise, the applicant's statement is due within 28 days of service of the reference notification under r 5(b) of the Procedure Rules, and the respondent's statement 28 days thereafter. There does not appear to be any requirement for the Adjudicator to draw these time limits to the attention of the parties. Invariably, however, the Adjudicator will do so, usually by making specific directions.

3.25 If the matter proceeds to a point at which the Adjudicator is invited to make a costs award (eg after the final hearing), costs are normally payable only from the time of submission of the Applicant's statement of case. The costs regime is covered in more detail below; it is important, however, that parties

---

13 The term 'file' is not used in the Procedure Rules; references are to serving documents on the Adjudicator.

14 Rules 12 and 13 of the Procedure Rules.

realise, or are informed, that their potential liability to pay costs commences at the point the Applicant's statement of case is submitted.

3.26 It is common for the preliminary directions made by the Adjudicator (as in the example at **Figure 3.3**) to include a requirement for the parties to serve, at the same time as their statements of case:[15]

- the list of documents upon which they seek to rely
- copies of those documents
- the list of documents in their possession but upon which they do not seek to rely.

These lists can either form part of the same document as the statement of case or be served separately. Copies of the documents upon which the party seeks to rely are generally attached to the statement of case.

3.27 The requirement to serve lists of documents effectively means that the parties are required to perform a mini-disclosure exercise shortly after the commencement of the Adjudication proceedings. There will generally be an opportunity for further disclosure and exchange of documents prior to the final hearing. Nonetheless, this preliminary direction imposes an important early duty (and opportunity) on the parties to define their cases with reference to the documents which will be relied upon at the final hearing.

Service of documents

3.28 Rule 50 of the Procedure Rules deals with service of documents and is set out in full in Appendix 3. The main requirements of r 50 to note are as follows.

- Every party must have a postal address in England and Wales for service, which can only be changed by service of a notice to that effect on the Adjudicator and the other parties.
- Documents may be served on parties by first class post to the service address or by leaving the document at the service address, or by Document Exchange.
- Documents may also be served on parties by fax and email but only if the relevant party has confirmed in advance that it will accept service by this method and has provided a fax number/email address. In the case of email, the recipient may also specify a format in which documents should be sent.
- Any document addressed to the Adjudicator must be sent by first class post to the address specified by the Adjudicator, or by such other method as the Adjudicator may specify.
- Rule 50(11) of the Procedure Rules contains a table setting out, according to method of service, when documents shall be deemed to have been served. These differ from the equivalent rules in CPR, Part 6.

---

15 And for r 27 of the Procedure Rules (disclosure and inspection of documents) to be modified accordingly.

Method of Service	Day of Service
first class post to a postal address in England and Wales	second working day after it was posted
leaving it at a postal address within England and Wales	working day after it was left
Document Exchange within England and Wales	second working day after it was left at the Document Exchange
fax	working day after transmission
email	working day after transmission

'Working day' is given its usual meaning by Rule 2 of the Procedure Rules. However, there is no clear indication of when the working day is deemed to end for the purpose of service. The Adjudicator's Office seem to regard 5pm as the relevant time, unlike the civil courts which regard 4.30pm (or sometimes 4pm) as the end of the day for service purposes. In general the Adjudicator's Office is amenable to receiving documents by email, if arranged beforehand, and this will often be the most convenient way for the parties to serve documents on the Adjudicator. Nonetheless, the Procedure Rules make it clear that first class post is the default method.

Statements of case

3.29   Since the advent of the Civil Procedure Rules, the term 'statement of case' has – officially if not in practice – replaced the older and more familiar term 'pleading' in litigation before the civil courts, being a generic term for particulars of claim, defence, reply and ancillary documents such as requests and replies made pursuant to CPR, Part 18. Statements of case in proceedings before the Adjudicator perform essentially the same function in that they enable the parties to set out the framework of the cases that they will ultimately present at the final hearing. All such documents are entitled '[Party's] Statement of Case'. There is no equivalent of the statement of case known as a 'reply' in civil proceedings, although under r 25 of the Procedure Rules the Adjudicator can order a party to reply to a statement of case or provide further information.

3.30   It is possible for a statement of case to be amended by means of an application to the Adjudicator, the procedure for which is covered below. This is all too common where one or both parties have drafted the statement of case without recourse to a legal professional and find, later in the Adjudication process, that the document represents their case inadequately. Whilst amendment can be a beneficial and necessary step, parties should be careful not to use it as a means to reply to matters set out in each other's (initial) statement of case as this could have cost implications, and may leave open the possibility of inconsistencies between the documents which could be exploited at the final hearing. If a party (presumably the applicant) wishes to reply to factual material contained in the opponent's statement of case, this can usually be done in witness evidence.

3.31   In addition to the party's name(s) and status in the proceedings, the heading of the statement of case should also contain the case reference, and the title number and property description of the title in respect of which the original application was made. All of this information can be found in the case summary.

3.32   The first section of the document requires the party to provide a name and address for service. If solicitors are instructed, their details should be set out here, including a reference. This is information which generally appears at the end of a statement of case in proceedings before the civil courts.

Applicant's statement of case

3.33   An example of an Applicant's statement of case is shown at **Figure 3.3**.

Figure 3.3 Applicant's statement of case

<u>**ADJUDICATOR TO HM LAND REGISTRY**</u>
<u>**CASE REFERENCE: REF/**</u>

TITLE NUMBER:
PROPERTY:

BETWEEN:

X LIMITED

                                                         <u>**APPLICANT**</u>

and

Mr SMITH

                                                         <u>**RESPONDENT**</u>

───

APPLICANT'S STATEMENT OF CASE

───

<u>**Name and Address for Service**</u>

This is the Statement of Case for X Limited, which is the Applicant. The address for service of documents is Jones & Jones, 1 Law Lane, Castletown, C1 1AA (DX 10000), Reference: ABC/DEF/1.

<u>**Reasons for Supporting the Application**</u>

(Figure 3.3 cont)

1. On [date], [names] were registered as freehold proprietors with title absolute of Title Number [no], being [address] (the "Property"). An official copy of this title is attached hereto marked EX1.

2. [name] had purchased the Property on [date] and was initially the sole freehold proprietor. The Property was registered following the transfer of legal ownership into the joint names of [names].

3. By transfer dated [date], [names] transferred the whole of their interest in the Property to X Limited ("X"), the Applicant. A copy of this transfer is attached hereto marked EX2.

4. By subsequent transfer, also dated [date], X transferred the whole of its legal interest in the Property to Y Limited ("Y"). A copy of this transfer is attached hereto marked EX3.

5. On [date], X and Y executed a Declaration of Trust which stated that Y '*declares that it holds the beneficial interest in the Property as nominee on behalf of X*'. A copy of this Declaration of Trust is attached hereto marked EX4.

6. Pending resolution of the present dispute, the Property remains registered in the names of [names]. At all material times, the Property has been used as commercial premises.

7. Since [date], the Respondent has been registered as freehold proprietor with title absolute of Title Number [no], being [land 1] and [land 2] (the latter piece of land not being relevant to this dispute). An official copy of this title is attached hereto marked EX5.

8. The Applicant's title and [land 1] are adjacent to each other and both have a frontage to [road]. The frontage of [land 1] consists of an open mouth behind which is a track leading away from the highway (the "Track").

1

(Figure 3.3 cont)

9. Immediately abutting the Property and an adjacent house, [house] (located behind the Property), is a small strip of land (the "Strip") which has at all material times been used for parking motor vehicles. Although it is unclear from the Land Registry plans, the Applicant believes that the Strip has been registered as part of [land 1].

10. The Applicant's case is that from [date] until the transfer of the Property to the Applicant in [date], [names] regularly and frequently parked up to two motor vehicles on the Strip. The usage was open and no permission was sought or given, nor was any payment made. No objection was received to the usage at any time.

11. The Applicant's case is that the portion of the Strip used by [names] measures approximately [cm] in width from the continuous wall of the Property and [house] and that it extends two car spaces in length (approximately [cm]) away from the highway frontage of the Property. The Applicant notes that the Strip continues beyond this point parallel to the wall of [house] and that there has been regular parking of a third car in that part of the Strip. However, that does not form part of this Application.

12. The position of the Strip and the parked vehicles can be seen from the photograph attached to the Statutory Declaration of [names] dated [date], a copy of which is attached hereto marked EX7.

13. Accordingly, it is averred that the Applicant is entitled to the benefit of the following easements, which have arisen by prescription following a period of usage of 20 years or more:

    (a) A right to park motor vehicles in a strip of land whose dimensions are approximately [cm] (length) x [cm] (width) from the corner of the Property abutting [road], as defined above;

    (b) A right to pass and re-pass on foot from the said strip of land to and from the entrance to the Property on [road];

2

(Figure 3.3 cont)

(c) A right to turn motor vehicles in that part of [land 1] adjacent to the said strip of land, for the purpose of entering and leaving the said strip.

14. For the avoidance of doubt, the Applicant avers that the parking of motor cars on the Strip has never caused any obstruction to the use of the Track; this can be seen from photograph (at EX7).

Facts upon which the Applicant intends to rely

15. [name] purchased the Property on [date] and used some or all of the Property as offices from [date] until at least [date]. The Applicant refers to the Statutory Declaration of [names] dated [date], a copy of which is attached hereto marked EX6. (The Applicant does not have the original of this document, which has been lodged with the Land Registry.)

16. Throughout the whole of this period, [name] openly parked a motor car on the Strip for up to [hours] a week without payment, permission or objection from any third party.

17. Throughout the whole of this period, [name], although not a legal owner of the Property until [date], openly parked a motor car on the Strip for up to [hours] a week without payment, permission or objection from any third party.

18. The specific motor vehicles parked on the Strip by [names] included *inter alia* the following: [cars].

19. In addition, throughout the period of [names'] ownership, the Strip was used by customers of the business being carried on from the Property for the purpose of parking motor cars, when space permitted.

20. It was the belief of [names] that the portion of the Strip used by them formed part of their title to the Property. On occasion, permission was given or refused by [name] to third parties seeking to part on the relevant portion of the

3

(Figure 3.3 cont)

Strip. For the avoidance of doubt, no application based on adverse possession is being advanced on the part of the Applicant.

BERTIE WOOSTER

Documents upon which the Applicant intends to rely

Description	Original/Copy	Date	Parties	Document No
Official Copy of Title No	copy			EX1
TR1 Form	original (copy supplied herewith)			EX2
TR1 Form	original (copy supplied herewith)			EX3
Declaration of Trust	original (copy supplied herewith)			EX4
Official Copy of Title No	copy			EX5
Statutory Declaration	copy (signed original filed at Land Registry)			EX6
Statutory Declaration	original (copy supplied herewith)			EX7

4

(Figure 3.3 cont)

Documents in the Applicant's Possession but upon which the Applicant does not intend to rely

Description	Original/Copy	Date	Parties	
Lease of the Property	original			

List of witnesses the Applicant intends to call

1. Mr Augustus Fink-Nottle

2. Miss Madeleine Bassett

3. Mrs Agatha Gregson

4. A representative of X Limited (name to be confirmed) will give evidence as to ownership of the Property.

Statement of Truth

[I believe] [The Applicant believes] that the facts contained in this Statement of Case are true.

Signed ……………………………………………………………………………..

Print Name(s) ……………………………………………………………………

[Position ……………………………………………………………………………..]

Date ………………………………………………………………………………

5

3.34 The main body of the document is split into two sections: (a) reasons for supporting the application and (b) facts upon which the applicant intends to rely. This is an attempt to create a distinction between argument and fact which is perhaps rather artificial and there will inevitably be some cross over and duplication between the two sections. Particulars of claim in proceedings before the civil courts would effectively combine the two sections, although there is a specific requirement under CPR, r 16.4 to plead the facts upon which the claimant relies.

3.35 The first matter which should be set out in the reasons for supporting the application is the proprietorship of the applicant and respondent, including title number, property description, and length and quality of ownership. It should be straightforward to identify, list and attach the documents evidencing title upon which the party will rely. These will potentially include official copies of the relevant titles (not necessarily limited to the titles of the applicant and respondent but often including one or more adjacent properties which may be affected by the dispute), historic conveyancing documents, plans, and photographs. It is normal for the applicant to include an official copy of the respondent's title (assuming that title is registered) even though this may not be a document on which the applicant relies.

3.36 The next matter which should be addressed is a comprehensive description of all the relevant parcels of land concerned in the dispute by reference to their registered titles, and their proximity to one another and the physical features on the ground. There is likely to be considerable saving of time and effort later in the Adjudication process if a detailed, clear, large-scale plan is prepared at this stage and annexed to the applicant's statement of case, preferably in a format which the respondent can use to illustrate or superimpose any areas of dispute. The plan need not be prepared by a surveyor, or be to scale, but an indication of measurements may be helpful depending on the nature of the dispute.

3.37 After these matters have been addressed, the statement of case should proceed to make the argument which the applicant is advancing. The drafting of the argument, particularly if undertaken by a legal professional, will probably read much like a statement of case in proceedings before the civil courts including, for example, anticipatory denials and alternative cases.

3.38 The 'facts upon which the applicant intends to rely' section, while inevitably overlapping to some extent with the previous section, is most logically approached as a chronological story of the factual background to the dispute. Clearly only matters relevant to the dispute should be included and points should be made as concisely as possible, as there will be an opportunity to expand in witness evidence later. However, care should be taken that the factual material contained in a statement of case will not be contradicted by witness evidence later in the process.

Respondent's statement of case

3.39 An example of a respondent's statement of case is shown at **Figure 3.4**.

Figure 3.4 Respondent's statement of case

<u>**ADJUDICATOR TO HM LAND REGISTRY**</u>
<u>**CASE REFERENCE: REF/**</u>

TITLE NUMBER:
PROPERTY:

BETWEEN:

Mr SMITH (1) and Mrs SMITH (2)

<u>**APPLICANTS**</u>

and

Mr JONES (1) and Mrs JONES (2)

<u>**RESPONDENTS**</u>

RESPONDENTS' STATEMENT OF CASE

<u>**Name and Address for Service**</u>

This is the Statement of Case for Mr and Mrs Jones, who are the Respondents. The address for service of documents is ABC Solicitors LLP, Justice Street, Middleton W1 1SS (Reference: XYZ/30).

<u>**Reasons for Opposing the Application**</u>

(Figure 3.4 cont)

1. The Respondents or members of the Respondents' family have at all material times been freehold proprietors of [address], now registered under freehold title number [no].

2. The Applicants or members of the Applicants' family have at all material times been freehold proprietors of [address] (the "Property").

3. Pursuant to a conveyance dated [date] and made between [names], the Respondents enjoy (the "Rights"):

   "a right of way over the yard at the rear of [property] to the wash-house at the rear of [property] AND ALSO a right of way to and up the steps at the rear of [property] … AND TOGETHER also with the right to the joint use of the wash-house at the rear of [property] aforesaid".

   The Rights are set out in the Property Register of [property].

4. In or around [date], it was verbally agreed (the "Verbal Agreement") between the First Respondent, on behalf of the Respondents, and the Applicants' predecessor in title that the Respondents' right of way to, and right of use of, the wash-house (the "Wash-house") as set out above, would be transferred to the adjacent dairy building (the "Dairy") following the partial demolition of the Wash-house. A key was provided to the Respondents for that purpose.

5. By entering into the Verbal Agreement, the Respondents relied on a representation by the Applicants' predecessor in title that they would have a right of way to, and right of use of, the Dairy. In reliance on that representation, the Respondents waived their rights in respect of the Wash-house, including the right to require the Wash-house to be rebuilt. The Applicants are now denying the existence of the Verbal Agreement and, thereby, the Respondents' rights in respect of the Dairy. It is averred that such denial is unconscionable and that the Applicants are estopped from so denying.

1

(Figure 3.4 cont)

6. Further and in the alternative, the Respondents' right of way subsists in its original form (in respect of the Wash-house) and has not been abandoned.

7. The Respondents therefore oppose the removal of the caution in respect of the Property.

Facts upon which the Respondents intend to rely

8. The Respondents reply to the Applicants' Statement of Case as follows, numbering the paragraphs from the beginning of that document.

9. Paragraphs 2 to 7 are admitted.

10. It is denied that the Wash-house was demolished with the consent of the Respondents' predecessor in title. Further, the demolition of the Wash-house was only partial, with 3 walls, a staircase and a walkway connecting to a gate remaining. It is averred that the Wash-house is capable of being rebuilt.

11. It is averred that, after partial demolition of the Wash-house, the Applicants' predecessor in title, [name], agreed with the Respondents' predecessor in title, [name], that she would do his washing and allow him to use the Dairy for storage.

12. Save for what is stated above regarding the extent of the Wash-house's demolition, Paragraph 10 is admitted.

13. Paragraphs 11 and 12 are denied. In or around [date], [name] spoke to [name], father of the Applicants, about use of the Dairy, believing that this was the Wash-house. [name] stated that the Wash-house had been demolished. Subsequently, the Verbal Agreement was reached (as set out above). It was also agreed by the Verbal Agreement that toilets, located on land belonging to [property] and in respect of which there was a right of way in favour of the Property, would be demolished and that all rights respecting the toilets in

2

46

(Figure 3.4 cont)

favour of the Property would cease, thus releasing the owner of the Property from his previous obligation to contribute to the upkeep of the toilets.

14. As to Paragraph 13, the Respondents rely on the Statutory Declaration of [name] which is cited in the caution entered against the Applicants' title.

15. In respect of Paragraph 14, it is averred that this is not relevant to the matter which the Adjudicator must decide nor does it demonstrate that the Respondents have no rights in respect of the Dairy. The Respondents have set out above their case on the Verbal Agreement.

16. Paragraph 15 is admitted.

17. Paragraph 16 is admitted, save that it is denied that the Respondents have made any untrue assertions in respect of the Property. The Respondents do not understand what the Applicants mean by "ownership rights" referred to in Paragraph 16 but it is specifically denied (if the same be alleged) that the Respondents have ever claimed to have title to the Property and the Respondents will rely on the letter from their former solicitors to the Applicants' solicitors dated [date] (attached to the Applicants' Statement of Case at EX4) which confirms that the Respondents merely assert rights over the Property.

18. In relation to Paragraph 17, the Respondents:

    (a) deny that the original structure of the Wash-house no longer remains, there being 3 walls, a staircase and a walkway connecting to a gate, and aver that the same is capable of being rebuilt;

    (b) aver that running water and/or power was supplied to both the Wash-house and the Dairy, and aver that it is possible to see the remains of a pipe and/or cable installed for this purpose.

19. In relation to Paragraph 18, the Respondents:

3

(Figure 3.4 cont)

(a) repeat what is said above about the Verbal Agreement and the unconscionable denial of the same by the Applicants;

(b) rely on the Statutory Declaration of [name] which is cited in the caution entered against the Applicants' title;

(c) aver that they would obtain a clear benefit from the use of a laundry room;

(d) deny that the letter at EX4 to the Applicants' Statement of Case supports the Applicants' assertion in this paragraph, since it states that the Respondents have indicated that they have rights to use (parts of) the Property.

20. Save for what is stated above regarding the extant parts of the Wash-house, Paragraphs 20 and 21 are admitted.

21. As to Paragraph 22, the parties have already expended considerable effort in trying to achieve an acceptable compromise, and the Respondents do not consider that a meeting would have advanced matters. The pending first registration of the Property will not register the rights that the Respondents say they have acquired in respect of the Dairy.

22. It is averred that the photographs referred to in Paragraph 23 show that parts of both buildings are still in existence and would be capable of being rebuilt and restored to their original uses.

23. The Respondents object to Paragraph 24 as it is inappropriate for the Applicants to seek to adduce the alleged views of the Land Registry on a point of law as facts upon which they rely in these proceedings. In any event, the Respondents rely on the letter to the Applicants' solicitors dated [date] in which he states, '*I do not feel that my letters ... support your contention that Land Registry "are agreeing that the easement to the wash house can no longer be exercised".*'.

4

(Figure 3.4 cont)

24. As to Paragraph 25:

    (a) in respect of the manner in which the Respondents have acquired rights over the Dairy, the Respondents repeat the matters set out above;

    (b) it is denied that the Respondents' rights exist pursuant to licence only or that any such licence has ever been revoked;

    (c) it is admitted that the Respondents have never used the Dairy for washing;

    (d) it is denied that the Wash-house was demolished with consent.

25. The Applicants are required to prove Paragraph 26.

26. The Respondents do not understand the first sentence of Paragraph 27. As to the remainder of that paragraph, the Respondents rely on the Statutory Declaration of [name] which is cited in the caution entered against the Applicants' title.

27. As to Paragraph 28, the Respondents aver that these rights of way subsisted to allow the owners of the Property access to the outside toilets (the "WCs") which had been in common ownership with the Property, and were demolished in [date]. In [date], the Respondents successfully applied for possessory title to the land on which the WCs had stood on the basis of adverse possession, the application not being opposed by the Applicants. In the premises, these rights of way are now obsolete.

28. As to Paragraph 29, the Respondents:

    (a) repeat the previous paragraph of this document;

5

(Figure 3.4 cont)

(b) deny that the extent of their storage facilities at [property] is a relevant factor in these proceedings or that they are thereby estopped from claiming further rights over the Dairy.

29. In respect of Paragraphs 30 to 32, the Respondents have set out their case above. Further submissions on the law will be made at the hearing of this matter.

30. In respect of Paragraphs 33 and 34, the Respondents repeat that the parties have already expended considerable effort in trying to achieve an acceptable compromise, and that thy do not consider that a meeting would have advanced matters.

HERCULE POIROT

Documents upon which the Respondents intend to rely

Description	Original/Copy	Date	Parties	Document No
Conveyance	copy			R1
Official Copy of Title No and Caution	copy			R2
Correspondence	copy	various		R3

6

(Figure 3.4 cont)

Documents in the Respondents' Possession but upon which they do not intend to rely

Description	Original/Copy	Date	Parties	

List of witnesses the Respondents intend to call

1. Captain Arthur Hastings

2. Miss Felicity Lemon

3. Inspector Japp

Statement of Truth

[I believe] [The Respondents believe] that the facts contained in this Statement of Case are true.

Signed ....

Print Name(s) ....

[Position ....]

Date ....

7

3.40   Much of what is said above about the applicant's statement of case will apply equally to the respondent's statement of case; only the differences are therefore noted.

3.41   Pursuant to the Rules, the respondent is required to list and attach all documents on which he relies even if they have already been listed in and attached to the applicant's statement of case. This will inevitably result in some duplication.

3.42   The respondent's statement of case is equivalent to a defence in proceedings before the civil courts and one way of drafting the document is to respond to the applicant's statement of case in the traditional manner of admitting, denying, or putting to proof each statement made in the applicant's statement of case, as well as setting out any necessary additional material required to elucidate the respondent's case. Alternatively, the respondent's statement of case can be pleaded without reference to the specific paragraphs of the applicant's statement of case. Whilst there is no presumption in the Procedure Rules, as in CPR, r 16.5(5), that the respondent's failure to address a specific issue in the applicant's statement of case amounts to an admission, it is important for obvious reasons that the respondent addresses the whole of the applicant's case insofar as the respondent is able to do so.

Lists of documents

3.43   There will ordinarily be two lists of documents appended to statements of case, assuming the preliminary directions require service of the lists at this stage as in the example above. The first – documents on which the party seeks to rely – will contain the documents attached to the statement of case. Documents typically attached to statements of case will include:

- official copies of the Register and filed plans;
- historic conveyancing documents (including attached plans);
- historic maps and plans not associated with conveyances, eg Ordnance Survey maps and tithe plans;
- photographs, both contemporary and historic – aerial photographs can be especially useful;
- surveyor's reports;
- Statutory Declarations, both historic and those submitted to the Land Registry in the course of the application;
- *relevant* grants of planning or other statutory permission.

3.44   Rule 47 of the Procedure Rules sets out the requirements of a document list. As in the examples of statements of case at **Figures 3.3** and **3.4**, there will typically be five columns:

- *Description* – a concise description of the type of document, for example
  - Official Copy of Title No X
  - Plan
  - Letter
  - Statutory declaration
- *Original or copy* – although all documents attached to the statement of case will be copies, the parties should record in the list whether they hold originals (if so, these should be available at trial) or merely copies, in which case the type of copy should be stated (certified copy, office copy, or other)

- *Date* – this can be a specific date, a year or, in relation to documents listed as a category, a generic description, eg 'various'
- *Parties* – particularly important for conveyancing documents, where the parties can be conveniently separated by numbers in parentheses, eg John Smith and Mary Smith (1) David Jones (2); alternatively this may be the author and recipient of a document such as a piece of correspondence
- *Document No* – a convenient system of referencing can be used; the precedent statement of case suggests 'EX1 [i.e. Exhibit 1], EX2 etc.' but it may be better to use App1, App2 etc. for the applicants' documents and R1, R2 etc. for the respondents' documents – the numbering will eventually be overtaken by the pagination of the hearing bundle in any event.

3.45   Rule 47(1B) provides that any description on a list of documents of a generic class of document must be sufficiently clear and precise for any party receiving the list to identify:

- the nature of the contents of each document included within that class of documents
- whether any particular document which exists is included within that class of documents.

The same process will then be repeated for the second list, namely documents in the party's possession but upon which the party does not intend to rely.

List of witnesses the party intends to call

3.46   Rule 14(1)(e) requires a statement of case to contain a list of witnesses that the party intends to call in support of that party's case. The Adjudicator will often also make a direction to that effect. As with the lists of documents, the requirement to serve a list of witnesses at the same time as a party's statement of case is an important difference when compared with the equivalent requirements in a typical civil trial process. The default rule is that a party must list *all* witnesses it intends to call and can only call additional witnesses with the permission of the adjudicator, ie by specific application.

3.47   Effectively this means that a party will normally have only 28 days, being the standard length of time for filing its statement of case, to identify witnesses, ascertain whether those witnesses are prepared to attend an adjudication for the purpose of giving oral evidence, and – ideally – take draft proofs of their evidence to ensure it will not conflict with the factual elements of the statement of case. However, it is only the list of witnesses which is required at this point: there is no requirement (as on a civil allocation questionnaire) to state which facts the witness is being called to attest to, let alone provide a witness statement. Although the list of witnesses should be as accurate as possible, it is better and quite permissible to err on the side of caution and list all individuals who might be called to give evidence even if it later transpires that some are unable to, or there is unnecessary duplication.

3.48   As in civil proceedings, it is vital that witnesses who have prepared a statement attend the adjudication for the purpose of cross-examination if any weight is to be given to their evidence. Witness evidence in general is covered in more detail below.

Statement of truth

3.49   This phrase, again familiar from civil proceedings, is defined in the 'Interpretation' section of the Procedure Rules[16] as follows:

> '(a) in the case of a witness statement, a statement signed by the maker of the statement that the maker of the statement believes that the facts stated in the witness statement are true; or
>
> (b) in the case of other documents, a statement that the party by whom or on whose behalf the document is submitted believes the facts stated in the document are true, signed by either:
>
>> (i)   the party by whom or on whose behalf the document is submitted; or
>>
>> (ii) that party's authorised representative, in which case the statement of truth must state the name of the representative and the relationship of the representative to the party.'

At its simplest, a Statement of Truth just needs to say, 'I believe that the facts contained in this Statement of Case are true', and be signed by the appropriate person as indicated above.

3.50   The statement of truth is a vital component of a statement of case. It is surprising on how many occasions unsigned statements of case, and witness statements, are included in the hearing bundle, though it is perhaps an inevitable consequence of modern document retrieval systems. Although it may seem to be a small detail, this invariably causes annoyance for the Adjudicator and the advocates who have to spend valuable time before or even during the hearing ensuring that properly signed copies are made available to all parties.

3.51   Practitioners increasingly require their clients to sign statements of truth on statements of case themselves and it is submitted that this is entirely appropriate, especially in view of the specific factual section included. A statement of case will often be treated as equivalent to a preliminary witness statement in cross-examination at the final hearing so it is vital that the facts are in order; requiring the party to sign the document may assist in concentrating his mind.

3.52   There is sometimes confusion among litigants-in-person between the meaning of statement of truth in the sense used above and its use by the Land Registry as a type of pro forma witness statement in support of applications (eg Form ST4). These Land Registry 'Statements of Truth' will inevitably feature on occasion as supporting documents in Adjudications.

Between statements of case and the hearing

3.53   As in a civil trial, there will generally be a period of several months between submission of the final statement of case and the final hearing. During this period, the Adjudicator will usually give further directions that enable the parties to get their cases ready for hearing. Some directions will be common to most Adjudications, and those will be considered first.

Witness evidence

3.54   Rule 26 of the Procedure Rules simply says that the Adjudicator may give directions requiring a party to provide a witness statement made by any

---

16 Rule 2 of the Procedure Rules.

witness on whose evidence that party intends to rely in the proceedings. The standard direction will be for the parties to exchange witness evidence on which they intend to rely by a particular date. Comment has already been made above that the parties should be careful to list all potential witnesses on their statements of case, and to ensure (so far as practicable) that the factual content of the statements of case will not contradict any later witness evidence. The observations made above about the importance of signed statements of truth apply equally to witness statements.

3.55   There is little that is distinctive about witness statements in proceedings before the Adjudicator compared to proceedings in the civil courts. Witness statements will be offered as a witness's evidence-in-chief at the final hearing. Adjudicators are often less inclined than judges to allow witnesses to expand on their evidence in-chief during the hearing, so it is vital that everything a witness wishes to say is contained in the witness statement.

3.56   It is somewhat concerning therefore that witness statements are often submitted – on behalf of parties who have legal representation – that provide only cursory treatment of the issues in dispute. An example would be where the issue is whether A has acquired an easement by some form of prescription over land of which B is the registered proprietor, and A's evidence on the point says nothing more than, 'I confirm that I have used the said right of way openly, and without force or permission, for a period exceeding 20 years'. Such wording may be acceptable on an application (as yet unopposed) to the Land Registry, which is probably its origin. In a witness statement for a contested action before the Adjudicator it is completely inadequate. A witness who has offered nothing more than those words in evidence may then be reliant on the 'right' questions being asked in cross-examination in order to have any opportunity to tell his story, which is extremely unsatisfactory.

3.57   It is essential for practitioners who take proofs of evidence, or otherwise assist witnesses of fact in preparation of their witness statements, to obtain as much detail as possible in relation to the matter(s) in dispute. Very often this will mean specific examples of the use of a claimed right of way, or instances of possession of a piece of land that are adverse to the title of the legal owner. Dates, times, places, and individuals who were present should be set out with as much precision as a combination of witness memory and contemporaneous documentation will allow. Frequencies of use should be estimated. Whilst there are no rules on how a witness statement should be set out, a chronological treatment will often be logical, in appropriate cases divided into the specific issues which the Adjudicator will be asked to address.

3.58   By contrast, a witness statement should not dwell on matters that are irrelevant to the issue(s) in the Adjudication. It will very often be tempting for witnesses to set out, or tell their legal adviser to set out, the entire history of a dispute with the owner of a neighbouring piece of land. There is nothing wrong with summarising the position in a couple of paragraphs to set the scene. But the Adjudicator is not likely to be interested in a detailed blow-by-blow account of historic arguments or disputes unless these are relevant, for example if they demonstrate that one party took steps to clarify the status of another party's usage of a piece of land. Detailed irrelevant material may also serve to highlight lack of detail on matters of relevance and lead to the inevitable conclusion that if a witness can remember irrelevant conversations in great detail, his lack of ability to remember how often he used a piece of land and for what, is telling.

3.59   There is no specific guidance in the Procedure Rules on the use of exhibits to witness statements. Parties often follow the practice of including one or more exhibits containing documents referred to in the witness statement. It is submitted that this practice should be avoided where those documents have already been included in a document list, in which case reference can be made to the document number.

3.60   Rule 49 of the Procedure Rules provides that no party may call an expert witness, or submit an expert's report as evidence, without the permission of the Adjudicator. It is suggested that a party wishing to rely on expert evidence – written or oral – should make an application to the Adjudicator at an early stage, before any costs are incurred.

Disclosure and inspection of documents

3.61   As stated above, it is common for the Adjudicator to direct that disclosure of a party's documents take place simultaneously with service of that party's statement of case. However, the default position is, as stated in r 27 of the Procedure Rules, that disclosure by all parties shall take place within 28 days after service of the respondent's statement of case. It is also not unusual for directions to be made that allow the parties to provide further disclosure of documents at a date after statements of case have been served, presumably because (at least for the applicant) it may only be after service of the final statement of case that it becomes obvious that a particular document needs to be relied upon or disclosed.

3.62   The specific requirements for disclosure and inspection pursuant to r 27 of the Procedure Rules are:

- the parties must include in their disclosure list (which complies with r 47 and is served on the Adjudicator and all other parties) documents which are in their possession and control and which:
  - that party intends to rely upon in the proceedings
  - adversely affect that party's own case
  - adversely affect another party's case
  - support another party's case
- the parties must send the Adjudicator copies of all of documents in their possession falling into the above categories
- in relation to documents listed in a party's statement of case:
  - permit other parties to inspect or take copies on reasonable notice and at a reasonable time and place
  - provide copies if requested by another party on payment by that party of reasonable copying costs

Thus a distinction is drawn between documents referred to in a party's statement of case, which any other party has a right to inspect, and other documents on a party's disclosure list, which apparently only the Adjudicator is entitled to see.

3.63   Rule 2(2) of the Procedure Rules says that a document is in a party's possession or control if:

- it is in his physical possession
- he has a right to possession of it
- he has a right to inspect or take copies of it.

3.64   Under r 28 of the Procedure Rules, the Adjudicator can require the attendance of any person to give evidence or produce any document specified by the Adjudicator which is in that person's possession or control. He does this by serving that person with a requirement notice, which must:

- be in writing
- identify the person who must comply with the requirement
- identify the matter to which the requirement relates
- state the nature of the requirement being imposed
- specify the time and place at which the person is required to attend and/ or produce any document
- include a statement of the possible consequences of any failure to comply.

3.65   The party on whose behalf the requirement notice is issued must serve it on the party who is to be required not less than seven working days before any required attendance. Any person who is not a party to the proceedings must be offered his travel expenses, and these must be paid not less than seven working days before any required attendance, unless refused.[17] The seven-working-day period can be shortened by mutual consent in which case a copy of the consent agreement must be served on the Adjudicator. Application can be made to the Adjudicator by the person who is the subject of the requirement to have the requirement varied or set aside.

3.66   The principles of requirement notices are similar to those of witness summonses or *sub poena* notices in civil proceedings. What is not clear is the nature of the possible consequences of a failure to comply referred to in r 28(3) (f) of the Procedure Rules. The Adjudicator has general powers under r 55 of the Procedure Rules to impose sanctions on *the parties* for non-compliance with directions, for example by cancelling or allowing an application in whole or in part. However, it is difficult to imagine what sanctions could be imposed on third parties since there is no equivalent of contempt of court in Adjudication proceedings. There is, as yet, no reported case on sanctions and non-compliance which offers any guidance on the matter.

Other interim directions

3.67   The Adjudicator may at any time, of his own motion or on the application of a party (on which see below) give further directions, which must be made in writing, dated and served on all parties including any non-party who made the application and, if applicable to him, the Registrar.[18]

3.68   Examples of interim directions the Adjudicator can make are:

- consolidation of proceedings
- requiring a party to clarify whether it intends to attend or be represented at a hearing, or to call witnesses
- permission to call an expert witness
- an adjournment
- setting aside or varying of existing directions

---

17 Presumably an estimate would suffice where necessary, together perhaps with an undertaking to make good any shortfall after the required attendance has been discharged.
18 Rules 20 and 21 of the Procedure Rules.

- requiring a party to provide one of various categories of clarification of further information:[19]
  - a statement of the facts in dispute or issues to be decided
  - a statement of the facts on which that party intends to rely and the allegations he intends to make
  - a summary of the arguments on which that party intends to rely
  - further information, responses to statements of case or supplementary statements.

3.69   It may be necessary during the course of proceedings for a party to be added or substituted for an existing party to the proceedings: r 24 of the Procedure Rules makes provision for this. The Adjudicator must give directions about the role and naming of the new party and how existing documents are to be served on that party. The new party then has 28 days from service of documents on him to serve the following documents on the Adjudicator and the other parties:

- his statement of case
- copies of documents in his possession or control which:
  - are central to his case
  - the Adjudicator or any other party will require in order to properly understand the new party's statement of case.

A continuing party may apply to the Adjudicator for leave to reply to any documents served by the new party and, if leave is granted, he must serve copies of the response on the Adjudicator and all other parties.

Applications

3.70   Rules 51 and 52 of the Procedure Rules provide a mechanism for the parties to make applications to the Adjudicator during the course of proceedings. Subject to the Adjudicator's power to dispense with any of the formal requirements, such applications must:

- be in writing and addressed to the Adjudicator
- state the name of the person on whose behalf the application is made
- state the nature of, and the reasons for, the application
- attach any evidence of consent to the application by any other parties.

3.71   The Adjudicator must serve notice on any party who has not consented to the application and will be affected by it, giving that party details of the application and of a specified period in which they are able to object to it, or make representations about it. There is a similar requirement if the Adjudicator decides to act of his own motion. In either case, however, the Adjudicator need not serve notice if he does not consider it appropriate or practicable to do so. An objection or representation is made by serving written notice, within the specified period, on the Adjudicator and all other persons who will be affected by the action.

3.72   The Adjudicator must consider all applications, objections and representations unless frivolous or vexatious, or made outside the specified time limit (in which case the Adjudicator has discretion to deal with the matter, but is not bound to). The Adjudicator must give a decision on the application, objection or representation to the person making the application, objection or representation and any other parties liable to be affected by it. Although

---

19   Rule 25 of the Procedure Rules.

the Adjudicator is not bound to give reasons for a decision on a procedural matter,[20] he commonly will do so.

Summary disposal

3.73   Rule 32A of the Procedure Rules provides a mechanism for summary disposal of proceedings. The test is very similar to that found in CPR, Part 24, namely that the Adjudicator may summarily dispose of the proceedings or any particular issue in the proceedings if:

(a)   he considers that the applicant or respondent has no real prospect of succeeding in the proceedings or on that issue; and

(b)   there is no other compelling reason why the proceedings or issue should not be disposed of summarily.

3.74   Except with the permission of the Adjudicator, an applicant may not apply for summary disposal until the respondent has served a statement of case or the time for doing so has expired. Presumably any application for permission would simply be included with the application for summary disposal. A respondent may apply for summary disposal at any time after the applicant has served a statement of case or the time for doing so has expired. If a respondent applies for summary disposal before filing his own statement of case, the time for filing that statement of case is extended to 28 days from the Adjudicator's decision on the summary disposal, or such other time as the Adjudicator directs.

3.75   As in civil proceedings, an application for summary disposal must be accompanied by a witness statement which states why the applicant believes the test has been satisfied.

3.76   The Adjudicator may allow or dismiss the application for summary disposal. If he summarily dismisses only part of the proceedings (for example, in relation to a particular issue), he must give case management directions as to the remainder.

Final hearing

3.77   There is a presumption[21] that a substantive decision will only be made following a hearing. However, the Adjudicator can make a substantive decision without a hearing – presumably as a result of considering the available documents if:

• he is satisfied there are no important public interest considerations that require a hearing in public, and

• he has served written notice on the parties of his intention or the fact that he has received an application requesting a substantive decision without a hearing, and
  – the parties agree to that course of action; or
  – the parties fail to object to that course of action within the specified time

• no notice by the Adjudicator is required if all the parties have requested a substantive decision without a hearing.

---

20   It is unlikely to be a 'substantive decision' or 'substantive order' within the meaning of r 2 of the Procedure Rules.

21   Rule 33(1) of the Procedure Rules.

Site inspections[22]

3.78   At any time the Adjudicator may serve a 'request for entry' requesting permission to enter onto and inspect property for the purposes of assisting in a determination of any of the matters in dispute. The request for entry is served on the party in occupation of, or who has ownership or control of, the relevant property and must specify a time for entry that, unless agreed otherwise in writing by the owner or occupier of the property, must not be earlier than seven days after service of the request for entry. The Adjudicator can take any refusal of such a request into account when making a substantive decision in the proceedings.

3.79   Although a request for entry can request entry at any time during the proceedings, it is most common for the Adjudicator to request entry immediately prior to the hearing, or at some point between the beginning and end of the hearing period. Even in the latter case, however, a site inspection does not form part of the hearing and is an informal occasion. When the Adjudicator serves the request for entry, he will generally ask the parties to confirm who if anyone will be attending the site inspection on behalf of each party: although it is not specifically set out in the Procedure Rules, the Adjudicator usually directs that the parties are entitled to be present along with their legal representatives.

3.80   Site inspections can be very useful from the point of view of the Adjudicator, as well as advocates who have not previously had the opportunity of seeing the property in question, which will usually be a property in respect of whose title an order is to be made at the conclusion of the hearing. Assuming that the parties have chosen to be present and/or represented at the site inspection, the Adjudicator will usually invite each party to point out any features of the property which they wish to bring to his attention while he walks around the property. This can often be a recipe for chaos. The (lay) parties may struggle to understand that the inspection is not part of the hearing, and is not an opportunity to give evidence or make submissions. Practitioners should warn their clients not to enter into arguments with their opponents on a site inspection; should this prove difficult, it may be better if the lay clients did not attend the site inspection. If a legal representative (generally the advocate) has not previously been on site, he may need to take hurried instructions from his clients concerning how the physical landscape relates to their case. He may need to do this discreetly while keeping up with the Adjudicator and listening carefully to any features which are being pointed out by another party. Although there are no rules about who may or may not speak during the informal site inspection, it is invariably better for the legal representatives to point out features to the Adjudicator having taken instructions from their clients. The Adjudicator will often take photographs of the site and may wish to spend some time looking round on his own. On a practical level, those attending site inspections will need to ensure that they dress appropriately for the conditions on the ground and are able to park somewhere, preferably not on the disputed land!

3.81   Although they do not have the status of evidence, references to site visits are frequently made during the hearing.

---

22   See r 30 of the Procedure Rules.

Skeleton arguments and hearing bundles

3.82 There is no general direction for the provision of skeleton arguments and hearing bundles under the Procedure Rules.[23] Usually, the Adjudicator makes directions about both well in advance of the hearing to enable all parties, and the Adjudicator, to have a thorough grasp of the cases being advanced by all parties well in advance of the hearing.

3.83 Normally all parties will be required to serve their skeleton arguments on all other parties and on the Adjudicator by at least seven days before the start of the hearing. In more complex cases, the skeletons may be required earlier than this. As in any civil case a skeleton should contain a summary of the argument which that party wishes to advance together with reference to relevant documents and facts. It should aim to 'define and confine' the issues to be decided by the Adjudicator. The Adjudicator usually requires a number of further documents from the advocate at the same time as the skeleton – unless lengthy, they can form part of the skeleton:

- list of issues to be decided – these should be enumerated as concisely as possible and ideally agreed with any other parties
- chronology of relevant events – ideally an agreed version should be produced, even if it contains items which are disputed and clearly labelled as such
- list of authorities relied upon – advocates should avoid citing authorities unnecessarily; many Adjudications turn entirely upon their facts and authorities are not required
- copies of any authorities cited.

3.84 It is suggested that permission is sought to serve the documents on the Adjudicator in electronic format in the first instance, with hard copies also being provided, or at least available at the hearing. The Adjudicator's Office is very helpful in this regard.

3.85 Preparation of hearing bundles will normally be the responsibility of the applicant unless the applicant is a litigant-in-person and another party is legally represented, in which case the legally represented party may be expected to undertake the task. A common direction is for the person preparing the bundles to write to the other parties 28 days before the hearing asking them to identify which documents they would like to have included, to which the other parties should reply no later than 21 days before the hearing. The bundles are then to be served no later than 14 days before the hearing so that the advocates are able to utilise them in the preparation of skeleton arguments.

3.86 The composition of a hearing bundle will be very similar to that of a civil trial, namely tabulated and paginated lever arch or ring binders containing statements of case, witness statements, any other relevant documents, and relevant correspondence. Care should be taken not to duplicate documents: for example, where the same document has been attached to multiple statements of case and/or witness statements, it should only be included once in the hearing bundle – if necessary it can be replaced by a note directing the user to the appropriate place. Only relevant correspondence should be included, in other words correspondence that has a bearing on the parties' cases (for example by containing an implied admission). Correspondence that relates to costs matters

---

23 Compare, for example, the very detailed guidance in the Chancery Guide.

should not be included nor, obviously, should any without prejudice material. It is absolutely vital that all the hearing bundles contain clear and legible copies of all documents, especially maps and plans of which colour copies must be provided where appropriate.

3.87   A copy of the hearing bundle should be served on each party, and two on the Adjudicator (one being for use by the witnesses at the hearing).

The hearing

3.88   The Adjudicator will have notified the parties of the date, time, location and length of the final hearing[24] by notice served no later than 28 days before the hearing (or sooner by agreement of all parties), possibly after requiring them to provide him with an estimated length of hearing under r 29 of the Procedure Rules. Rule 31 of the Procedure Rules allows the Adjudicator to dispose of any particular matter as a preliminary issue.

3.89   Unless held at the Adjudicator's London Hearing Centre,[25] hearings normally take place at the premises of a court or other tribunal. The Adjudicator's Office effectively books a court room and provides its own staff, so the local court staff may be unaware that the Adjudication is taking place and it will not necessarily have been listed in accordance with the normal local arrangements. This may cause difficulties with opening the court room early to allow parties to take their positions. Legal representatives may therefore want to check arrangements in advance with the court staff.

3.90   If any party does not attend the hearing after having been served with notice of it, the Adjudicator must adjourn the hearing[26] unless he is not satisfied that the reasons for the absence are justified, or the absent party consents, or it would be unjust to adjourn the hearing.

3.91   Parties may represent themselves at the hearing, or they may be represented or assisted by any person whether or not legally qualified.[27] The Adjudicator may however refuse to permit a particular person to conduct such representation or assistance if he is satisfied that there is sufficient reason for doing so.

3.92   Save for the overriding objective, there are no rules that provide guidance as to how a contested hearing should be conducted. Almost always, it will follow the format of a normal civil trial:

- there may be a brief opening statement by one or more of the parties;
- the applicant's evidence will be given in chief by means of the written statements of each witness together with any questions of clarification allowed;
- each of the applicant's witnesses will be cross-examined in turn, if required, followed by any required re-examination;
- the process will be repeated for the respondent's witnesses;
- the respondent will make a closing speech;
- the applicant will make a closing speech.

---

24   Rule 34 of the Procedure Rules.
25   6th Floor Victory House, 34 Kingsway, London WC2B 6EX.
26   Rule 38 of the Procedure Rules.
27   Rule 35 of the Procedure Rules.

3.93 Witnesses will normally give evidence on oath, standing (or sitting) in a traditional witness box. The relevant party's legal representatives (or the party if none) should ascertain in advance what form of oath they wish to take and provide this information to the Adjudicator's staff. It is important to reiterate that witnesses must attend the hearing for the purposes of cross-examination if any weight is to be given to their evidence. It is also vital that witnesses have read and understood their written statements prior to the hearing and that they understand how to navigate around those statements and the hearing bundle. Any mistakes in the witness statements should be identified and corrected at an early stage. It is not normal in Adjudication proceedings for witnesses to wait outside the court room to be called, although an oral application can be made to the Adjudicator if this is felt to be necessary. As stated previously, there is a reluctance to allow supplemental questions in chief at all, especially for the respondent's witnesses since, unless they could be recalled, the applicant's witnesses would not have opportunity to comment on the new evidence.

3.94 The Adjudicator's decision (which will be a 'substantive decision' within the meaning of r 2 of the Procedure Rules) will usually be reserved although r 39 of the Procedure Rules does allow an oral decision to be given at the conclusion of the hearing. It can take up to several months[28] for a reserved decision to appear.

3.95 The decision will usually be in two parts: a substantive order and written reasons.

3.96 An example of a substantive order is at **Figure 3.5**.

---

28   No time limit is specified by the Procedure Rules.

Figure 3.5 Substantive order

REF

THE ADJUDICATOR TO HER MAJESTY'S LAND REGISTRY
LAND REGISTRATION ACT 2002

IN THE MATTER OF A REFERENCE FROM HM LAND REGISTRY

BETWEEN

APPLICANT

and

RESPONDENTS

Property Address:

Made by: Mr Orr sitting as Deputy Adjudicator to HM Land Registry

---

ORDER

The Adjudicator to HM Land Registry orders that:

1.   The Chief Land Registrar do cancel the original Application made by the Applicant in

     form AP1 dated the   for the alteration of Title No.   so

     far as effect has not hitherto been given to the application;

(Figure 3.5 cont)

2. The Applicant shall within 21 days from service of this order serve on the Adjudicator and the Respondents his submissions in writing (if any) as to why he should not pay the costs of the Respondents and as to the basis and manner of the assessment of costs;

3. The Respondents shall within 21 days after service of the Applicant's submissions serve on the Adjudicator and the Applicant their submissions (if any) in response to the submissions of the Applicant.

Dated this

BY ORDER OF THE ADJUDICATOR TO HM LAND REGISTRY

3.97   The substantive order must be in writing, be dated, sealed, state the name of the person who has made the order, state the substantive decision that has been reached, state any steps that must be taken to give effect to the substantive decision, and state the possible consequences of any party's failure to comply. The substantive order must be served by the Adjudicator on every party and, to the extent that it requires him to take any action, on the Registrar.

Typically the substantive order will require the Registrar to give effect to, or cancel, an application either absolutely or in some qualified manner.

3.98   The Adjudicator must also give the reasons for his substantial decision in writing to all parties. These form the Adjudicator's judgment and will usually be contained in a separate document to the substantial order. Such judgments are usually comprehensive and will often include a detailed summary of the facts, the cases presented by both parties, the documents, any site visit that has taken place, and the relevant law, before giving a reasoned decision. The growing number of Adjudicator's decisions thus forms an important contribution to the jurisprudence of real property law.

Costs

3.99   Rules 42 and 43 of the Procedure Rules deal with costs. The issue of costs will not generally arise until after the Adjudicator's substantive decision has been given. The substantive decision will often contain directions for the parties to make submissions on costs and may give an indication of what costs order the Adjudicator considers should be made. The Adjudicator can also make a costs order of his own motion. The Procedure Rules give the Adjudicator wide discretion as to what costs order should be made – in coming to a decision, he must have regard to 'all the circumstances', which is defined by Rule 42 as including conduct of the parties, relative success in the proceedings, and any representations made. A costs order could require one party to pay another party's costs *in toto* or limited to a fixed sum or proportion, or to costs from a particular date.

3.100   The Adjudicator can order costs to be assessed summarily[29] or by assessment in a specified manner in the absence of agreement, and can assess those costs on the standard or indemnity basis – these terms have the same meaning as in civil proceedings, namely:

- standard – only costs which have been reasonably and proportionately incurred will be allowed, and any doubt is to be resolved in favour of the paying party;
- indemnity – all costs reasonably incurred will be allowed and any doubt is to be resolved in favour of the receiving party.

3.101   Representations on costs by the parties will usually take place on paper. There may be as many as six stages to go through before the matter is concluded:

- party A applies for costs in principle
- party B resists the application
- party A responds to party B
- [decision of the Adjudicator on the principle of costs in favour of Party A]
- party A submits a bill of costs
- party B raises points of objection
- party A responds to party B's points of objection
- [decision by the Adjudicator on *quantum* of costs].

---

29 The Adjudicator may direct the receiving party to submit a CPR Form N260 if summary assessment is ordered.

3.102   The Adjudicator also has power under r 43 to order costs thrown away against a party's legal representative. Such an order will be made in circumstances where a party has incurred costs unnecessarily as a result of that legal representative's neglect or delay and it is just in all the circumstances for that legal representative to compensate the party in question for the whole or part of those costs.

3.103   All costs orders must be served on the affected parties in writing.

Appeals[30]

3.104   Appeals from decisions of the Adjudicator lie to the High Court, sitting at the Royal Courts of Justice or one of the regional District Registries with chancery jurisdiction.

3.105   The Adjudicator may grant permission to appeal but must first allow the parties an opportunity to make representations (unlike civil proceedings, where it is generally only the applicant who has *locus standi* on a permission application). Permission can also be sought from the High Court directly. If permission is sought from the Adjudicator (and granted), he has the power to stay the whole or part of his decision pending the outcome of any appeal. If the applicant desires this, he must specifically apply for a stay giving reasons. Written notice must be served by the Adjudicator on all affected parties of any decision to grant permission or to stay a decision in whole or in part.

---

30   Rules 44 and 45 of the Procedure Rules

Chapter 4

Alteration and rectification of the Register

4.01   Most references to the Adjudicator from the Land Registry will have as their source an application to amend the Register in some way, to which an objection has been made. This chapter considers the special rules that apply when a proposed amendment is classed as an 'alteration' or 'rectification' of the Register. *Note that 'rectification' of the Register in this context is entirely distinct from rectification of a document, a distinctive original jurisdiction which the Adjudicator exercises in parallel to the High Court.*

4.02   A major principle underlying the new regime introduced by LRA 2002 is that registration as proprietor – rather than possession – of a piece of land should be the key to proprietary rights. LRA 2002, s 58 states that a legal estate will be vested in a person upon his registration as the proprietor of that legal estate, even if it would not otherwise so vest. This new emphasis on the Register itself as a guarantee and a source of proprietary rights has, on the one hand, increased the importance of ensuring that the Register is accurate and, on the other hand, necessitated a special protocol to be utilised on those occasions when the Register does not reflect the reality.

4.03   It is in that context that Sch 4 to LRA 2002 exists to make provision for alteration of the Register and to introduce the concept of rectification. The full text of Sch 4 can be seen in Appendix 1. Schedule 4 distinguishes between alteration (i) pursuant to a court order and (ii) otherwise than pursuant to a court order, which in practice means by the registrar. In the context of a disputed application to the Land Registry, the decision as to whether to alter the Register or not is effectively made by the Adjudicator, who makes an order requiring the Registrar to allow a particular application or not.

4.04   Both the court and the Registrar can make orders for alteration of the Register for the following reasons:[1]

- Correcting a mistake.
  Examples would be the correction of a typographical error made by the Land Registry, the inclusion of an erroneous entry, the registration of an individual as proprietor where the land in question had already been conveyed to someone else, or the first registration of someone whose predecessor's title had already been barred by adverse possession.
- Bringing the register up to date.
  Examples would be where a document effecting a disposition of the land had been rectified and there was a need to update/amend the details of the proprietor accordingly, where such a document had been rescinded and the previously named proprietor was to be restored (both these examples would not be 'mistakes' within the meaning of the previous section as the relevant entry was correct at the time it was made) or where the land was found to be the subject of (for example) an easement arising by prescription or implied grant.

---

1   LRA 2002, Sch 4, paras 2 and 5.

- Giving effect to any estate, right or interest excepted from the effect of registration.
  These exceptions are set out in LRA 2002, ss 9–12.

4.05 In addition to the above, the Registrar alone has the additional power to alter the Register for the purpose of removing a superfluous entry, in other words one that has ceased to apply. An example would be the removal of an obsolete restriction or charge placed on the title by a mortgage lender.

4.06 All of the above are examples of 'alteration' of the Register. Paragraph 1 of Sch 4 to LRA 2002 introduces, within the 'alteration' category, the new sub-set of 'rectification'. For an alteration to be also a rectification it must (a) involve the correction of a mistake and (b) prejudicially affect the title of a registered proprietor. Instances of rectification, being corrections of a mistake, may allow an individual to make a claim under the Land Registry's indemnity policy as provided in LRA 2002, Sch 8. Note that rectification of the Register does *not* take effect retrospectively.

4.07 The special provisions relating to rectification of the Register, in so far as they apply to the Registrar's powers, are set out in LRA 2002, Sch 6, para 6(2). Essentially, rectification can only be ordered in one of three circumstances:

- where the registered proprietor consents;
- where the registered proprietor has by fraud or lack of proper care caused or contributed to the mistake; or
- if it would for any other reason be unjust for the alteration not to be made.

4.08 Paragraph 6(2) of Sch 4 only applies to land which is in the possession of a registered proprietor. In this respect, LRA 2002, s 131(1) states:

'For the purposes of [LRA 2002], land is in the possession of a proprietor of a registered estate if it is physically in his possession or in that of a person who is entitled to be registered as the proprietor of the registered estate.'

Land is physically in someone's possession if that person exercises an appropriate degree of physical control over it, depending on the factual circumstances, as set out in *JA Pye (Oxford) Limited v Graham*.[2]

4.09 If the application for rectification does satisfy one or more of the conditions set out in Sch 4, para 6(2), para 6(3) provides that the application must be approved, unless there are exceptional circumstances which justify not making the alteration.

4.10 The 'exceptional circumstances' criterion could perhaps be regarded as something of a *carte blanche* for the Registrar's/Adjudicator's discretion and the LRA 2002 gives no guidance on how it is to be interpreted.

4.11 An example of the potential application of the 'exceptional circumstances' criterion can be seen in the following recently decided (unreported) case. A registered proprietor (A) was repeatedly assured by the Land Registry, despite his own misgivings, that a specific parcel of land (L) fell within his own registered title and that, under the new regime introduced

---

2   [2003] 1 AC 419, approving the dictum of Slade J in *Powell v McFarlane* (1977) 38 P & CR 452 at 470–1.

by LRA 2002, that title was indefeasible. In reliance on those assurances, and a complete lack of interest from the adjacent landowner (B) when the matter was mentioned to B, A built upon part of L and used the remainder of L for access. B later applied to register himself as proprietor of L based on historic conveyancing documents which did indeed prove B's title. The case was clearly one of rectification since it involved the correction of a mistake and was prejudicial to the registered proprietor of L. A did not consent to the application, and there was no suggestion that he had contributed to the mistake by fraud or carelessness. The matter went before the Adjudicator, who held that A's title should not be rectified. It was, however, unclear whether this was because B had failed to overcome the threshold of para 6(2) – namely that it would be unjust for the alteration not to be made – or because A succeeded under para 6(3), there being exceptional circumstances which justified not making the order. The Adjudicator appears to have conducted a balancing exercise taking both sections into account and decided that on the exceptional facts of the case, A's title should not be rectified. As a result of the decision, B was, presumably, entitled to make a claim against the Land Registry's indemnity policy under the Sch 8 provisions on the basis that A had been incorrectly registered as proprietior of L and this caused B loss.

4.12   Costs in successful rectification cases would normally be covered by the indemnity provisions of Sch 8, being part of the loss suffered. Schedule 4, para 9 makes specific provisions about costs in non-rectification cases. The Registrar is given the power to pay such amount as he thinks fit in respect of costs or expenses reasonably incurred by a person in connection with the alteration:

- if incurred with the consent of the Registrar; or
- if the costs/expenses had to be incurred urgently and it was not practicable to apply for the Registrar's consent; or
- the Registrar has subsequently approved the costs/expenses.

Chapter 5

The Adjudicator's powers on a reference

5.01   The establishment of the Adjudicator has resulted in a large volume of litigation relating to the law of land registration and real property being diverted from the courts to the Adjudicator by means of references from the Land Registry. In this chapter the important question of the difference in the Adjudicator's powers on a reference compared to those of a court is considered.

5.02   References from the Land Registry comprise the vast majority of the Adjudicator's case load. As examined in Chapter 3, parties will usually be thrust straight into adjudication proceedings following an application to the Land Registry which has been objected to, where the objection cannot be disposed of summarily by the Land Registry, or by agreement. The purpose of the reference, and of the adjudication which results, is to determine what effect should be given to a particular application or objection and how, if at all, the Register should be amended to reflect this. However, if the matter proceeds to a contested hearing, the Adjudicator will almost always be determining matters of fact and law which go beyond the details that will be entered on the Register.

5.03   In *The Chief Land Registrar v Silkstone and Others*,[1] the Court of Appeal gave crucial guidance as to the procedure before the Adjudicator and the parameters within which the Adjudicator operates. In particular, the Court held that the Adjudicator has the jurisdiction to determine the merits underlying the application unless he refers the issue to the court to be determined.[2] Thus a factual issue decided by the Adjudicator would appear to be *res judicata* for the purpose of any future court proceedings, subject to any appeal.

5.04   The question follows as to why the Adjudicator does not simply take over from the courts of first instance as the primary arbiter of real property disputes that take place in respect of registered land. The obvious point is that parties cannot elect to start proceedings before the Adjudicator; proceedings can only commence by reference from the Land Registry. However, parties will often be aware before making an application to the Land Registry whether or not it is likely to be disputed and, if they are knowledgeable in the field and/or being properly advised, it will be obvious that a particular dispute is likely to be referred to the Adjudicator. It is therefore important for parties to be aware of the limits to the Adjudicator's powers on a Land Registry reference.

5.05   In Chapter 3, the view was expressed that the case summary prepared by the Land Registry is of considerable importance since it effectively defines the subject of the reference, and thus the Adjudicator's jurisdiction in relation to a particular reference. The case summary itself will succinctly encapsulate the matters in dispute from the original application to the Land Registry and the objection(s) to it. Certainly the Adjudicator does not have the overarching powers of the court effectively to make any order that is deemed to be just,

---

1   [2011] EWCA Civ 801.
2   See especially [48], per Rimer LJ.

including any order of its own motion. The statutory source of the Adjudicator's principal jurisdiction provides only for the resolution of the matter referred by the Land Registry. So parties who contemplate taking a course which is likely to result in a reference to the Adjudicator should first of all be aware that they are not likely to be able to expand the reference to encompass other, related, areas of dispute. It would of course be possible for an application to be made at case management stage for multiple disputed applications to be joined for the purpose of a final hearing.

5.06   It may, however, happen that the parties reach a final hearing and, whether as a result of a mistake, oversight, or otherwise, there is some technical omission in the original application to the Land Registry and/or the case summary which leaves open the possibility that the Adjudicator may not technically have the power to determine the whole of the dispute between the parties. In this case, it is suggested that there may be benefit in the Adjudicator's being invited to determine the whole of the factual dispute between the parties even if the Adjudicator's power to make an order in relation to the entire dispute is circumscribed by the application.

5.07   An example of this would be where the area of land defined in the application did not encompass the entirety of the land over which there was a dispute. This may be because of a badly drawn plan or because a particular title number was inadvertently omitted. Any findings of fact by the Adjudicator in relation to the land omitted from the ambit of the application are likely to be persuasive and, if necessary could be prayed in aid of a further application or court proceedings.

5.08   Nonetheless, it is important for practitioners to recognise that, because the Adjudicator's jurisdiction is not an original one, the Adjudicator has no power to allow the scope of the reference, once made, to be widened. Although amendments to statements of case and other documents can be allowed in accordance with the Procedure Rules, this will not achieve a widening of the reference in the same way as would amendments to court pleadings.

5.09   Practitioners should also be aware that the only powers that the Adjudicator has on a reference are to instruct the Registrar to give effect to or reject an application in whole or in part, and to award costs in relation to the proceedings before the Adjudicator (not the Land Registry). The Adjudicator cannot give any other form of relief, as has already been highlighted in Chapters 2 and 3. For that reason, parties will still need to commence court proceedings notwithstanding the likely higher cost of those proceedings if they are seeking injunctive or declaratory relief, damages, or an order for sale. There is, however, no reason why an application for rectification of a document which the Adjudicator has power to rectify cannot be commenced (this is the Adjudicator's only source of original jurisdiction) and then joined with a related Land Registry reference.

5.10   In appropriate circumstances, the Adjudicator will direct one of the parties to commence court proceedings. This may save the parties the expense of an adjudication resulting in a factual determination and appropriate amendment to the Register, followed by further court proceedings to obtain relief. See Chapter 3 for the relevant procedure.

5.11   An example would be where A and B, who are not married to each other, cohabit in a property as man and wife. The property is held in A's sole name. After a number of years the relationship breaks down. B applies to the

Land Registry to protect her interest in the property based on resulting trust (contributions to the purchase price), constructive trust (numerous discussions throughout the relationship that the property would be 'theirs') and proprietary estoppel (B's selling her own property to move in with A on the strength of a representation that the quasi-marital home would be 'theirs'). A objects to B's application and the matter is referred to the Adjudicator. There are numerous factual and legal disputes in B's application which can be resolved by the Adjudicator. However, the Adjudicator has no power to order a sale of the property under s 14 of the Trusts of Land and Appointment of Trustees Act 1996, which is what B really wants. It would be more cost effective for the parties to be directed to commence court proceedings, as the court is in a position to determine the matter and grant the appropriate relief at the same time. Once the matter has been determined factually by the court, the Adjudicator's function will then be simply to instruct the Registrar to make any appropriate amendments to the Register, and to deal with any outstanding costs.

Chapter 6

The Adjudicator online

6.01   A substantial amount of material pertinent to hearings before the Adjudicator can be found online. In the first years of the Adjudicator's existence, there was a dedicated website at www.ahmlr.gov.uk. This has now been superseded by, and incorporated into, the 'Tribunals' section of the Ministry of Justice website, at http://www.justice.gov.uk/tribunals/ahmlr, as shown in **Figure 6.1**.

Figure 6.1 AHMLR website

Tribunals Service | Feedback | Search | Contact us

Tribunals Service
Adjudicator to HM Land Registry

Approved by the Plain English Campaign
Wednesday 23 January 2013

About us   Decisions   Forms & Guidance   Rules & Legislation   Hearing Centre   Useful links

You are here > Home > Forms & Guidance

In this section

Forms
Explanatory Leaflet
Mock Statements
Flowcharts
Appeals & Stays

Forms & Guidance

Forms

Use this form if you want to correct a document that relates to registered land
ALR Rectification Application Form (45kb)

Use this form if someone else wants to correct a document and you don't agree
ALR Objection to Rectification Application Form (35kb)

Explanatory Leaflet

This leaflet aims to give you helpful information on what we do. It is not a substitute for the Act or the Rules and has no legal power. If you are not sure about your position or your options, you should contact us or get professional legal advice.

A Short Guide for Users (92kb)
This version of the guide covers cases received by the Adjudicator on or before 31 December 2007

Short guide for users for cases commencing January 2008 (92kb)
This version of the guide covers cases received by the Adjudicator on or after 1 January 2008 but before 25 August 2008

Short guide for users for cases commencing after 25 August 2008 (96kb)
This version of the guide covers cases received by the Adjudicator on or after 25 August 2008

Guidance to the amended Practice and Procedure Rules (71kb)

Back to top

Mock Statements

Mock Statement of Case – Applicant (118kb)
Mock Statement of Case – Applicant (received after 25 August 2008) (61kb)
Mock Statement of Case – Respondent (115kb)
Mock Statement of Case – Respondent (received after 25 August 2008) (61kb)
Mock Witness Statement (30kb)

Back to top

Flowcharts

The flowcharts below are intended to explain the process of an appeal. Further information can be obtained from your local Citizens Advice Bureau

Adjudicator intends to direct the applicant to commence court proceedings (56kb)
Where either party has already commenced court proceedings (76kb)
Case retained by the Adjudicator, statement of case procedure (62kb)
Extension of time procedure (21kb)

Back to top

Appeals & Stays

This document was last updated on 6 December 2006

Information on Appeals & Stays (25kb)

6.02   The new website appears, at the time of writing, to be something of a work in progress. In particular, a preserved 'snapshot' of the old website is available via a link from the new website to the National Archives website – this can be accessed via the new website or directly at http://webarchive.nationalarchives.gov.uk/20110119215424/http://www.ahmlr.gov.uk/formsguidance.htm, as shown in **Figure 6.2**.

Figure 6.2 Archived website

6.03   Essentially the same information is contained on both versions of the website, although the old website is no longer being updated. Presumably the link is a temporary solution until the new website takes its final shape.

6.04   The main sources of information available online are set out below. Unless otherwise stated, references are to the new website shown in Figure 6.1. The effective homepage, which is accessed via the 'Adjudicator to HM Land Registry' tab on the left-hand side of the website gives some brief details about the Adjudicator and the relationship with the Land Registry.

ACCESSING INFORMATION

6.05   Much of the remaining information is presently accessed via the 'Appeals' tab on the left-hand side of the website and this is indicated in the text below.

Explanatory leaflets (via Appeals tab)

6.06   A useful starting point for a practitioner who is new to this area or a litigant in person is the Short Guide for Users. This comes in a .PDF document of less than 1mb or 20 pages. There are three versions depending on the date on which the relevant proceedings were received by the Adjudicator:

- on or before 31 December 2007;
- from 1 January 2008 until 24 August 2008 inclusive;
- from 25 August 2008.

6.07   The Guide contains a summary of the procedure used in reference and rectification cases together with a short glossary and contact details. As the website preamble states, however, it is not a substitute for the relevant legislation. The different versions of the Guide are largely a result of the 2008 amendments to the Procedure Rules.

6.08   The Procedure Rules (as amended) can also be found in this section of the website in a .PDF document marked as 'Guidance to the Amended Practice and Procedure Rules'. This is a composite copy of the Procedure Rules prepared by the Adjudicator's office – it does not contain any 'guidance' as such – which is useful because there is no 'official' document containing the amended rules.

Mock statements of case (via Appeals tab)

6.09   The website contains mock statements of case for applicant and respondent, again divided into those applicable before and after the 2008 amendments to the Procedure Rules came into force. The mock statements are based on an adverse possession claim and are useful templates for those who have not previously drafted such documents. Further examples are at Figure 3.4 and Figure 3.5 in Chapter 3.

Flowcharts (via Appeals tab)

6.10   The basic adjudication procedure can be unfamiliar territory for many experienced practitioners. To assist, the website includes a series of flowcharts illustrating the basic steps to be taken at various stages:

- when the applicant is directed to commence court proceedings;
- when either party has already commenced court proceedings;
- statement of case procedure where cases are retained by the Adjudicator;
- procedure for extension of time.

Forms (via Appeals tab, also via Forms tab on right-hand side)

6.11   This section gives access to the specimen Rectification Application Form and the specimen Objection to Rectification Application Form. The forms are in .PDF format and cannot presently be completed electronically.

6.12   The Rectification Application Form is the only originating process that can be submitted to the Adjudicator directly.

Appeals and stays (via Appeals tab)

6.13   There is a short note containing information on appeals and stays. See further Chapter 3 for the relevant procedure.

Venues

6.14   This tab gives details of the London Hearing Centre at Victory House, Kingsway including directions by road, rail, underground and bus.

6.15   At the time of writing, there is a link to the old Tribunals' Service 'venue finder' for venues outside London where the user is invited to search by postcode. However, this proves unhelpful in identifying any actual venues, at least as far as the Adjudicator is concerned! As explained in Chapter 3, current practice for references seems to be for the Adjudicator's Office to hire a room in the nearest venue operated by HM Courts and Tribunals Service to the land which is the subject of the reference.

Decisions

6.16   This is a very useful feature of the Adjudicator's online service, since it provides a fully referenced and searchable bank of decisions. To quote directly from the site:

'Only a small proportion of the decisions of the Adjudicator are included on this website. They are added only if the Adjudicator considers that either

(1)   they contain a statement of law or practice that is of general interest, and may be of assistance to other parties using the website or

(2)   they decide points of law which have not, so far as the Adjudicator has been able to ascertain, been the subject of any other decision or

(3)   they are in some other way of general importance.'

6.17   Cases can be searched by the Adjudicator's name, date, case reference, or by the following specific categories, each of which is divided into relevant sub-categories:

- adverse possession;
- alteration and rectification of the Register;
- beneficial interests, trusts and restrictions;
- boundary disputes;
- charges and charging orders;
- compulsory purchase;
- contracts and options;
- costs;
- deeds;
- easements and profits à prendre;
- estoppel;
- evidence;
- fraud, forgery, duress and undue influence;
- highways and public rights of way;
- leases and licences;
- manorial rights;
- practice and procedure;
- restrictive covenants;
- rivers, waterways and foreshore;
- rectification or setting aside of documents;
- Network Access Agreements.

It is also possible to search by the name of applicant or respondent, or by key words from the decision notes which are set out on the Decision Summary page.

6.18   A successful search will produce a list of results in tabular form with details of the decision date, case reference, Adjudicator's name, and categories. It is then possible to click to see the Decision Summary, which gives details of the applicant and respondent, and notes on the decision – generally key words and phrases which enable the decision to be identified on a search. The decision itself can then be viewed, in read-only 'Word' format.

Rules and legislation

6.19   The website contains links to the following legislation (at www. legislation.gov.uk):

- Land Registration Act 2002
- Land Registration Rules 2003 (as amended)
- Adjudicator to HM Land Registry (Practice & Procedure) Rules 2003
- Adjudicator to Her Majesty's Land Registry (Practice and Procedure) (Amendment) Rules 2008
- Network Access Appeal Rules 2008.

As stated above, the unofficial amended (ie composite) version of the Procedure Rules is available only via the 'Appeals' tab.

Related pages

6.20   On the right-hand side of the website are two links to 'related pages'. The first, marked Forms, contains the rectification forms which can also be accessed via the 'Appeals' tab.

6.21   The second, marked 'Contacts', gives contact details for public enquiries, and also contains links to the following general HM Courts and Tribunals Service publications in .PDF format:

- 'I want to complain – what to I do?' (Leaflet EX343)
- Complaint Form (EX343a) (which can be completed electronically but not saved)
- Customer Service Standards.

The archived site

6.22   The archived site – available via a link in the right-hand side of the main website – largely duplicates information available on the main website save that it is no longer updated. However, the following additional material is available:

- Mock Witness Statement (via Forms & Guidance tab) – this is necessarily sketchy but contains some important pointers;
- a 'Useful Links' tab which contains links to, and summaries of, Land Registry and justice-related websites; however (as per the warning at the top of the page), some of the links are out-of-date or do not function properly within the archived site.

Chapter 7

Adverse possession

INTRODUCTION

7.01   Cases involving adverse possession often fall to be considered by the Adjudicator. For example, a person in possession of unregistered land can apply for first registration on the grounds of holding a possessory title.[1] Similarly an objection can be made to an application for first registration of land on the grounds that another holds possessory title.[2] Boundary disputes also regularly involve a consideration of adverse possession in determining where exact boundaries lie.[3] When called upon to settle such disputes, the Adjudicator will follow the law as laid down by common law and statute.

7.02   LRA 2002 significantly changed the law of adverse possession. However, many disputes inevitably stem from actions before LRA 2002 came into force,[4] and these are still subject to the previous legal regime. Knowledge of both regimes is essential for the property law practitioner, as is an understanding of how the Adjudicator determines what constitutes 'adverse possession'.

THE MEANING OF 'ADVERSE POSSESSION'

7.03   The meaning of adverse possession is essentially the same under both regimes,[5] subject to some minor exceptions.[6]

7.04   Adverse possession is possession by a party which is inconsistent with and in denial of the title of the true owner.[7] The term 'adverse' means that possession must be without the consent or license of the true owner or enabled by a contractual instrument or trust. Such possession will involve the dispossession or discontinuance of possession by the owner and the commencement of possession by the squatter.

7.05   To establish adverse possession the squatter must demonstrate two things:

- factual possession;
- *animus possidendi* (intention to possess).[8]

---

1   See eg *Rees v Devon County Council & Brayford Parish Council* [2009] REF/2007/1185.
2   See eg *Abbs & Marie v Eldridge & Eldridge* [2011] REF/2010/1166.
3   See eg *Crosdil v Hodder* [2011] REF/2009/1177.
4   On 13 October 2003.
5   LRA 2002, Sch 6, para 11 and Limitation Act 1980, s 15.
6   These include the rules as to successive squatters and acknowledgment of title (considered below). See also LRA 2002, Sch 6, para 11.
7   *Wilson v Martin's Exors* [1933] 1 EGLR 178 at 179.
8   *Powell v McFarlane* (1977) 38 P & CR 452 at 470.

Factual possession

7.06   Factual possession requires an appropriate degree of physical control of the land. It must be a single possession which can be by either one squatter or several squatters consecutively.[9] Further, the possession must be exclusive; the squatter cannot be in possession simultaneously with the owner. The squatter must deal with the land as an owner would be expected to do.[10]

7.07   An obvious indicator of factual possession is the physical enclosure of the land;[11] however, this is neither indispensable nor conclusive. Other indicators of factual possession include cultivating or farming the land; however, what constitutes factual possession will vary greatly depending on the characteristics of the land in question.[12] The resources of a squatter are irrelevant.[13]

7.08   Another common consideration is whether the squatter, by his actions, clearly manifests his intention to possess the land.[14]

Intention to possess

7.09   As well as factually possessing the land, the squatter must intend to possess the land. This state of mind is known as *animus possidendi*. The squatter must have an intention to exclude the world at large, including the owner, so far as is reasonably practicable and so far as the law will allow.[15] This intention only has to be for the time being, so it does not have to cover all future circumstances. For example, a squatter who would be willing to pay for the land if requested to do so in the future is not incapable of being in adverse possession.[16]

7.10   The squatter need not have an intention to own the land, the intention to possess is sufficient.[17] Similarly, the focus is placed on the intention to possess, not dispossess.[18] Accordingly, the requisite intention can be established in a situation where a squatter mistakenly believes he is the true owner of the land.

7.11   The standard which the Adjudicator will apply in determining whether or not the squatter has evidenced the necessary factual possession and intention to possess is a relatively high one. Clear and affirmative evidence is required.[19] Should the squatter's actions be open to an interpretation other than his intention to possess, he will not be deemed to have the requisite *animus possidendi*.

---

9   See para **7.35** below for the rules on successive squatters.
10   *Ibid.*
11   *Seddon v Smith* (1877) 36 LT 168.
12   *Powell v McFarlane* (1977) 38 P & CR 452 at 471.
13   *West Bank Estates* [1967] 1 AC 665 at 678B.
14   *Lambeth LBC v Blackburn* [2001] 82 P & CR 494 at 499.
15   *Powell v McFarlane* (1977) 38 P & CR 452 at 470.
16   *Ocean Estates v Pinder* [1969] 2 AC 19 at 24.
17   *JA Pye (Oxford) Ltd v Graham* [2002]UKHL 30 at [42].
18   *Hughes v Cork* [1994] E.G.C.S. 25, per Beldam LJ.
19   *Powell v McFarlane* (1977) 38 P & CR 452 at 472.

THE CONSEQUENCES OF ADVERSE POSSESSION

The 'old' regime (before LRA 2002)

7.12   Section 15 of the Limitation Act 1980 provides:

'No action shall be brought by any person to recover any land after the expiration of twelve years from the date on which the right of action accrued to him ...'

Section 17 of the Limitation Act 1980 provides:

'At the expiration of the period prescribed by this Act for any person to bring an action to recover land ... the title of that person to the land shall be extinguished.'

Thus, in the case of unregistered land, where a squatter has adversely possessed land for 12 years, the true owner's title is extinguished and the squatter acquires possessory title capable of registration.[20] Once the true owner's title is extinguished, it cannot be revived by regaining possession. It is important to remember that the title is extinguished only as against the squatter, not third parties.

7.13   For registered land, the effect of adversely possessing the land is slightly different. LRA 1925, s 75 provides:

'(1) The Limitation Acts shall apply to registered land in the same manner and to the same extent as those Acts apply to land not registered, except that where, if the land were not registered, the estate of the person registered as proprietor would be extinguished, such estate shall not be extinguished but shall be deemed to be held by the proprietor for the time being in trust for the person who, by virtue of the said Acts, has acquired title against any proprietor, but without prejudice to the estates and interests of any other person interested in the land whose estate or interest is not extinguished by those Acts.

(2) Any person claiming to have acquired a title under the Limitation Acts to a registered estate in the land may apply to be registered as proprietor thereof.'

The trust instrument was used because, where land is registered, the owner's title cannot be extinguished until the register has been altered. The trust ensured, however, that, until the register was altered, the original owner no longer retained beneficial title to the land; this lay with the squatter.

7.14   However, this state of affairs was deemed unsatisfactory as the register became unreliable. This consideration influenced a radical restructuring of the rules of adverse possession and the LRA 2002 introduced a new regime. Before looking at the new regime, it is necessary to consider the transitional arrangements put in place.

Transitional arrangements

7.15   The regime for unregistered land was unchanged by LRA 2002, save for one modification. This change deals with the situation where the paper

---

20   LRA 2002, s 3(2).

owner sells unregistered land. Under LRA 1925 the registered proprietor would take subject to a squatter's possessory title.[21] This remained the case until three years after LRA 2002 came into force.[22] After this date,[23] a possessory title only overrides a first registration where the squatter is in actual occupation[24] or the purchaser has notice of the occupation.[25]

7.16   As regards registered land, LRA 2002, Sch 12 provides:

'(1)   Where a registered estate in land is held in trust for a person by virtue of section 75(1) of the Land Registration Act 1925 immediately before the coming into force of section 97,[26] he is entitled to be registered as the proprietor of the estate.

(2)   A person has a defence to any action for the possession of land (in addition to any other defence he may have) if he is entitled under this paragraph to be registered as the proprietor of an estate in the land.

(3)   Where in an action for possession of land a court determines that a person is entitled to a defence under this paragraph, the court must order the registrar to register him as the proprietor of the estate in relation to which he is entitled under this paragraph to be registered ...'[27]

Thus any person who can show that he was in adverse possession of land for 12 years or more prior to 3 October 2003 is entitled to be registered as owner.

The 'new' regime

7.17   LRA 2002 imposed a new adverse possession regime for registered land. The rules are contained primarily in Sch 6 to LRA 2002. However, the starting point is to be found in s 96 which provides:

'(1)   No period of limitation under section 15 of the Limitation Act 1980 (time limits in relation to recovery of land) shall run against any person, other than a chargee, in relation to an estate in land or rentcharge the title to which is registered.

...

(3)   Accordingly, section 17 of that Act (extinction of title on expiry of time limit) does not operate to extinguish the title of any person where, by virtue of this section, a period of limitation does not run against him.'

Thus the automatic acquisition of possessory title after 12 years of adverse possession is no longer possible. A squatter is however, able to apply for registration in accordance with the provisions of Sch 6 to LRA 2002.

Schedule 6 to LRA 2002

7.18   The most obvious change made to the law of adverse possession by Sch 6 is that the limitation period for registered land is reduced from 12 to 10 years:

---

21   LRA 1925, s 70(1), (6).
22   LRA 2002, Sch 12, para 7.
23   Ie after 3 October 2006.
24   LRA 2002, s 11(4)(b).
25   LRA 2002, s 11(4)(c).
26   This section came into force on 3 October 2003.
27   Paragraph 18.

'1(1)A person may apply to the registrar to be registered as the proprietor of a registered estate in land if he has been in adverse possession of the estate for the period of ten years ending on the date of the application ...'[28]

7.19 Another key change is that the adverse possession has to be proximate to the application for registration. Previously, one would only need to prove that at some point in the past the squatter had enjoyed 12 consecutive years of adverse possession, even if such possession had ended. Under Sch 6, unless a squatter has been evicted (other than pursuant to a judgment for possession) by the registered owner in the period of six months immediately prior to the date of an application made under para 1(1), he will not be able to make an application for registration if he has relinquished possession.[29]

7.20 A squatter who is a defendant in proceedings which involve asserting a right to possession of the land in question will not be able to make an application under para 1(1).[30] Similarly, a squatter is unable to make an application where judgment for possession has been given against him in the last two years.[31]

7.21 Should a squatter make an application to become the registered proprietor under para 1(1), the registrar must give notice of the application to the list of persons detailed in para 2(1), which includes the registered proprietor and any registered chargees.[32] Such notice must inform these parties that unless they require the application to be dealt with under Sch 6, para 5, the applicant is entitled to be registered as the new proprietor of the estate.[33] Essentially this means that unless one of the parties given notice of the application objects to the application, it will succeed. The objection must be made by 12 noon on the 65th business day after the date of notice.[34]

7.22 Any objection must be contained within Form NAP, which will be included within the registrar's notice.[35]

7.23 Where the applicant is registered in the absence of objections, he will take the property free of any registered charges.[36]

Objecting to an application for registration

7.24 Many applications will be objected to under para 4. Where an objection has been lodged the applicant is only entitled to be registered if one of the following three conditions applies:

'5(2)The first condition is that—
    (a) it would be unconscionable because of an equity by estoppel for the registered proprietor to seek to dispossess the applicant, and
    (b) the circumstances are such that the applicant ought to be registered as the proprietor.

---

28   LRA 2002, Sch 6, para 1(1).
29   *Ibid,* para 1(2).
30   *Ibid,* para 1(3)(a).
31   *Ibid,* para 1(3)(b).
32   *Ibid,* para 2.
33   *Ibid,* para 2(2) and para 4.
34   LRR 2003, r 189.
35   *Ibid,* r 190.
36   LRA 2002, Sch 6, para 9(3).

(3) The second condition is that the applicant is for some other reason entitled to be registered as the proprietor of the estate.

(4) The third condition is that –

(a) the land to which the application relates is adjacent to land belonging to the applicant,

(b) the exact line of the boundary between the two has not been determined under rules under section 60,

(c) for at least ten years of the period of adverse possession ending on the date of the application, the applicant (or any predecessor in title) reasonably believed that the land to which the application relates belonged to him, and

(d) the estate to which the application relates was registered more than one year prior to the date of the application.'[37]

If none of these circumstances is made out then the application will be rejected. If the application is successful on one of the above grounds then the applicant will take subject to any interest affecting the estate.[38]

Estoppel

7.25   An example of an application which may succeed on grounds of estoppel is where a squatter mistakenly builds on a neighbour's land, thinking it to be his own, and the neighbour, despite realising the squatter's mistake, acquiesces in it.[39]

7.26   In practice, para 5(2) is of little significance; if an applicant can establish proprietary estoppel he has no need to rely on the provisions for adverse possession and can bring court proceedings in the usual manner. However, making an application to the Adjudicator may prove a less expensive route of achieving the desired result.

7.27   If the Adjudicator determines that an equity by estoppel does arise, however, the circumstances do not justify the registration of the squatter as proprietor; LRA 2002, s 110(4) allows for the Adjudicator to grant a lesser remedy.[40]

'Some other reason'

7.28   There are no limitations as to what this 'other reason' might be, however the Adjudicator has considered what types of application will qualify as displaying 'some other reason' for entitlement to registration under para 5(3), and in the case of *Crosdil v Hodder*[41] the Adjudicator stated that:

'It is worth noting that para 14.43 of the Law Commission Report No 271 (2001) gives two examples where the condition might be satisfied. The first is where the applicant is entitled to the land under the will or intestacy of the deceased proprietor but is on the land without the consent of the deceased's personal representatives, and the second is where the applicant contracted to buy the land and paid the purchase price, but the land was never transferred to him ...'

---

37 *Ibid,* para 5.
38 *Ibid,* para 9(2).
39 (2001) Law Com Final Report No 271, para 14.40.
40 LRA 2002, s 110(4).
41 *Crosdil v Hodder* [2011] REF/2009/1177.

The Adjudicator went on to use this information to explain how para 5(3) should be applied:

> '... It can of course be said that in both these instances the claimant or applicant can obtain a remedy without having to rely on adverse possession. But the examples given tend to suggest that this condition was intended to be interpreted narrowly.'[42]

Paragraph 5(3) will therefore apply where a squatter who has been in adverse possession for 10 or more years is also entitled to be registered for some other reason (other than proprietary estoppel). Again, court proceedings could be issued to consider his 'other reason' for entitlement, but applying under the adverse possession regime means that all his reasons for entitlement, including having adverse possession, can be dealt with in the same forum.

Boundary disputes

7.29   The purpose of para 5(4) is to deal with the situation where the legal boundaries do not match exactly with physical boundaries as laid out on the ground.

7.30   If the exact boundary has been determined under LRA 2002, s 60 the squatter's application will fail. However, the wording of para 5(4) suggests that any determination of boundary not made in accordance with s 60 (ie before the enactment of LRA 2002) will not result in the failure of the squatter's application.

7.31   The Adjudicator has given guidance on how a squatter's 'reasonable belief' will be judged:

> 'The question is not whether a better-informed or advised person might have come to a different view [of ownership]. It is whether the Applicants' belief was reasonable or unreasonable.'[43]

The reasonable belief needs to be held for 10 years, although the period of adverse possession may exceed this. However, unsurprisingly, there is no requirement that the belief should persist up to the date of the application.[44]

Further applications for registration

7.32   If an applicant's first application is rejected he has the ability to re-apply after a further two years have elapsed.[45] However, this second application cannot be made if the applicant is a defendant in proceedings which involve asserting a right to possession of the land in question, a judgment for possession of the land in question has been given against him in the past two years or if he has been evicted from the land pursuant to a judgment for possession.[46]

7.33   If an applicant has remained in adverse possession and is able to make this second application, he is entitled to be entered in the register as the new proprietor of the estate. The new rules thus give the registered owner, or other

---

42   *Ibid,* at para 30.
43   *Osborne v Lawton, Noyes & Fawcett* [2011] REF/2010/1066 at para 9.
44   *Davies v John Wood Property Plc* [2010] REF/2008/0528 at para 48.
45   LRA 2002, Sch 6, para 6(1).
46   LRA 2002, Sch 6, para 6(2).

interested party, two years to regain possession of the land before the squatter is entitled to be registered. This encourages an owner not to sleep on his rights and ensures that land remains economically viable.

Interruption of the 12 year period

7.34   Before the introduction of the new regime, a period of adverse possession would be interrupted by a written acknowledgment by the squatter of the owner's title.[47] However, under the new regime such an acknowledgment will not cause time to run afresh.[48] This safeguard is no longer required as an owner will no longer be subject to automatic extinguishment of his title after a prolonged period of adverse possession. Any acknowledgment may still be relevant, however, in determining whether a squatter has the necessary intention to possess.

Successive squatters

7.35   Under the old regime periods of adverse possession by successive squatters could be aggregated provided there was no break in possession.[49] The new regime, however, states that a person is regarded as having been in adverse possession where:

- he is the successor in title to an estate in land, during any period of adverse possession by a predecessor in title to that estate; or
- during any period of adverse possession by another person which comes between, and is with, periods of adverse possession of his own.[50]

For example, if A dispossesses the owner, O, and enjoys possession for six years and is in turn dispossessed by B who enjoys possession for a further four years, B has not enjoyed possession for the requisite 10 year period unless he is the successor in title to A. If A then dispossessed B, A would be entitled to apply for registration under the second condition above even though A personally has not been in adverse possession for the full 10 years.

---

47 Limitation Act 1980, s 29.
48 Of course, it may still be of consideration when dealing with unregistered land, a chargee of a registered title or registered titles where the limitation period had not expired before 13 October 2003 (ie situations where the new regime does not apply). See REF/2008/1668/1669.
49 Limitation Act 1980. Sch 1, para 8(2).
50 LRA 2002, Sch 6, para 11(2).

Chapter 8

Boundary disputes

8.01   Boundary disputes are some of the most fiercely contested and emotive of all disputes involving property.[1] This is especially true where the dispute is between the owners of neighbouring residential properties. The dispute may arise as a result of the erection of a new garden fence, the moving of an existing fence, the cutting down of a hedge, or some other perceived encroachment onto the neighbour's property. The actual amount of land in dispute will very often be miniscule, with the alternative versions of the boundary perhaps differing by a matter of inches only. In fact, such disputes are typically reflective of a long history of poor neighbour relations which eventually crystallises legally with the perceived encroachment.

8.02   Whether the parties end up before a court, or before the Adjudicator, in many cases the costs of the proceedings will far outweigh any legal benefit to be gained, although, given the emotive nature of the disputes, parties may regard even pyrrhic victories as justifying the means. As Sedley LJ put it in *Strachey v Ramage*:[2]

> 'When Lord Hoffmann ... spoke of litigation conducted with the zeal of Fortinbras's army, he will have had in mind ... the little patch of ground That hath no profit in it but the name. In the present case a poorly drawn conveyance left in doubt the ownership of a patch of ground a fraction of an acre in size. Neither party, so far as one can tell, needed to own it in order to enjoy the use of the rest of their land, though both found its use convenient. Whichever of them held title to it, an easement of use or access should have satisfied the other's needs. But instead of reaching a compromise along these lines, war was declared. Unlike Old Caspar after Blenheim, we can now tell who won; but whether the expenditure on law and lawyers, vastly exceeding the value of the piece of land, has been worthwhile one has to doubt.'

8.03   Historically, and in the case of unregistered land, the boundary of a property would be identified from its title deeds. There would be two chief means of identification:

- the 'parcels clause', a verbal description of the property by reference to physical features on the ground;
- one or more plans on which the property boundary was marked, usually – though not always – in relation to the surrounding plots of land.

8.04   The parcels clause and plan(s) are normally to be found in conveyances, being the documents which actually effect the transfer of land. Later conveyances commonly refer to a plan, or a form of wording, which appear in an earlier document. Interpretation issues will arise if the parcels clause and plan are inconsistent. For example, if the parcels clause refers to land which is 'shown for identification purposes only' on the plan then there

---

1   Although the courts draw a distinction between a 'boundary dispute' and a 'property dispute': *Lee v Barrey* [1957] Ch 251 and *Strachey v Ramage* [2008] EWCA Civ 384.
2   [2008] EWCA Civ 384 at [54].

is likely to be a presumption that the wording of the parcels clause prevails. Problems may arise, however, where the parcels clause refers to land 'more particularly delineated' on the plan, which would seem to suggest that the plan is to be preferred. The plan may, however, be of insufficient scale or detail to enable it to be of much use in construing the parcels clause. In the event of a dispute, a judicial determination would take into account all of the available evidence together with features present on the ground.

8.05 The most straightforward way, from a legal point of view, to determine the exact nature of a boundary is for the neighbouring landowners to enter into a boundary agreement. Such an agreement is exempt from the formalities of LP(MP)A 1989, s 2 as it is not a 'contract for the sale or other disposition of an interest in land'. However, the drawing up of a boundary agreement is likely to involve some expense, for example, the instruction of a surveyor and a solicitor, so it is comparatively rare in ordinary residential cases.

8.06 Assuming no boundary agreement exists, when land is registered for the first time, the Land Registry prepares a document known as the 'filed plan' from the available deeds and documents. The filed plan shows the delineation of the registered title, usually enclosed by a red line, in relation to the neighbouring land and public highways. Although the plan is relatively large scale (commonly 1:1250 on modern filed plans), the thickness of the red line precludes the filed plan's use to determine the boundary with any degree of precision. The 'boundaries rule' has evolved as a result – this says that a boundary set out on a filed plan is in the nature of a general boundary only and is now enshrined in LRA 2002, s 60 which provides:

'(1) The boundary of a registered estate as shown for the purposes of the register is a general boundary, unless shown as determined under this section.

(2) A general boundary does not determine the exact line of the boundary.

(3) Rules may make provision enabling or requiring the exact line of the boundary of a registered estate to be determined and may, in particular, make provision about
   (a) the circumstances in which the exact line of a boundary may or must be determined,
   (b) how the exact line of a boundary may be determined,
   (c) procedure in relation to applications for determination, and
   (d) the recording of the fact of determination in the register or the index maintained under section 68.

(4) Rules under this section must provide for applications for determination to be made to the registrar.'

8.07 It is thus possible to apply to the Land Registry for a determination of the exact line of the boundary. LRR 2003, r 118 provides the mechanism for doing so:

'(1) A proprietor of a registered estate may apply to the registrar for the exact line of the boundary of that registered estate to be determined.

(2) An application under paragraph (1) must be made in Form DB and be accompanied by
   (a) a plan, or a plan and a verbal description, identifying the exact line of the boundary claimed and showing sufficient surrounding physical features to allow the general position of the boundary to be drawn on the Ordnance Survey map, and
   (b) evidence to establish the exact line of the boundary.'

8.08 The Registrar will consider the evidence submitted with an application and may instruct a surveyor to attend at the property and prepare a report. By LRR 2003, r 119(1), the Registrar must then be satisfied that:

'(a) the plan, or plan and verbal description, supplied in accordance with rule 118(2)(a) identifies the exact line of the boundary claimed,

(b) the applicant has shown an arguable case that the exact line of the boundary is in the position shown on the plan, or plan and verbal description, supplied in accordance with rule 118(2)(a), and

(c) he can identify all the owners of the land adjoining the boundary to be determined and has an address at which each owner may be given notice.'

8.09 If these conditions are satisfied, then the Registrar must give notice of the application to the owners of any land adjoining the boundary, except for any owner who has already entered into a boundary agreement. LRR 2003, r 119 provides further details of the mechanism by which adjoining owners may object to an application and the consequences if they do not do so. Applications which are objected to will, where the objections remain unresolved, ultimately be referred to the Adjudicator in the usual way. In addition to applications specifically to determine the extent of the boundary, boundary disputes may come to be before the Adjudicator as the result of a reference by the Registrar of another type of disputed application, for example an application for first registration or an application to be registered as proprietor on the grounds of adverse possession. Boundary disputes may also overlap with other areas of litigation which do not fall within the Adjudicator's jurisdiction, such as damages claims in the torts of nuisance or trespass.

8.10 The first step parties should take when preparing for a contested boundary dispute is to make a comprehensive search for all pre-registration deeds which contain descriptions of the boundary by way of parcels clauses or plans. These should be exhibited to the statement of case in the usual way, although the majority will presumably already have been included in the Land Registry application. In particular, parties should:

• check whether there has been any existing agreement or determination in relation to part, or the whole, of the boundary;

• ensure that they follow up references to parcels clauses and/or plans from previous conveyancing documents;

• reproduce plans in sufficient clarity and with the original colour coding;

• where it would be helpful, map historic plans on to a large scale diagram of the present day features on the ground and/or an aerial photograph; if possible, one composite document should be produced and marked up;

• take clear photographs and mark their position on a diagram or panoramic photograph;

• ensure that all diagrams, plans and photographs contain accurate scaled measurements – for obvious reasons, this is especially important in boundary dispute cases;

• consider disclosing any expert reports that have been obtained.

8.11 Historic evidence of the locality, such as old maps or tithe plans, is unlikely to assist in the precise determination of a boundary since (to the extent that it would otherwise be helpful) the scale is likely to be insufficiently large. Similarly, parties should not rely too heavily on historic photographs although, where evidence from deeds is lacking, they can sometimes provide crucial missing links.

Chapter 9

Easements

INTRODUCTION

9.01   The existence and creation of easements has become one of the most litigated areas of property law in recent years. There are, perhaps, a number of reasons for this: a greater awareness on the part of ordinary people as to their 'rights' (or potential rights), a greater willingness to litigate, and relatively greater affluence than in the past. All of these could be said to be reasons for the growth in any area of litigation. Litigation in relation to easements, however, may commonly have another element – that of a tactical ploy to frustrate, or reduce the value of, development of land by a neighbour, landowner, or property developer. For that reason, it is suggested that practitioners are likely to come across this species of property litigation with increasing frequency and that a sizeable proportion of such disputes are likely to be decided by the Adjudicator.

9.02   When dealing with any claim relating to an easement, an understanding of the law relating to easements will be crucial. There are several specialist works which should always be consulted if possible.[1] This chapter aims to provide a summary of the main aspects of the substantive law on easements for those unfamiliar with the area, before considering the subject in the context of the Adjudicator's jurisdictions to rectify documents, and to hear references from the Land Registry.

9.03   The law surrounding easements has recently attracted the attention of the Law Commission.[2] One of the main proposals is that the rules on implication of easements should be simplified with a single statutory test being put in their place. The law in this area may therefore change in the foreseeable future although there is as yet no draft bill.

SUBSTANTIVE LAW

9.04   An easement is a species of right which one landowner may acquire over the land of another. Examples of easements are:

- pedestrian right of way;
- right of vehicular access;
- right to park (or wash, etc) a car;
- right of light;
- right of structural support.

9.05   Profits *à prendre* are similar species of rights to easements: as the name implies, these are usually rights to take something from the land of another, for example, the right to take fish from a river or pond. For simplicity's sake this

---

1   *Gale on Easements* (12th edn, 2012); Sara, *Boundaries and Easements* (5th edn, 2011); and the relevant chapters in Megarry & Wade, *The Law of Real Property* (8th edn, 2012).
2   Law Com No 327 (2011).

chapter will consider easements only, but much of what is said applies equally to profits *à prendre*.

9.06   There are certain conditions which must be satisfied before an easement can come into existence. Essentially there are four characteristics that are essential to an easement.

There must be a dominant and a servient tenement

9.07   Lord Cairns LJ in *Rangeley v Midland Railway Company*[3] said: 'There can be no easement properly so called unless there is both a servient and a dominant tenement … There can be no such thing.'

9.08   If A owns Plot 1 and grants a right to use a path across Plot 1 to the owner for the time being of a neighbouring plot, Plot 2, then an easement in favour of Plot 2 is capable of subsisting with Plot 1 as the servient tenement and Plot 2 as the dominant tenement.

However, if A grants such a right to B, who owns no land, B acquires merely a licence to walk over Plot 1. The right granted to B could not subsist as an easement as the requirement for a dominant tenement would not be made out.

9.09   On any transfer of the dominant tenement the benefit of the easement will pass to successive proprietors in land, ensuring that the owner for the time being can enjoy it.

9.10   Where a tenement is severed, the benefit of an easement will pass with each severed part as long as the severed part is accommodated by the easement and the severance does not increase the burden on the servient tenement.

An easement must accommodate the dominant tenement

9.11   The right must accommodate and benefit the dominant land; it is not sufficient that the right should afford the owner for the time being some personal advantage (*Hill v Tupper*[4]). No right can qualify as an easement unless it can be shown that the right confers a significant benefit on the dominant land as distinct from offering some merely personal advantage or convenience to the dominant owner.

9.12   In *Moncrieff v Jamieson*[5] Lord Hope emphasised that the essence of an easement is that it 'exists for the reasonable and comfortable enjoyment of the dominant tenement'.

9.13   In order to support the claim that a right accommodates the dominant tenement, the servient land must be sufficiently closely situated to confer a practical benefit on the dominant land. For example, there cannot be an easement over land in Kent appurtenant to an estate in Northumberland (*Bailey v Stephens*[6]). This does not mean that an easement cannot exist unless the dominant and servient tenements are contiguous. An easement can still exist, even when separated by land, provided that it is near enough for the dominant tenement to receive benefit (*Pugh v Savage*[7]).

---

3   (1867–8) LR 3 Ch App 306 CA in Chancery.
4   (1863) 2 Hurl. & C. 121.
5   [2007] UKHL 42.
6   (1862) 12 CB NS 91.
7   [1970] 2 QB 373.

Dominant and servient tenements must not be owned by the same person

9.14 A person cannot meaningfully have rights against himself. However, it has been held that this requirement for diversity of occupation is satisfied between landlord and tenant.

9.15 It is possible that a tenant may be granted an easement over other land owned by his landlord. For example, A and B, as joint freehold owners of Plot 1, could be granted an easement over the neighbouring land, Plot 2, which A and Z hold as leasehold.

A right over land cannot amount to an easement unless it is capable of forming the subject matter of a grant

9.16 There must be a capable grantor and grantee. The right must be capable of being granted by deed and therefore must usually be within the general nature of rights capable of being created as easements and must be sufficiently definite. The right must not impose any positive burden on the servient owner nor must it deprive the servient owner of all beneficial proprietorship:

> 'If the right granted in relation to the area over which it is to be exercised is such that it would leave the servient owner without any reasonable use of his land, whether for parking or anything else, it could not be an easement though it might be some larger or different right.' (*London & Blenheim Estates Ltd v Ladbroke Retail Parks Ltd*[8])

Creation of easements

9.17 Easements are most frequently created on a sale of part of a piece of land belonging to the seller.

9.18 Easements are either legal or equitable. A legal easement must be equivalent to either a fee simple or a term of years and it is usually created by deed; however, it may be acquired by prescription or statute.

9.19 An equitable easement may arise if there has been a failure to observe the formalities necessary to create a legal easement, or if an easement is granted which is not equivalent to either a fee simple or a term of years.

9.20 In most cases, the easement will be created expressly either by the seller in his own favour over the part of his land being sold or in favour of the buyer over the part of land being retained by the seller.

9.21 Where there is no express reservation or grant, certain easements may be created by implication or may be acquired by prescription.

9.22 Easements can be created by one of the following means:

- statute
- express grant or reservation
- implied grant or reservation
- section 62 of the Law of Property Act 1925
- prescription
- equity.

8 [1994] 1 WLR 31.

Statute

9.23   Easements can be created pursuant to statute, and are often created in favour of various service utilities which supply and maintain gas, water or electricity. Another example would be a statute giving a right of support to a canal constructed under statutory powers.

9.24   These easements are often an exception to the general principle which requires that an easement must satisfy the test of having a specific dominant tenement. Various statutory undertakers are also indirectly empowered by statute to enable the creation of easements or way-leaves for the supply of vital commodities.

9.25   Easements can be created in the course of compulsory purchase of land. For instance, the body purchasing the land under a statutory power may need additional rights over adjoining land in order to carry out the purpose for which the land is being purchased. In *Newcomen v Coulson*[9] the rights created were easements in the ordinary sense of the word. These are usually incidents annexed to the land purchased and bind successors in title to the land in respect of which the right is created by deed.

9.26   Statutory undertakers of land may need, for example, to install pipes and cables on private land and will usually include the power from enabling statues to enter the relevant land for the purposes of installation, repair and replacement (see ss 47 and 50 of the Countryside and Rights of Way Act 2000).

Express grant or reservation

9.27   At common law, an easement can only be generated expressly by deed, usually by express grant or reservation contained in a conveyance or transfer. Easements are also contained in leases and separate deeds of easement can be executed. The intention of the grant of an easement must be clear.

9.28   A grant arises, where A, the landowner of Plot 1, creates in favour of B, the owner of Plot 2, an easement over Plot 1. A reservation arises where A disposes of part of his land to B on terms that A shall retain an easement over the land transferred to B. The easement is subsequently created in favour of A, the transferor of the land.

9.29   Sara, *Boundaries and Easements*,[10] summarises in this way the approach to be taken to construction of an express grant of a right of way:

> 'Where there is an express grant, the physical extent of the right of way is essentially a matter of construction. In construing the grant the court will take note both of the words of the grant and the physical extent of the way at the date of the grant. The usual way of expressing the extent of a right of way in a grant is either by defining the width or by referring to a plan … if there is any ambiguity or uncertainty the court will be quick to look at the circumstances of the grant and the physical extent of the way at the time of the grant.
>
> The basic rule as set out in *Robinson v Bailey* [1948] 2 All ER 791 is that a right of way will be for all purposes for which the way can be conveniently enjoyed unless there is something in the words of the grant or the surrounding circumstances which indicate that it is to be more restrictively construed.'

9   (1877) LR 5 ChD 133 CA.
10   (5th edn, 2011).

Construction of an express grant of a right of way is thus essentially a matter of applying common sense in construing the wording of the grant subject to (a) any assistance that may be derived from a relevant plan and (b) any argument that, at the time the grant was made, the site was physically restricted in some way that is likely to have informed the intention of the grantor and/or the actual use which the grantee would have been able to make of the easement.

9.30 A grant is normally incorporated in a transfer of a freehold estate or a grant of a leasehold estate where it is intended that the new estate owner and successors in title will enjoy certain rights over the land retained by the transferor or lessor.

9.31 There is no requirement at common law that the grant should make explicit reference to the dominant tenement or in any other way identify the land benefited by the easement. However, the court will examine all the relevant evidence and circumstances in order to determine whether there was a dominant tenement and whether it benefited from the purported easement. It is a statutory requirement of registration that the burden of any legal easement created out of a registered estate be entered in the register which identifies the servient estate or affected portion.[11]

Implied grant or reservation

9.32 There are several ways in which an easement may arise by means of implied grant or reservation.

9.33 One of the most common ways in which such an easement may arise is by necessity. An example of an easement arising by necessity would be where a grantor grants a plot of land with the result that the grantor is prevented from accessing some other part of his own land. In these circumstances (for example where the retained land is completely surrounded by the land that has been disposed of), there may be an implied reservation by necessity, in favour of the retained land, of a right of way over the land disposed of, otherwise there would be no means of access to the retained land from outside the retained land. The rule is one of construction of the relevant grant and will depend upon the intention of the parties as implied from the circumstances.

9.34 A right of way by necessity may only be implied if there is no other realistic possibility of access to the retained land at the time of the grant. A right of way by necessity will not exist where it would simply be inconvenient to use an alternative.

9.35 Easements are implied much more readily in favour of a grantee, on the principle that a grant must be construed in the amplest rather than the narrowest way.

9.36 A further way in which an easement can arise by implication is an easement giving effect to intended use; an express grant of the land will often be accompanied by an implied grant of easements. The grantee must show that at the date of the grant, the parties had an intention that the property should be used in a definitive and particular manner and that the implied easement is to give rise to this purpose (*Moncrieff v Jamieson*[12]).

11 Land Registration Rules 2003, r 84(2).
12 [2007] UKHL 42.

9.37   This rule, together with the rule in *Wheeldon v Burrows*,[13] has been considered to be 'no more than examples of the application of a general and well established principle which applies to contracts, whether relating to grants of land or other arrangements. That principle is that the law will imply a term into a contract, where, in the light of the terms of the contract, such a term would have been regarded as reasonably necessary or reasonably obvious to the parties' (*Moncrieff v Jamieson*).

9.38   Easements necessary for the enjoyment of some right expressly granted may be implied, such as a right to use stairs on the letting of a flat in a tower block, or a right of way to a spring, on the grant of an easement to draw water from it.

9.39   The rule in *Wheeldon v Burrows* determines what easements are implied in favour of the grantee of one part of a holding against the owner of the remainder and represents a branch of the general rule against derogation from the grant. It relates not to the transmission of existing easements over the land or third party land, but to the translation into easements of rights over the grantor's retained land which are necessary to the proper enjoyment of the land granted. It is necessary to look at the grantor's previous use of the land and to allow the grantee to take easements corresponding to the facilities that the grantor found necessary. Prior to the grant, rights cannot have been easements as there was common ownership. These are called 'quasi-easements'.

9.40   *Wheeldon v Burrows* was a case where a long line of earlier authorities was summed up in a general rule (concerning an implied reservation rather than an implied grant). The rule for implied grant was set out by way of contrast. The case laid down that upon the grant of part of a tenement, there would pass to the grantee as easements all quasi-easements over the land retained which:

- were continuous and apparent;
- were necessary for the reasonable enjoyment of the land granted; and
- had been, and were at the time of the grant, used by the grantor for the benefit of the land retained.

Section 62 of the Law Property Act 1925

9.41   Of similar effect is s 62 of the Law of Property Act 1925. Section 62 applies to both registered and unregistered land and was designed to make it unnecessary to set out the full effects of every conveyance by the use of general words. If no contrary intention is expressed, every conveyance of land passes, inter alia, 'all … liberties, privileges, easements, rights, and advantages whatsoever, appertaining or reputed to appertain to the land, or any part thereof, or at the time of conveyance … enjoyed with … the land or any part thereof'.

9.42   Examples of conveyances are mortgages, leases and assets, but not mere contracts. See further Chapter 10.

9.43   Examples of rights which s 62 will convert into full easements are:
- a licence;
- a right that was accustomed to be exercised but the origin of which was perhaps unknown;
- a right that was reputed to be exercised with a particular property;
- a continuous and apparent quasi-easement.

13   (1879) LR 12 Ch D 31.

For s 62 to be effective in respect of such a right, it must have been enjoyed at the time when the conveyance was made. It does not matter whether the user is continuous and permanent or permissive and precarious. It is the fact that the right has been enjoyed and not the legal basis upon which the right has been asserted which is material.

9.44   A landlord about to renew a lease should take care first to revoke any licences which have been given to the tenant and prevent any further enjoyment of them, otherwise s 62 may convert them into easements.

9.45   Section 62 cannot create as an easement a right which is incapable of being an easement.

9.46   Section 62 is also subject to any contrary intention which may be implied from the circumstances pertaining at the time of the grant.

Prescription

9.47   Easements arising by prescription are probably the most fertile source of litigation despite (or perhaps because) they typically depend upon a reconstruction of a factual scenario which has arisen over a specified period of time.

9.48   There are three means by which an easement may arise by prescription:

- *Common law* – this requires a continuous period of 20 years which can technically be defeated by showing that at some period since time immemorial (1189) the right did not/could not have existed.
- *Lost modern grant* – this is a legal fiction which achieves essentially the same result as common law prescription by presuming that a grant of an easement was made before the 20-year period of user began – whether or not the right existed in 1189 is irrelevant although it can still be defeated by showing that there was nobody who could lawfully have made the grant throughout the entire period when it could have been made.
- *Prescription Act 1832* – this put prescription on a statutory footing (although it did not replace the previous methods), with particular periods specified for easements and profits *à prendre* – the main difficulty with the Act is that the periods have to be enjoyed up to the bringing of an action and will not otherwise crystallise.

9.49   The doctrine of prescription is an ancient one. Lord Hoffmann said in *R v Oxfordshire CC (ex parte Sunningwell PC)*:[14]

'Any legal system must have rules of prescription which prevent the disturbance of long established de facto possession.'

9.50   Section 2 of the Prescription Act 1832 (as amended) provides:

'No claim which may be lawfully made at common law, by custom, prescription, or grant, to any way or other easement, or to any watercourse, or the use of any water to be enjoyed or derived upon, over, or from any land or water of our said Lord the King, or being parcel of the Duchy of Lancaster or of the Duchy of Cornwall, or being the property of any ecclesiastical or law person, or body corporate, when such way or other matter as herein last

14   [2000] 1 AC 335.

before mentioned shall have been actually enjoyed by any person claiming right thereto without interruption for the full period of 20 years, shall be defeated or destroyed by showing only that such way or other matter was first enjoyed at any time prior to such period of 20 years, but nevertheless such claim may be defeated in any other way by which the same is now liable to be defeated; and where such way or other matter as herein last before mentioned shall have been so enjoyed as aforesaid for the full period of 40 years, the right thereto shall be deemed absolute and infeasible, unless it shall appear that the same was enjoyed by some consent or agreement expressly given or made for that purpose by deed or writing.'

9.51 The Prescription Act 1932 requires that the easement 'shall have been actually enjoyed by any person claiming the right thereto.' From this statutory provision, the following elements can be distilled:

- continuity;
- openness;
- absence of force;
- enjoyment 'by a person claiming right thereto';
- actual or imputed knowledge of the servient owner;
- absence of permission; and
- legality.

Some time ago, the Law Reform Committee[15] reported that the law of prescription is unsatisfactory and out of date, and that it needs extensive reform. A majority of the committee recommended its total abolition, but a strong minority recommended that *in lieu* of all existing forms of prescription there should be an improved Prescription Act for easements, though not for profits, based on a 12 year period of the user. As with the more recent proposals of the Law Commission, there has been as yet no movement on this issue by parliament.

EASEMENTS AT THE LAND REGISTRY

9.52 Upon first registration, the Land Registry will translate the information held within conveyancing deeds associated with the property and estate, into one of the registered titles governed by LRA 2002. Information will be taken from pre-registration conveyances, contacts, transfer documents (including assents), results from searches under the Land Charges Act 1972, plans, and property questionnaires.

9.53 On any first registration, the process applied by the Land Registry will be to determine the nature of the property and priority of rights, interests and charges that have accumulated around any unregistered land and which must therefore be reflected on the Land Register.

9.54 The register kept at the Land Registry shows the true state of the title.[16] On application to the Land Registry, an official copy of that title and/or its filed plan will be provided on payment of a fee.[17]

---

15 14th Report, Cmnd 3100 (1966).
16 LRA 2002, s 58(1). In other words, the fact that a proprietor is registered means that the registered estate is deemed to be vested in him – a significant change brought in by LRA 2002.
17 The most convenient method of obtaining these documents is now online, via the Land Registry website (www.landregistry.gov.uk).

9.55   The register is divided into three elements, the purpose of which is considered briefly here:

- Property Register
- Proprietorship Register
- Charges Register.

Property Register

9.56   The property register describes the estate in land which is registered and can be either freehold or leasehold land and identifies the property with a short description, including the postal address, together with reference to the plan that shows the physical area of the land which is the subject of the registration. The plan is known as a 'filed plan' and is usually in the format of an Index map, based on the Ordnance Survey, showing the extent of land. The boundaries shown on the plan will only show a general indication of the position of the boundaries; however, the right does exist for the landowner to have the boundaries fixed by the registry.[18] Here, evidence from pre-registration documents may be required to determine and prove the exact position of the boundaries.

9.57   The property register also records other features of the land, such as easements, covenants, rights or privileges over other land which *benefit* the estate comprised within the title. In the matter of easements, the key element registered within the property register, is the benefit associated with the easement.

Example

'IT IS HEREBY AGREED AND DECLARED as follows:

The Purchaser and its successors in title of the property shall not by implication or otherwise be entitled to any right of light or air or other easement (other than those hereby expressly granted) which would in any way prejudicially affect or restrict the use of the neighbouring or adjoining land of the Vendor or any part thereof for building developments or other purposes.

All rights in the nature of easements or quasi-easements existing as between the Property and the neighbouring or adjoining land of the vendor shall continue to be enforceable by and as between the respective owners of the properties aforesaid PROVIDED that the Purchaser and its successors in title shall not by virtue of this provision be required or obliged to supply water gas or electricity to the neighbouring or adjoining land of the Vendor or any part thereof.'

Proprietorship Register

9.58   The purpose of the proprietorship register is to record the class of title and it clearly identifies the registered proprietor's full name and address. This part will contain any entries that affect the right of disposal. An entry may also be entered to bind the current proprietor, for example where the owner entered

---

18 LRA 2002, s 60(3) and (4) and Land Registration Rules 2003, rr 118–122.

into a personal covenant, such as an indemnity covenant binding only on him and not on future successors in title.

Charges Register

9.59   The purpose of the charges register is to record details of charges or incumbrances which currently affect title. The charges register also records other features of the land, such as easements, covenants, rights or privileges over other land which *burden* the estate comprised within the title. In the matter of easements, the key element registered within the property register, is the burden associated with the easement.

Example

'EXCEPTING AND RESERVING unto the Vendor and its successors in title owners or occupiers for the time being of the adjoining or neighbouring land of the Vendor following rights namely:

the right to connect into and thereafter to use for all purposes all existing drains sewers surface water pipes gas water and other pipes electric cables now laid or within eighty years from the date hereof to be laid in replacement thereof in on or under the Property

the right to enter upon the Property for the purpose of maintaining and repairing such services PROVIDED nevertheless that those exercising that right shall do so causing as little damage as possible and the surface of the land shall be restored and made good as soon as possible.'

In the case of unregistered land, similar wording will appear on the pre-registration deeds/conveyancing documents.

EASEMENTS BEFORE THE ADJUDICATOR

9.60   Chapter 2 sets out the sources of the Adjudicator's jurisdiction and powers. The Adjudicator's power under LRA 2002, s 108(2) to rectify a document falling within that subsection naturally encompasses the wording of easements, presumably by express grant or reservation.

9.61   However the bulk of the Adjudicator's work relating to easements arises under the LRA 2002, s 73(7) reference procedure. Typical cases will be references from applications to the Land Registry for entry onto the Register of the benefit and burden of an easement that is said to have arisen by prescription, or that is recorded in an earlier conveyancing document but whose wording not been transferred onto the Register (in which case the application will be one of alteration and usually, if it prejudicially affects the title of a registered owner of land, rectification – see Chapter 4). It is not necessary for both the servient and dominant tenements to be registered land – only one must be.

9.62   The majority of easement references will involve disputes of fact as to whether or how the easement has arisen. Careful evidence will normally need to be given by both parties, but especially the party alleging the existence of the easement. It is not sufficient, in a prescription case, simply to say that one has used the easement for an unbroken period of 20 years without secrecy, force, or permission. Particular aspects of the law of prescription will need to be addressed in the evidence:

- *Frequency*
  Occasional use of a claimed right may not be sufficient to found an easement by prescription so if possible regular frequent usage should be demonstrated (references should be made to dates and times in the case of a right of way, for example).
- *Quality*
  Just because a right has arisen in some form does not mean that it will be available at all times and for all purposes. A right of vehicular access, for example, may be restricted to particular times, or to a particular frequency if that is all the evidence of prescription supports.
- *Abandonment*
  Once an easement has arisen by prescription, it can be abandoned again. There is no hard and fast rule as to the amount of time that must elapse for the right to be abandoned and it will be a matter of fact in each case. If, for example, a right of way has crystallised after 20 years' usage, it is unlikely to be abandoned by non-user for one year, but 20 years' lack of use may well support a presumption that it has been abandoned.
- *Acquiescence*
  The creation of an easement will be defeated if it can be shown that it took place with permission. However, even if permission was granted, an easement may still arise if usage by the potentially dominant owner exceed the terms of that permission and the servient owner did nothing about it. It may be risky, for example, to rely on a historic conversation between the parties (or their predecessors in title) in which specific permission was given in order to support an argument that no rights can have arisen at all.

Chapter 10

Beneficial interests in property

INTRODUCTION

10.01   As a result of social changes in British society since the end of the Second World War, patterns of land ownership have changed dramatically. First, there has been a rise in the number of people owning their own property, often with the assistance of a mortgage, who previously would have rented property without any particular aspiration to ownership of land. The second sea change has been the rise in legal co-ownership of property, initially by married couples but increasingly by couples who co-habit but are not married. The distinction between the two is important because the latter do not enjoy the protections which the law affords to married couples, although for many years the Law Commission has been pressing for change in the law to reflect the fact that more and more couples are choosing to live together without getting married. Nonetheless, at the present time, the distinction remains an important one in so far as it concerns mutual rights to co-owned property. As far as registered land is concerned, legal co-ownership is reflected by the inclusion of the legal proprietors' names in the Proprietorship Register.

10.02   The third change relevant to the growth in litigation in this area is the increase in cases where an individual who is not a legal owner of land asserts a beneficial interest in that land on one of a number of recognised bases.

10.03   Land which is the subject of co-ownership – whether legal or beneficial – is said to be held on a trust for the co-owners, who are the beneficiaries of that trust. Prior to 1997, there were two species of trust that could be created: a trust for sale, and a settlement. The Trusts of Land and Appointment of Trustees Act 1996 (ToLATA 1996) has modified the previous law so that only one form of trust of land – usually referred to as a trust of land – can be created from the day that ToLATA 1996 came into force, 1 January 1997. Examples of the previous species of trust still exist, although they will inevitably dwindle over time. Here we consider only trusts of land since these are the type of real property trust that will most commonly arise in practice before the Adjudicator. Litigation about beneficial interests in property is usually concerned either with proving the existence of such interests, or calculating their size.

10.04   If land is held by co-owners as joint tenants, the co-owners all own a single share jointly. That single share can be severed by one of a number of acts and there is a strong presumption that, upon severance of the joint tenancy, the co-owners will hold in equal shares. However unless and until severance of the joint tenancy takes place, the size of shares is unlikely to have any practical effect since the entirety of the land will ultimately pass to the survivor of the co-owners outside the estate(s) of the other(s).

10.05   Proceedings which involve a dispute about beneficial interests in registered land will thus usually be in respect either of land which is legally held by one or more tenants in common, or of land which is held by a single registered proprietor and over which some other party seeks to assert a beneficial interest. That registered co-owners hold as tenants in common will normally be indicated by the appearance of the following wording on the Proprietorship Register:

> 'No disposition by a sole proprietor of the registered estate (except a trust corporation) under which capital money arises is to be registered unless authorised by an order of the court.'

Such wording is not necessary in the case of joint tenants who hold the land in one share only and so could not dispose of the land without the consent of all co-owners.

10.06 The starting point for calculation of the size of the respective interests is the familiar maxim that 'equity follows the law'. In other words, the presumption is that registered co-owners will hold in equal shares – most commonly there are two and they hold in 50:50 shares – and a sole registered proprietor will hold 100 per cent of his registered title. These presumptions as to ownership can be rebutted by evidence to the contrary.

10.07 Most commonly, a party attempts to rebut the presumptions as to beneficial ownership by asserting the existence of one of three forms of trust: express, (implied) resulting or (implied) constructive.

EXPRESS TRUSTS

10.08 An express trust of land will be created where the parties have entered into a written declaration of trust setting out the manner in which the beneficial shares in the property are to be held. Historically such documents were unusual but, for the reasons set out above, it is now increasingly common to find a declaration of trust document being executed when land is purchased for occupation by more than one adult individual. Such a declaration may take the form of a discrete document executed by the trustees at the same time as the transfer document, although the modern form of Land Registry transfer forms (TR1, TP1 etc) incorporate a panel where joint purchasers can insert both the manner of their co-ownership (joint tenancy or tenancy in common) and, if the latter, the shares in which the property is to be held.

10.09 An express declaration of trust may be executed at any time after the purchase of property, for example upon a subsequent marriage or co-habitation, and may simply confirm the *status quo*, namely that the beneficial shares in a property follow the pattern of legal ownership. The declaration could be used, for example, by one half of a newly co-habiting couple to disclaim any interest in an existing property owned by the other co-habitee.

10.10 If there is a document purporting to execute an express trust, there is unlikely to be any question for the Adjudicator to determine about the size of the shares in which the property is held. There may, however, be an allegation that the execution of the document was brought about through forgery, duress or undue influence, and these will be issues of fact for the Adjudicator to determine.

RESULTING TRUSTS

10.11 The second category of trust is a resulting trust. A resulting trust is presumed in favour of Party A where Party A has provided the funds for the purchase of property which is then held in the name of Party B. Party B is said to hold the property on trust for Party A. Similarly, where a property is held in the joint names of Parties A and B but the legal shares are not reflected by the parties' contributions to the purchase price, the property will, broadly speaking, be held on resulting trust by A and B for themselves in the shares in which they actually contributed to the purchase.

10.12   The leading case on resulting trusts, *Lloyds Bank v Rosset*,[1] confirmed that only direct contributions to the purchase price of the property are likely to be sufficient to imply a resulting trust. In particular, contributions to mortgage repayments are not likely to be sufficient as they amount merely to repayments of a personal debt.

CONSTRUCTIVE TRUSTS

10.13   Because of the difficulties in asserting the existence of a resulting trust, by far the largest category of beneficial interests being asserted come under the banner of the constructive trust, most commonly the 'common intention' constructive trust. The essential principle of this type of trust is that the property is held on trust for the beneficiaries as the result of a common intention on which the party or parties asserting ownership against the legal owner has relied to his or their detriment. The common intention may have been expressly discussed between the parties (for example during one or more conversations), or it may be implied from their behaviour.

10.14   The English courts have taken a stricter approach to developing jurisprudence in this area than, for example, the Australian courts which have developed the notion of a 'remedial' constructive trust, designed as a remedy to achieve a fair outcome between the parties. English law still requires the court to reach a result based on a determination of what the parties intended, or would have intended if they had thought about the question.

10.15   The recent cases of *Stack v Dowden*[2] (in the House of Lords) and *Jones v Kernott*[3] (in the Supreme Court) have – depending on one's viewpoint – either clarified or failed to clarify the law in this area. What seems to be clear, however, is that a wide range of matters can be taken into account during a judicial determination of beneficial interests based on a common intention constructive trusts scenario. The first question is whether the parties had any actual discussions about the manner in which they were to hold the beneficial shares. If no such discussions took place, or if they cannot be relied upon, then the whole manner in which co-habiting parties conducted their lives may be relevant, including household expenditure, contribution to the mortgage and any extensions to the property, and the bringing up of children. The aim of the judicial process is to analyse the parties' behaviour to try and determine what their intentions were.[4]

10.16   If attempting to demonstrate the existence of a common intention constructive trust, it will be important for the party asserting a beneficial

---

1   [1990] UKHL 14, *per* Lord Bridge of Harwich.
2   [2007] UKHL 17.
3   [2011] UKSC 53.
4   *Jones* makes a distinction between 'inferring' and 'imputing' the parties' intentions but the distinction between the two may be of little practical importance.

share contrary to the manner in which the legal shares are held to demonstrate detrimental reliance as a result of his belief in the constructive trust. This may have come about through, for example, his selling an existing property and investing the proceeds in renovations or household expenditure in the property in which he then co-habits. The test for detrimental reliance is essentially the same as that in proprietary estoppel cases.[5]

10.17   Beneficial interest cases will commonly arise before the Adjudicator following the entry of a restriction at the Land Registry in Form RX1 by the person asserting the beneficial interest. It is necessary for the party asserting an interest to set out in some detail on Form RX1 the precise basis on which the interest is said to have arisen and the Land Registry will only enter the restriction if this step has been undertaken. An unresolved objection to the restriction will then result in the matter being referred to the Adjudicator in the usual way.

10.18   The Adjudicator will resolve the factual dispute between the parties in the same way as a court. Parties should accordingly give careful thought from the beginning about preparation of the case and the evidence that will be required.

10.19   The first task for the party asserting the beneficial interest will be to set out clearly the basis on which the beneficial interest is said to have arisen. This should already have been done in the application made to the Land Registry. Although it will be quite common to set out particulars of the interest being asserted in more detail in the Applicant's statement of case, parties should be aware that any documents that have been before the Land Registry can normally be included in the hearing bundle for the Adjudication, and can therefore be put in cross examination. It is therefore vital to formulate the case carefully at the time that the RX1 is submitted: the asserting party must be clear from the beginning what interest is being claimed, and what evidence will be relied upon.

10.20   Assuming that the matter proceeds to a full determination before the Adjudicator, the parties will require the same evidence as for a trial in the High Court. This is likely to involve careful witness evidence about the dates, circumstances and content of any conversations in which discussions took place about shared ownership of property as well as any conversations from which details of such ownership might be implied. The parties will usually wish to put in evidence receipts for any expenditure, household bills, bank statements and other financial material to support (or negate) a conclusion that responsibility for finances was shared. Also relevant may be past history of property ownership, particularly if it is alleged that funds had their source in a previous house.

10.21   The Adjudicator will undertake a determination of the existence and size of beneficial interests in the same way as a court. However, as noted elsewhere in this work, he has none of the powers under ToLATA 1996 to order sale of property or consequential orders. Nonetheless, his factual judicial determination will be binding in the same way as any first instance decision.

---

5   See further *Cobbe v Yeoman's Row Management Ltd* [2008] UKHL 55.

Appendix 1

Land Registration Act 2002 (extracts)

PART 8
ELECTRONIC CONVEYANCING

91 Electronic dispositions: formalities

(1) This section applies to a document in electronic form where—

    (a)   the document purports to effect a disposition which falls within subsection (2), and

    (b)   the conditions in subsection (3) are met.

(2) A disposition falls within this subsection if it is—

    (a)   a disposition of a registered estate or charge,

    (b)   a disposition of an interest which is the subject of a notice in the register, or

    (c)   a disposition which triggers the requirement of registration, which is of a kind specified by rules

(3) The conditions referred to above are that—

    (a)   the document makes provision for the time and date when it takes effect,

    (b)   the document has the electronic signature of each person by whom it purports to be authenticated,

    (c)   each electronic signature is certified, and

    (d)   such other conditions as rules may provide are met.

(4) A document to which this section applies is to be regarded as—

    (a)   in writing, and

    (b)   signed by each individual, and sealed by each corporation, whose electronic signature it has

(5) A document to which this section applies is to be regarded for the purposes of any enactment as a deed.

(6) If a document to which this section applies is authenticated by a person as agent, it is to be regarded for the purposes of any enactment as authenticated by him under the written authority of his principal.

(7) If notice of an assignment made by means of a document to which this section applies is given in electronic form in accordance with rules, it is to be regarded for the purposes of any enactment as given in writing.

(8) The right conferred by section 75 of the Law of Property Act 1925 (c. 20) (purchaser's right to have the execution of a conveyance attested) does not apply to a document to which this section applies

[(9) In relation to the execution of a document by a company in accordance with section 44(2) of the Companies Act 2006 (signature on behalf of the company)—

(a) subsection (4) above has effect in relation to paragraph (a) of that provision (signature by two authorised signatories) but not paragraph (b) (signature by director in presence of witness);

(b) the other provisions of section 44 apply accordingly (the references to a document purporting to be signed in accordance with subsection (2) of that section being read as references to its purporting to be authenticated in accordance with this section);

(c) where subsection (4) above has effect in relation to a person signing on behalf of more than one company, the requirement of subsection (6) of that section is treated as met if the document specifies the different capacities in which the person signs][1]

[(9A) If subsection (3) of section 29C of the Industrial and Provident Societies Act 1965 (execution of documents) applies to a document because of subsection (4) above, subsection (5) of that section (presumption of due execution) shall have effect in relation to the document with the substitution of "authenticated" for "signed".][2]

(10) In this section, references to an electronic signature and to the certification of such a signature are to be read in accordance with section 7(2) and (3) of the Electronic Communications Act 2000 (c. 7).

Notes
1   Substituted subject to savings specified in SI 2008/948 arts 11 and 12 by Companies Act 2006 (Consequential Amendments etc) Order 2008, SI 2008/948, Sch 1(2), para 224 (6 April 2008).
2   Added by Co-operatives and Community Benefit Societies Act 2003, s 5(8) (20 October 2003).

Commencement
Pt 8, s 91(1)–(10): 13 October 2003 (SI 2003/1725, art 2(1)).

Extent
Pt 8, s 91(1)–(10): England, Wales.

92 Land registry network

(1) The registrar may provide, or arrange for the provision of, an electronic communications network for use for such purposes as he thinks fit relating to registration or the carrying on of transactions which—

(a) involve registration, and
(b) are capable of being effected electronically.

(2) Schedule 5 (which makes provision in connection with a network provided under subsection (1) and transactions carried on by means of such a network) has effect.

Commencement
Pt 8, s 92(1)–(2): 13 October 2003 (SI 2003/1725, art 2(1)).

Extent
Pt 8, s 92(1)–(2): England, Wales.

93 Power to require simultaneous registration

(1) This section applies to a disposition of—

(a) a registered estate or charge, or
(b) an interest which is the subject of a notice in the register, where the disposition is of a description specified by rules

(2) A disposition to which this section applies, or a contract to make such a disposition, only has effect if it is made by means of a document in electronic form and if, when the document purports to take effect—

(a)   it is electronically communicated to the registrar, and
(b)   the relevant registration requirements are met.

(3) For the purposes of subsection (2)(b), the relevant registration requirements are—

(a)   in the case of a registrable disposition, the requirements under Schedule 2, and
(b)   in the case of any other disposition, or a contract, such requirements as rules may provide.

(4) Section 27(1) does not apply to a disposition to which this section applies

(5) Before making rules under this section the [Secretary of State][1] must consult such persons as he considers appropriate.

(6) In this section, "disposition", in relation to a registered charge, includes postponement.

Notes
1   Words substituted by Transfer of Functions (Her Majesty's Land Registry, the Meteorological Office and Ordnance Survey) Order 2011, SI 2011/2436, Sch 2(1), para 4(2)(d) (9 November 2011).

Commencement
Pt 8, s 93(1)–(6): 13 October 2003 (SI 2003/1725, art 2(1)).

Extent
Pt 8, s 93(1)–(6): England, Wales.

94 Electronic settlement

The registrar may take such steps as he thinks fit for the purpose of securing the provision of a system of electronic settlement in relation to transactions involving registration.

Commencement
Pt 8, s 94: 13 October 2003 (SI 2003/1725, art 2(1)).

Extent
Pt 8, s 94: England, Wales.

95 Supplementary

Rules may—

(a)   make provision about the communication of documents in electronic form to the registrar;
(b)   make provision about the electronic storage of documents communicated to the registrar in electronic form.

Commencement
Pt 8, s 95(a)–(b): 13 October 2003 (SI 2003/1725, art 2(1)).

Extent
Pt 8, s 95(a)–(b): England, Wales.

PART 9
ADVERSE POSSESSION

96 Disapplication of periods of limitation

(1) No period of limitation under section 15 of the Limitation Act 1980 (c. 58) (time limits in relation to recovery of land) shall run against any person, other than a chargee, in relation to an estate in land or rentcharge the title to which is registered.

(2) No period of limitation under section 16 of that Act (time limits in relation to redemption of land) shall run against any person in relation to such an estate in land or rentcharge.

(3) Accordingly, section 17 of that Act (extinction of title on expiry of time limit) does not operate to extinguish the title of any person where, by virtue of this section, a period of limitation does not run against him.

Commencement
Pt 9, s 96(1)–(3): 13 October 2003 (SI 2003/1725, art 2(1)).

Extent
Pt 9, s 96(1)–(3): England, Wales.

97 Registration of adverse possessor

Schedule 6 (which makes provision about the registration of an adverse possessor of an estate in land or rentcharge) has effect.

Commencement
Pt 9, s 97: 13 October 2003 except in relation to provisions specified in SI 2003/1725, art 2(2)(b); 13 October 2004 in relation to provisions specified in SI 2003/1725, art 2(2)(b) (SI 2003/1725, art 2(2)(b)).

Extent
Pt 9, s 97: England, Wales.

98 Defences

(1) A person has a defence to an action for possession of land if—

    (a)   on the day immediately preceding that on which the action was brought he was entitled to make an application under paragraph 1 of Schedule 6 to be registered as the proprietor of an estate in the land, and

    (b)   had he made such an application on that day, the condition in paragraph 5(4) of that Schedule would have been satisfied.

(2) A judgment for possession of land ceases to be enforceable at the end of the period of two years beginning with the date of the judgment if the proceedings in which the judgment is given were commenced against a person who was at that time entitled to make an application under paragraph 1 of Schedule 6.

(3) A person has a defence to an action for possession of land if on the day immediately preceding that on which the action was brought he was entitled to make an application under paragraph 6 of Schedule 6 to be registered as the proprietor of an estate in the land.

(4) A judgment for possession of land ceases to be enforceable at the end of the period of two years beginning with the date of the judgment if, at the end of that period, the person against whom the judgment was given is entitled to make an

application under paragraph 6 of Schedule 6 to be registered as the proprietor of an estate in the land.

(5) Where in any proceedings a court determines that—

(a) a person is entitled to a defence under this section, or

(b) a judgment for possession has ceased to be enforceable against a person by virtue of subsection (4), the court must order the registrar to register him as the proprietor of the estate in relation to which he is entitled to make an application under Schedule 6.

(6) The defences under this section are additional to any other defences a person may have.

(7) Rules may make provision to prohibit the recovery of rent due under a rentcharge from a person who has been in adverse possession of the rentcharge.

Commencement
Pt 9, s 98(1)–(1)(b): 13 October 2004 (SI 2003/1725, art 2(2)(a)).
Pt 9, s 98(2)–(7): 13 October 2003 (SI 2003/1725, art 2(1)).

Extent
Pt 9, s 98(1)–(7): England, Wales.

PART 10
LAND REGISTRY

Administration

99 The land registry

(1) There is to continue to be an office called Her Majesty's Land Registry which is to deal with the business of registration under this Act.

(2) The land registry is to consist of—

(a) the Chief Land Registrar, who is its head, and

(b) the staff appointed by him; and references in this Act to a member of the land registry are to be read accordingly.

(3) The [Secretary of State][1] shall appoint a person to be the Chief Land Registrar.

(4) Schedule 7 (which makes further provision about the land registry) has effect.

Notes
1   Words substituted by Transfer of Functions (Her Majesty's Land Registry, the Meteorological Office and Ordnance Survey) Order 2011, SI 2011/2436, Sch 2(1), para 4(2)(e) (9 November 2011).

Commencement
Pt 10, s 99(1)–(4): 13 October 2003 (SI 2003/1725, art 2(1)).

Extent
Pt 10, s 99(1)–(4): England, Wales.

100 Conduct of business

(1) Any function of the registrar may be carried out by any member of the land registry who is authorised for the purpose by the registrar.

(2) The [Secretary of State]¹ may by regulations make provision about the carrying out of functions during any vacancy in the office of registrar.

(3) The [Secretary of State]¹ may by order designate a particular office of the land registry as the proper office for the receipt of applications or a specified description of application.

(4) The registrar may prepare and publish such forms and directions as he considers necessary or desirable for facilitating the conduct of the business of registration under this Act.

Notes
1 Words substituted by Transfer of Functions (Her Majesty's Land Registry, the Meteorological Office and Ordnance Survey) Order 2011, SI 2011/2436, Sch 2(1), para4(2)(f) (9 November 2011).

Commencement
Pt 10, s 100(1)–(4): 13 October 2003 (SI 2003/1725, art 2(1)).

Extent
Pt 10, s 100(1)–(4): England, Wales.

101 Annual report

(1) The registrar must make an annual report on the business of the land registry to the [Secretary of State]¹.

(2) The registrar must publish every report under this section and may do so in such manner as he thinks fit.

(3) The [Secretary of State]¹ must lay copies of every report under this section before Parliament.

Notes
1 Words substituted by Transfer of Functions (Her Majesty's Land Registry, the Meteorological Office and Ordnance Survey) Order 2011, SI 2011/2436, Sch 2(1), para 4(2)(g) (9 November 2011).

Commencement
Pt 10, s 101(1)–(3): 13 October 2003 (SI 2003/1725, art 2(1)).

Extent
Pt 10, s 101(1)–(3): England, Wales.

Fees and indemnities

102 Fee orders

The [Secretary of State]¹ may with the advice and assistance of the body referred to in section 127(2) (the Rule Committee), and the consent of the Treasury, by order—

(a) prescribe fees to be paid in respect of dealings with the land registry, except under section 69(3)(b) or 105;
(b) make provision about the payment of prescribed fees.

Notes
1 Words substituted by Transfer of Functions (Her Majesty's Land Registry, the Meteorological Office and Ordnance Survey) Order 2011, SI 2011/2436, Sch 2(1), para 4(2)(h) (9 November 2011).

Commencement
Pt 10, s 102(a)–(b): June 27, 2003 (SI 2003/1612, art 2).

Extent
Pt 10, s 102(a)–(b): England, Wales.

103 Indemnities

Schedule 8 (which makes provision for the payment of indemnities by the registrar) has effect.

Commencement
Pt 10, s 103: 13 October 2003 (SI 2003/1725, art 2(1)).

Extent
Pt 10, s 103: England, Wales.

Miscellaneous

104 General information about land

The registrar may publish information about land in England and Wales if it appears to him to be information in which there is legitimate public interest.

Commencement
Pt 10, s 104: 13 October 2003 (SI 2003/1725, art 2(1)).

Extent
Pt 10, s 104: England, Wales.

105 Consultancy and advisory services

(1) The registrar may provide, or arrange for the provision of, consultancy or advisory services about the registration of land in England and Wales or elsewhere.

(2) The terms on which services are provided under this section by the registrar, in particular terms as to payment, shall be such as he thinks fit.

Commencement
Pt 10, s 105(1)–(2): 13 October 2003 (SI 2003/1725, art 2(1)).

Extent
Pt 10, s 105(1)–(2): England, Wales.

106 Incidental powers: companies

(1) If the registrar considers it expedient to do so in connection with his functions under section 69(3)(a), 92(1), 94 or 105(1) or paragraph 10 of Schedule 5, he may—

   (a) form, or participate in the formation of, a company, or
   (b) purchase, or invest in, a company.

(2) In this section— "company" means a company [as defined in section 1(1) of the Companies Act 2006][1]; "invest" means invest in any way (whether by acquiring assets, securities or rights or otherwise).

(3) This section is without prejudice to any powers of the registrar exercisable otherwise than by virtue of this section.

Notes
1   Words substituted by Companies Act 2006 (Consequential Amendments, Transitional Provisions and Savings) Order 2009, SI 2009/1941, Sch 1, para 193(2) (1 October 2009).

Commencement
Pt 10, s 106(1)–(3): 13 October 2003 (SI 2003/1725, art 2(1)).

Extent
Pt 10, s 106(1)–(3): England, Wales.

PART 11
ADJUDICATION

107 The adjudicator

(1) The Lord Chancellor shall appoint a person to be the Adjudicator to Her Majesty's Land Registry.

(2) To be qualified for appointment under subsection (1), a person must [satisfy the judicial-appointment eligibility condition on a 7-year basis][1]

(3) Schedule 9 (which makes further provision about the adjudicator) has effect.

Notes
1   Words substituted subject to transitional provisions specified in SI 2008/1653, art 3 by Tribunals, Courts and Enforcement Act 2007, Sch 10(1), para 35(2) (21 July 2008: substitution has effect subject to transitional provisions specified in SI 2008/1653, art 3).

Commencement
Pt 11, s 107(1)–(3): 28 April 2003 (SI 2003/1028, art 2(a)).

Extent
Pt 11, s 107(1)–(3): England, Wales.

108 Jurisdiction

(1) The adjudicator has the following functions—

    (a)   determining matters referred to him under section 73(7), and
    (b)   determining appeals under paragraph 4 of Schedule 5.

(2) Also, the adjudicator may, on application, make any order which the High Court could make for the rectification or setting aside of a document which—

    (a)   effects a qualifying disposition of a registered estate or charge,
    (b)   is a contract to make such a disposition, or
    (c)   effects a transfer of an interest which is the subject of a notice in the register.

(3) For the purposes of subsection (2)(a), a qualifying disposition is—

    (a)   a registrable disposition, or
    (b)   a disposition which creates an interest which may be the subject of a notice in the register.

(4) The general law about the effect of an order of the High Court for the rectification or setting aside of a document shall apply to an order under this section.

Commencement
Pt 11, s 108(1)–(4): 13 October 2003 (SI 2003/1725, art 2(1)).

Extent
Pt 11, s 108(1)–(4): England, Wales.

109 Procedure

(1) Hearings before the adjudicator shall be held in public, except where he is satisfied that exclusion of the public is just and reasonable.

(2) Subject to that, rules may regulate the practice and procedure to be followed with respect to proceedings before the adjudicator and matters incidental to or consequential on such proceedings.

(3) Rules under subsection (2) may, in particular, make provision about—

    (a) when hearings are to be held,

    (b) requiring persons to attend hearings to give evidence or to produce documents,

    (c) the form in which any decision of the adjudicator is to be given,

    (d) payment of costs of a party to proceedings by another party to the proceedings, and

    (e) liability for costs thrown away as the result of neglect or delay by a legal representative of a party to proceedings.

Commencement
Pt 11, s 109(1)–(3)(e): 13 October 2003 (SI 2003/1725, art 2(1)).

Extent
Pt 11, s 109(1)–(3)(e): England, Wales.

110 Functions in relation to disputes

(1) In proceedings on a reference under section 73(7), the adjudicator may, instead of deciding a matter himself, direct a party to the proceedings to commence proceedings within a specified time in the court for the purpose of obtaining the court's decision on the matter.

(2) Rules may make provision about the reference under subsection (1) of matters to the court and may, in particular, make provision about—

    (a) adjournment of the proceedings before the adjudicator pending the outcome of the proceedings before the court, and

    (b) the powers of the adjudicator in the event of failure to comply with a direction under subsection (1).

(3) Rules may make provision about the functions of the adjudicator in consequence of a decision on a reference under section 73(7) and may, in particular, make provision enabling the adjudicator to determine, or give directions about the determination of—

    (a) the application to which the reference relates, or

    (b) such other present or future application to the registrar as the rules may provide.

(4) If, in the case of a reference under section 73(7) relating to an application under paragraph 1 of Schedule 6, the adjudicator determines that it would be unconscionable because of an equity by estoppel for the registered proprietor to seek to dispossess the applicant, but that the circumstances are not such that the applicant ought to be registered as proprietor, the adjudicator—

    (a) must determine how the equity due to the applicant is to be satisfied, and

    (b) may for that purpose make any order that the High Court could make in the exercise of its equitable jurisdiction.

Commencement
Pt 11, s 110(1)–(4)(b): 13 October 2003 (SI 2003/1725, art 2(1)).

Extent
Pt 11, s 110(1)–(4)(b): England, Wales.

111 Appeals

(1) Subject to subsection (2), a person aggrieved by a decision of the adjudicator may appeal to the High Court.

(2) In the case of a decision on an appeal under paragraph 4 of Schedule 5, only appeal on a point of law is possible.

(3) If on an appeal under this section relating to an application under paragraph 1 of Schedule 6 the court determines that it would be unconscionable because of an equity by estoppel for the registered proprietor to seek to dispossess the applicant, but that the circumstances are not such that the applicant ought to be registered as proprietor, the court must determine how the equity due to the applicant is to be satisfied.

Commencement
Pt 11, s 111(1)–(3): 13 October 2003 (SI 2003/1725, art 2(1)).

Extent
Pt 11, s 111(1)–(3): England, Wales.

112 Enforcement of orders etc

A requirement of the adjudicator shall be enforceable as an order of the court.

Commencement
Pt 11, s 112: 13 October 2003 (SI 2003/1725, art 2(1)).

Extent
Pt 11, s 112: England, Wales.

113 Fees

The Lord Chancellor may by order—

    (a)   prescribe fees to be paid in respect of proceedings before the adjudicator;
    (b)   make provision about the payment of prescribed fees.

Commencement
Pt 11, s 113(a)–(b): 13 October 2003 (SI 2003/1725, art 2(1)).

Extent
Pt 11, s 113(a)–(b): England, Wales.

114 Supplementary

Power to make rules under this Part is exercisable by the Lord Chancellor.

Commencement
Pt 11, s 114: 13 October 2003 (SI 2003/1725, art 2(1)).

Extent
Pt 11, s 114: England, Wales.

SCHEDULE 4
ALTERATION OF THE REGISTER

Section 65

Introductory

1   In this Schedule, references to rectification, in relation to alteration of the register, are to alteration which—

(a) involves the correction of a mistake, and

(b) prejudicially affects the title of a registered proprietor.

Commencement
Sch 4, para 1(a)–(b): 13 October 2003 (SI 2003/1725, art 2(1)).

Extent
Sch 4, para 1(a)–(b): England, Wales.

Alteration pursuant to a court order

2   (1) The court may make an order for alteration of the register for the purpose of—

(a) correcting a mistake,

(b) bringing the register up to date, or

(c) giving effect to any estate, right or interest excepted from the effect of registration.

(2) An order under this paragraph has effect when served on the registrar to impose a duty on him to give effect to it.

Commencement
Sch 4, para 2(1)–(2): 13 October 2003 (SI 2003/1725 art 2(1)).

Extent
Sch 4, para 2(1)–(2): England, Wales.

3   (1) This paragraph applies to the power under paragraph 2, so far as relating to rectification.

(2) If alteration affects the title of the proprietor of a registered estate in land, no order may be made under paragraph 2 without the proprietor's consent in relation to land in his possession unless—

(a) he has by fraud or lack of proper care caused or substantially contributed to the mistake, or

(b) it would for any other reason be unjust for the alteration not to be made.

(3) If in any proceedings the court has power to make an order under paragraph 2, it must do so, unless there are exceptional circumstances which justify its not doing so.

(4) In sub-paragraph (2), the reference to the title of the proprietor of a registered estate in land includes his title to any registered estate which subsists for the benefit of the estate in land.

Commencement
Sch 4, para 3(1)–(4): 13 October 2003 (SI 2003/1725, art 2(1)).

Extent
Sch 4, para 3(1)–(4): England, Wales.

4   Rules may—

(a)   make provision about the circumstances in which there is a duty to exercise the power under paragraph 2, so far as not relating to rectification;

(b)   make provision about the form of an order under paragraph 2;

(c)   make provision about service of such an order.

Commencement
Sch 4, para 4(a)–(c): 13 October 2003 (SI 2003/1725, art 2(1)).

Extent
Sch 4, para 4(a)–(c): England, Wales.

Alteration otherwise than pursuant to a court order

5   The registrar may alter the register for the purpose of—

(a)   correcting a mistake,

(b)   bringing the register up to date,

(c)   giving effect to any estate, right or interest excepted from the effect of registration, or

(d)   removing a superfluous entry.

Commencement
Sch 4, para 5(a)–(d): 13 October 2003 (SI 2003/1725, art 2(1)).

Extent
Sch 4, para 5(a)–(d): England, Wales.

6   (1) This paragraph applies to the power under paragraph 5, so far as relating to rectification.

(2) No alteration affecting the title of the proprietor of a registered estate in land may be made under paragraph 5 without the proprietor's consent in relation to land in his possession unless—

(a)   he has by fraud or lack of proper care caused or substantially contributed to the mistake, or

(b)   it would for any other reason be unjust for the alteration not to be made.

(3) If on an application for alteration under paragraph 5 the registrar has power to make the alteration, the application must be approved, unless there are exceptional circumstances which justify not making the alteration.

(4) In sub-paragraph (2), the reference to the title of the proprietor of a registered estate in land includes his title to any registered estate which subsists for the benefit of the estate in land.

Commencement
Sch 4, para 6(1)–(4): 13 October 2003 (SI 2003/1725, art 2(1)).

Extent
Sch 4, para 6(1)–(4): England, Wales.

7   Rules may—

(a)   make provision about the circumstances in which there is a duty to exercise the power under paragraph 5, so far as not relating to rectification;

(b)   make provision about how the register is to be altered in exercise of that power;

(c)   make provision about applications for alteration under that paragraph, including provision requiring the making of such applications;

(d)   make provision about procedure in relation to the exercise of that power, whether on application or otherwise.

Commencement
Sch 4, para 7(a)–(d): 13 October 2003 (SI 2003/1725, art 2(1)).

Extent
Sch 4, para 7(a)–(d): England, Wales.

Rectification and derivative interests

8   The powers under this Schedule to alter the register, so far as relating to rectification, extend to changing for the future the priority of any interest affecting the registered estate or charge concerned.

Commencement
Sch 4, para 8: 13 October 2003 (SI 2003/1725, art 2(1)).

Extent
Sch 4, para 8: England, Wales.

Costs in non-rectification cases

9   (1) If the register is altered under this Schedule in a case not involving rectification, the registrar may pay such amount as he thinks fit in respect of any costs or expenses reasonably incurred by a person in connection with the alteration which have been incurred with the consent of the registrar.

(2) The registrar may make a payment under sub-paragraph (1) notwithstanding the absence of consent if—

(a)   it appears to him—
    (i)   that the costs or expenses had to be incurred urgently, and
    (ii)   that it was not reasonably practicable to apply for his consent, or
(b)   he has subsequently approved the incurring of the costs or expenses.

Commencement
Sch 4, para 9(1)–(2)(b): 13 October 2003 (SI 2003/1725, art 2(1)).

Extent
Sch 4, para 9(1)–(2)(b): England, Wales.

SCHEDULE 5
LAND REGISTRY NETWORK

Section 92

Access to network

1   (1) A person who is not a member of the land registry may only have access to a land registry network under authority conferred by means of an agreement with the registrar.

(2) An agreement for the purposes of sub-paragraph (1) ("network access agreement") may authorise access for—

(a)   the communication, posting or retrieval of information,

(b)   the making of changes to the register of title or cautions register,

(c)   the issue of official search certificates,

(d)   the issue of official copies, or

(e)   such other conveyancing purposes as the registrar thinks fit.

(3) Rules may regulate the use of network access agreements to confer authority to carry out functions of the registrar.

(4) The registrar must, on application, enter into a network access agreement with the applicant if the applicant meets such criteria as rules may provide.

Commencement
Sch 5, para 1(1)–(4): 13 October 2003 (SI 2003/1725, art 2(1)).

Extent
Sch 5, para 1(1)–(4): England, Wales.

Terms of access

2   (1) The terms on which access to a land registry network is authorised shall be such as the registrar thinks fit, subject to sub-paragraphs (3) and (4), and may, in particular, include charges for access.

(2) The power under sub-paragraph (1) may be used, not only for the purpose of regulating the use of the network, but also for—

(a)   securing that the person granted access uses the network to carry on such qualifying transactions as may be specified in, or under, the agreement,

(b)   such other purpose relating to the carrying on of qualifying transactions as rules may provide, or

(c)   enabling network transactions to be monitored.

(3) It shall be a condition of a network access agreement which enables the person granted access to use the network to carry on qualifying transactions that he must comply with any rules for the time being in force under paragraph 5.

(4) Rules may regulate the terms on which access to a land registry network is authorised.

Commencement
Sch 5, para 2(1)–(4): 13 October 2003 (SI 2003/1725, art 2(1)),

Extent
Sch 5, para 2(1)–(4): England, Wales.

Termination of access

3   (1) The person granted access by a network access agreement may terminate the agreement at any time by notice to the registrar.

(2) Rules may make provision about the termination of a network access agreement by the registrar and may, in particular, make provision about—

(a)   the grounds of termination,

(b)   the procedure to be followed in relation to termination, and

(c)   the suspension of termination pending appeal.

(3) Without prejudice to the generality of sub-paragraph (2)(a), rules under that provision may authorise the registrar to terminate a network access agreement if the person granted access—

(a) fails to comply with the terms of the agreement,

(b) ceases to be a person with whom the registrar would be required to enter into a network access agreement conferring the authority which the agreement confers, or

(c) does not meet such conditions as the rules may provide.

Commencement
Sch 5, para 3(1)–(3)(c): 13 October 2003 (SI 2003/1725, art 2(1)).

Extent
Sch 5, para 3(1)–(3)(c): England, Wales.

Appeals

4   (1) A person who is aggrieved by a decision of the registrar with respect to entry into, or termination of, a network access agreement may appeal against the decision to the adjudicator.

(2) On determining an appeal under this paragraph, the adjudicator may give such directions as he considers appropriate to give effect to his determination.

(3) Rules may make provision about appeals under this paragraph.

Commencement
Sch 5, para 4(1)–(3): 13 October 2003 (SI 2003/1725, art 2(1)).

Extent
Sch 5, para 4(1)–(3): England, Wales.

Network transaction rules

5   (1) Rules may make provision about how to go about network transactions

(2) Rules under sub-paragraph (1) may, in particular, make provision about dealings with the land registry, including provision about—

(a) the procedure to be followed, and

(b) the supply of information (including information about unregistered interests).

Commencement
Sch 5, para 5(1)–(2)(b): 13 October 2003 (SI 2003/1725, art 2(1)).

Extent
Sch 5, para 5(1)–(2)(b): England, Wales.

Overriding nature of network access obligations

6   To the extent that an obligation not owed under a network access agreement conflicts with an obligation owed under such an agreement by the person granted access, the obligation not owed under the agreement is discharged.

Commencement
Sch 5, para 6: 13 October 2003 (SI 2003/1725, art 2(1)).

Extent
Sch 5, para 6: England, Wales.

Do-it-yourself conveyancing

7   (1) If there is a land registry network, the registrar has a duty to provide such assistance as he thinks appropriate for the purpose of enabling persons engaged in qualifying transactions who wish to do their own conveyancing to do so by means of the network.

(2) The duty under sub-paragraph (1) does not extend to the provision of legal advice.

Commencement
Sch 5, para 7(1)–(2): 13 October 2003 (SI 2003/1725, art 2(1)).

Extent
Sch 5, para 7(1)–(2): England, Wales.

Presumption of authority

8   Where—

(a)   a person who is authorised under a network access agreement to do so uses the network for the making of a disposition or contract, and

(b)   the document which purports to effect the disposition or to be the contract—

(i)   purports to be authenticated by him as agent, and

(ii)   contains a statement to the effect that he is acting under the authority of his principal,

he shall be deemed, in favour of any other party, to be so acting.

Commencement
Sch 5, para 8(a)–(b)(ii): 13 October 2003 (SI 2003/1725, art 2(1)).

Extent
Sch 5, para 8(a)–(b)(ii): England, Wales.

Management of network transactions

9   (1) The registrar may use monitoring information for the purpose of managing network transactions and may, in particular, disclose such information to persons authorised to use the network, and authorise the further disclosure of information so disclosed, if he considers it is necessary or desirable to do so.

(2) The registrar may delegate his functions under sub-paragraph (1), subject to such conditions as he thinks fit.

(3) In sub-paragraph (1), "monitoring information" means information provided in pursuance of provision in a network access agreement included under paragraph 2(2)(c).

Commencement
Sch 5, para 9(1)–(3): 13 October 2003 (SI 2003/1725, art 2(1)).

Extent
Sch 5, para 9(1)–(3): England, Wales.

Supplementary

10   The registrar may provide, or arrange for the provision of, education and training in relation to the use of a land registry network.

Commencement
Sch 5, para 10: 13 October 2003 (SI 2003/1725, art 2(1)).

Extent
Sch 5, para 10: England, Wales.

11   (1) Power to make rules under paragraph 1, 2 or 3 is exercisable by the [Secretary of State][1].

(2) Before making such rules, the [Secretary of State][1] must consult such persons as he considers appropriate.

(3) In making rules under paragraph 1 or 3(2)(a) , the [Secretary of State][1] must have regard, in particular, to the need to secure—

    (a)   the confidentiality of private information kept on the network,
    (b)   competence in relation to the use of the network (in particular for the purpose of making changes), and
    (c)   the adequate insurance of potential liabilities in connection with use of the network.

Notes
1   Words substituted by Transfer of Functions (Her Majesty's Land Registry, the Meteorological Office and Ordnance Survey) Order 2011, SI 2011/2436, Sch 2(1), para 4(2)(n) (9 November 2011).

Commencement
Sch 5, para 11(1)–(3)(c): 13 October 2003 (SI 2003/1725, art 2(1)).

Extent
Sch 5, para 11(1)–(3)(c): England, Wales.

12   In this Schedule—

"land registry network" means a network provided under section 92(1);
"network access agreement"has the meaning given by paragraph 1(2);
"network transaction" means a transaction carried on by means of a land registry network;
"qualifying transaction" means a transaction which—

    (a)   involves registration, and
    (b)   is capable of being effected electronically.

Commencement
Sch 5, para 12 definition of "land registry network"– definition of "qualifying transaction" (b): 13 October 2003 (SI 2003/1725, art 2(1)).

Extent
Sch 5, para 12 definition of "land registry network"– definition of "qualifying transaction" (b): England, Wales.

SCHEDULE 6
REGISTRATION OF ADVERSE POSSESSOR

Section 97

Right to apply for registration

1   (1) [Subject to paragraph 16, a][1] person may apply to the registrar to be registered as the proprietor of a registered estate in land if he has been in adverse possession of the estate for the period of ten years ending on the date of the application.

(2) [Subject to paragraph 16, a]² person may also apply to the registrar to be registered as the proprietor of a registered estate in land if—

    (a)   he has in the period of six months ending on the date of the application ceased to be in adverse possession of the estate because of eviction by the registered proprietor, or a person claiming under the registered proprietor,

    (b)   on the day before his eviction he was entitled to make an application under sub-paragraph (1), and

    (c)   the eviction was not pursuant to a judgment for possession.

(3) However, a person may not make an application under this paragraph if—

    (a)   he is a defendant in proceedings which involve asserting a right to possession of the land, or

    (b)   judgment for possession of the land has been given against him in the last two years

(3) For the purposes of sub-paragraph (1), the estate need not have been registered throughout the period of adverse possession.

Notes
1   Words inserted by Cross-Border Mediation (EU Directive) Regulations 2011, SI 2011/1133, Pt 3, reg 50 (20 May 2011).
2   Words inserted by Cross-Border Mediation (EU Directive) Regulations 2011, SI 2011/1133, Pt 3, reg 51 (20 May 2011).

Commencement
Sch 6, para 1(1)–(4): 13 October 2003 (SI 2003/1725, art 2(1)).

Extent
Sch 6, para 1(1)–(4): England, Wales.

Notification of application

2   (1) The registrar must give notice of an application under paragraph 1 to—

    (a)   the proprietor of the estate to which the application relates,
    (b)   the proprietor of any registered charge on the estate,
    (c)   where the estate is leasehold, the proprietor of any superior registered estate,
    (d)   any person who is registered in accordance with rules as a person to be notified under this paragraph, and
    (e)   such other persons as rules may provide.

(2) Notice under this paragraph shall include notice of the effect of paragraph 4.

Commencement
Sch 6, para 2(1)–(2): 13 October 2003 (SI 2003/1725, art 2(1)).

Extent
Sch 6, para 2(1)–(2): England, Wales.

Treatment of application

3   (1) A person given notice under paragraph 2 may require that the application to which the notice relates be dealt with under paragraph 5.

(2) The right under this paragraph is exercisable by notice to the registrar given before the end of such period as rules may provide.

Commencement
Sch 6, para 3(1)–(2): 13 October 2003 (SI 2003/1725, art 2(1)).

Extent
Sch 6, para 3(1)–(2): England, Wales.

4   If an application under paragraph 1 is not required to be dealt with under paragraph 5, the applicant is entitled to be entered in the register as the new proprietor of the estate.

Commencement
Sch 6, para 4: 13 October 2003 (SI 2003/1725, art 2(1)).

Extent
Sch 6, para 4: England, Wales.

5   (1) If an application under paragraph 1 is required to be dealt with under this paragraph, the applicant is only entitled to be registered as the new proprietor of the estate if any of the following conditions is met.

(2) The first condition is that—

- (a)   it would be unconscionable because of an equity by estoppel for the registered proprietor to seek to dispossess the applicant, and
- (b)   the circumstances are such that the applicant ought to be registered as the proprietor.

(3) The second condition is that the applicant is for some other reason entitled to be registered as the proprietor of the estate.

(4) The third condition is that—

- (a)   the land to which the application relates is adjacent to land belonging to the applicant,
- (b)   the exact line of the boundary between the two has not been determined under rules under section 60,
- (c)   for at least ten years of the period of adverse possession ending on the date of the application, the applicant (or any predecessor in title) reasonably believed that the land to which the application relates belonged to him, and
- (d)   the estate to which the application relates was registered more than one year prior to the date of the application.

(5) In relation to an application under paragraph 1(2), this paragraph has effect as if the reference in sub-paragraph (4)(c) to the date of the application were to the day before the date of the applicant's eviction.

Commencement
Sch 6, para 5(1)–(3): 13 October 2003 (SI 2003/1725, art 2(1)).
Sch 6, para 5(4)–(5): 13 October 2004 (SI 2003/1725, art 2(2)(b)).

Extent
Sch 6, para 5(1)–(5): England, Wales.

Right to make further application for registration

6   (1) Where a person's application under paragraph 1 is rejected, he may make a further application to be registered as the proprietor of the estate if he is in adverse possession of the estate from the date of the application until the last day of the period of two years beginning with the date of its rejection.

[(1A) Sub-paragraph (1) is subject to paragraph 16,]¹

(2) However, a person may not make an application under this paragraph if—

    (a) he is a defendant in proceedings which involve asserting a right to possession of the land,

    (b) judgment for possession of the land has been given against him in the last two years, or

    (c) he has been evicted from the land pursuant to a judgment for possession.

Notes
1   Added by Cross-Border Mediation (EU Directive) Regulations 2011, SI 2011/1133, Pt 3, reg 52 (20 May 2011).

Commencement
Sch 6, para 6(1)–(2)(c): 13 October 2003 (SI 2003/1725, art 2(1)).

Extent
Sch 6, para 6(1)–(2)(c): England, Wales.

7   If a person makes an application under paragraph 6, he is entitled to be entered in the register as the new proprietor of the estate.

Commencement
Sch 6, para 7: 13 October 2003 (SI 2003/1725 art, 2(1)).

Extent
Sch 6, para 7: England, Wales.

Restriction on applications

8   (1) No one may apply under this Schedule to be registered as the proprietor of an estate in land during, or before the end of twelve months after the end of, any period in which the existing registered proprietor is for the purposes of the Limitation (Enemies and War Prisoners) Act 1945 (8 & 9 Geo. 6 c. 16)—

    (a) an enemy, or

    (b) detained in enemy territory.

(2) No-one may apply under this Schedule to be registered as the proprietor of an estate in land during any period in which the existing registered proprietor is—

    (a) unable because of mental disability to make decisions about issues of the kind to which such an application would give rise, or

    (b) unable to communicate such decisions because of mental disability or physical impairment.

(3) For the purposes of sub-paragraph (2), "mental disability" means a disability or disorder of the mind or brain, whether permanent or temporary, which results in an impairment or disturbance of mental functioning.

(4) Where it appears to the registrar that sub-paragraph (1) or (2) applies in relation to an estate in land, he may include a note to that effect in the register.

Commencement
Sch 6, para 8(1)–(4): 13 October 2003 (SI 2003/1725, art 2(1)).

Extent
Sch 6, para 8(1)–(4): England, Wales.

Effect of registration

9   (1) Where a person is registered as the proprietor of an estate in land in pursuance of an application under this Schedule, the title by virtue of adverse possession which he had at the time of the application is extinguished.

(2) Subject to sub-paragraph (3), the registration of a person under this Schedule as the proprietor of an estate in land does not affect the priority of any interest affecting the estate.

(3) Subject to sub-paragraph (4), where a person is registered under this Schedule as the proprietor of an estate, the estate is vested in him free of any registered charge affecting the estate immediately before his registration.

(4) Sub-paragraph (3) does not apply where registration as proprietor is in pursuance of an application determined by reference to whether any of the conditions in paragraph 5 applies.

Commencement
Sch 6, para 9(1)–(4): 13 October 2003 (SI 2003/1725, art 2(1)).

Extent
Sch 6, para 9(1)–(4): England, Wales.

Apportionment and discharge of charges

10   (1) Where—

  (a)   a registered estate continues to be subject to a charge notwithstanding the registration of a person under this Schedule as the proprietor, and
  (b)   the charge affects property other than the estate,

the proprietor of the estate may require the chargee to apportion the amount secured by the charge at that time between the estate and the other property on the basis of their respective values.

(2) The person requiring the apportionment is entitled to a discharge of his estate from the charge on payment of—

  (a)   the amount apportioned to the estate, and
  (b)   the costs incurred by the chargee as a result of the apportionment.

On a discharge under this paragraph, the liability of the chargor to the chargee is reduced by the amount apportioned to the estate.

(4) Rules may make provision about apportionment under this paragraph, in particular, provision about—

  (a)   procedure,
  (b)   valuation,
  (c)   calculation of costs payable under sub-paragraph (2)(b), and
  (d)   payment of the costs of the chargor.

Commencement
Sch 6, para 10(1)–(4)(d): 13 October 2003 (SI 2003/1725, art 2(1)).

Extent
Sch 6, para 10(1)–(4)(d): England, Wales.

Meaning of "adverse possession"

11   (1) A person is in adverse possession of an estate in land for the purposes of this Schedule if, but for section 96, a period of limitation under section 15 of the Limitation Act 1980 (c. 58) would run in his favour in relation to the estate.

(2) A person is also to be regarded for those purposes as having been in adverse possession of an estate in land—

  (a) where he is the successor in title to an estate in the land, during any period of adverse possession by a predecessor in title to that estate, or
  (b) during any period of adverse possession by another person which comes between, and is continuous with, periods of adverse possession of his own.

(3) In determining whether for the purposes of this paragraph a period of limitation would run under section 15 of the Limitation Act 1980, there are to be disregarded—

  (a) the commencement of any legal proceedings, and
  (b) paragraph 6 of Schedule 1 to that Act.

Commencement
Sch 6, para 11(1)–(3)(b): 13 October 2003 (SI 2003/1725, art 2(1)).

Extent
Sch 6, para 11(1)–(3)(b): England, Wales.

Trusts

12   A person is not to be regarded as being in adverse possession of an estate for the purposes of this Schedule at any time when the estate is subject to a trust, unless the interest of each of the beneficiaries in the estate is an interest in possession.

Commencement
Sch 6, para 12: 13 October 2003 (SI 2003/1725 art 2(1)).

Extent
Sch 6, para 12: England, Wales.

Crown foreshore

13   (1) Where—

  (a) a person is in adverse possession of an estate in land,
  (b) the estate belongs to Her Majesty in right of the Crown or the Duchy of Lancaster or to the Duchy of Cornwall, and
  (c) the land consists of foreshore,

paragraph 1(1) is to have effect as if the reference to ten years were to sixty years.

(2) For the purposes of sub-paragraph (1), land is to be treated as foreshore if it has been foreshore at any time in the previous ten years.

(3) In this paragraph, "foreshore" means the shore and bed of the sea and of any tidal water, below the line of the medium high tide between the spring and neap tides.

Commencement
Sch 6, para 13(1)–(3): 13 October 2003 (SI 2003/1725, art 2(1)).

Extent
Sch 6, para 13(1)–(3): England, Wales.

Rentcharges

14   Rules must make provision to apply the preceding provisions of this Schedule to registered rentcharges, subject to such modifications and exceptions as the rules may provide.

Commencement
Sch 6, para 14: 13 October 2003 (SI 2003/1725, art 2(1)).

Extent
Sch 6, para 14: England, Wales.

Procedure

15   Rules may make provision about the procedure to be followed pursuant to an application under this Schedule.

Commencement
Sch 6, para 15: 13 October 2003 (SI 2003/1725 art 2(1)).

Extent
Sch 6, para 15: England, Wales.

[Extension of time limits because of mediation in certain cross-border disputes][1]

Notes
1   Added by Cross-Border Mediation (EU Directive) Regulations 2011, SI 2011/1133, Pt 3, reg 53 (20 May 2011).

[16.—   (1) In this paragraph—

   (a) "Mediation Directive" means Directive 2008/52/EC of the European Parliament and of the Council of 21 May 2008 on certain aspects of mediation in civil and commercial matters,
   (b) "mediation"has the meaning given by article 3(a) of the Mediation Directive,
   (c) "mediator"has the meaning given by article 3(b) of the Mediation Directive, and
   (d) "relevant dispute" means a dispute to which article 8(1) of the Mediation Directive applies (certain cross-border disputes).

(2) Sub-paragraph (3) applies where—

   (a) a period of time is prescribed by paragraph 1(1), 1(2)(a) or 6(1) in relation to the whole or part of a relevant dispute,
   (b) a mediation in relation to the relevant dispute starts before the period expires, and
   (c) if not extended by this paragraph, the period would expire before the mediation ends or less than eight weeks after it ends.

(3) The period expires instead at the end of eight weeks after the mediation ends (subject to sub-paragraph (4)).

(4) If a period has been extended by this paragraph, sub-paragraphs (2) and (3) apply to the extended period as they apply to a period mentioned in sub-paragraph (2)(a).

(5) Where more than one period applies in relation to a relevant dispute, the extension by sub-paragraph (3) of one of those periods does not affect the others

(6) For the purposes of this paragraph, a mediation starts on the date of the agreement to mediate that is entered into by the parties and the mediator.

(7) For the purposes of this paragraph, a mediation ends on date of the first of these to occur—

(a) the parties reach an agreement in resolution of the relevant dispute,
(b) a party completes the notification of the other parties that it has withdrawn from the mediation,
(c) a party to whom a qualifying request is made fails to give a response reaching the other parties within 14 days of the request,
(d) the parties, after being notified that the mediator's appointment has ended (by death, resignation or otherwise), fail to agree within 14 days to seek to appoint a replacement mediator,
(e) the mediation otherwise comes to an end pursuant to the terms of the agreement to mediate.

(8) For the purpose of sub-paragraph (7), a qualifying request is a request by a party that another (A) confirm to all parties that A is continuing with the mediation.

(9) In the case of any relevant dispute, references in this paragraph to a mediation are references to the mediation so far as it relates to that dispute, and references to a party are to be read accordingly.][1]

Notes
1   Added by Cross-Border Mediation (EU Directive) Regulations 2011, SI 2011/1133, Pt 3, reg 53 (20 May 2011).

Extent
Sch 6, para 16(1)–(9): England, Wales.

SCHEDULE 8
INDEMNITIES

Section 103

Entitlement

1   (1) A person is entitled to be indemnified by the registrar if he suffers loss by reason of—

(a) rectification of the register,
(b) a mistake whose correction would involve rectification of the register,
(c) a mistake in an official search,
(d) a mistake in an official copy,
(e) a mistake in a document kept by the registrar which is not an original and is referred to in the register,
(f) the loss or destruction of a document lodged at the registry for inspection or safe custody,
(g) a mistake in the cautions register, or
(h) ailure by the registrar to perform his duty under section 50.

(2) For the purposes of sub-paragraph (1)(a)—

   (a) any person who suffers loss by reason of the change of title under section 62 is to be regarded as having suffered loss by reason of rectification of the register, and

   (b) the proprietor of a registered estate or charge claiming in good faith under a forged disposition is, where the register is rectified, to be regarded as having suffered loss by reason of such rectification as if the disposition had not been forged.

(3) No indemnity under sub-paragraph (1)(b) is payable until a decision has been made about whether to alter the register for the purpose of correcting the mistake; and the loss suffered by reason of the mistake is to be determined in the light of that decision.

Commencement
Sch 8, para 1(1)–(3): 13 October 2003 (SI 2003/1725, art 2(1)).

Extent
Sch 8, para 1(1)–(3): England, Wales.

Mines and minerals

2   No indemnity is payable under this Schedule on account of—

   (a) any mines or minerals, or

   (b) the existence of any right to work or get mines or minerals,

unless it is noted in the register that the title to the registered estate concerned includes the mines or minerals.

Commencement
Sch 8, para 2(a)–(b): 13 October 2003 (SI 2003/1725, art 2(1)).

Extent
Sch 8, para 2(a)–(b): England, Wales.

Costs

3   (1) In respect of loss consisting of costs or expenses incurred by the claimant in relation to the matter, an indemnity under this Schedule is payable only on account of costs or expenses reasonably incurred by the claimant with the consent of the registrar.

(2) The requirement of consent does not apply where—

   (a) the costs or expenses must be incurred by the claimant urgently, and

   (b) it is not reasonably practicable to apply for the registrar's consent.

(3) If the registrar approves the incurring of costs or expenses after they have been incurred, they shall be treated for the purposes of this paragraph as having been incurred with his consent.

Commencement
Sch 8, para 3(1)–(3): 13 October 2003 (SI 2003/1725, art 2(1)).

Extent
Sch 8, para 3(1)–(3): England, Wales.

4   (1) If no indemnity is payable to a claimant under this Schedule, the registrar may pay such amount as he thinks fit in respect of any costs or expenses reasonably incurred by the claimant in connection with the claim which have been incurred with the consent of the registrar.

(2) The registrar may make a payment under sub-paragraph (1) notwithstanding the absence of consent if—

   (a)   it appears to him—
         (i)   that the costs or expenses had to be incurred urgently, and
         (ii)   that it was not reasonably practicable to apply for his consent, or
   (b)   he has subsequently approved the incurring of the costs or expenses.

Commencement
Sch 8, para 4(1)–(2)(b): 13 October 2003 (SI 2003/1725 art 2(1)).

Extent
Sch 8, para 4(1)–(2)(b): England, Wales.

Claimant's fraud or lack of care

5   (1) No indemnity is payable under this Schedule on account of any loss suffered by a claimant—

   (a)   wholly or partly as a result of his own fraud, or
   (b)   wholly as a result of his own lack of proper care.

(2) Where any loss is suffered by a claimant partly as a result of his own lack of proper care, any indemnity payable to him is to be reduced to such extent as is fair having regard to his share in the responsibility for the loss.

(3) For the purposes of this paragraph any fraud or lack of care on the part of a person from whom the claimant derives title (otherwise than under a disposition for valuable consideration which is registered or protected by an entry in the register) is to be treated as if it were fraud or lack of care on the part of the claimant.

Commencement
Sch 8, para 5(1)–(3): 13 October 2003 (SI 2003/1725, art 2(1)).

Extent
Sch 8, para 5(1)–(3): England, Wales.

Valuation of estates etc.

6   Where an indemnity is payable in respect of the loss of an estate, interest or charge, the value of the estate, interest or charge for the purposes of the indemnity is to be regarded as not exceeding—

   (a)   in the case of an indemnity under paragraph 1(1)(a), its value immediately before rectification of the register (but as if there were to be no rectification), and
   (b)   in the case of an indemnity under paragraph 1(1)(b), its value at the time when the mistake which caused the loss was made.

Commencement
Sch 8, para 6(a)–(b): 13 October 2003 (SI 2003/1725, art 2(1)).

Extent
Sch 8, para 6(a)–(b): England, Wales.

Determination of indemnity by court

7 (1) A person may apply to the court for the determination of any question as to—

(a) whether he is entitled to an indemnity under this Schedule, or
(b) the amount of such an indemnity.

(2) Paragraph 3(1) does not apply to the costs of an application to the court under this paragraph or of any legal proceedings arising out of such an application.

Commencement
Sch 8, para 7(1)–(2): 13 October 2003 (SI 2003/1725, art 2(1)).

Extent
Sch 8, para 7(1)–(2): England, Wales.

Time limits

8 For the purposes of the Limitation Act 1980 (c. 58)—

(a) a liability to pay an indemnity under this Schedule is a simple contract debt, and
(b) the cause of action arises at the time when the claimant knows, or but for his own default might have known, of the existence of his claim.

Commencement
Sch 8, para 8(a)–(b): 13 October 2003 (SI 2003/1725, art 2(1)).

Extent
Sch 8, para 8(a)–(b): England, Wales.

Interest

9 Rules may make provision about the payment of interest on an indemnity under this Schedule, including—

(a) the circumstances in which interest is payable, and
(b) the periods for and rates at which it is payable.

Commencement
Sch 8, para 9(a)–(b): 13 October 2003 (SI 2003/1725 art 2(1)).

Extent
Sch 8, para 9(a)–(b): England, Wales.

Recovery of indemnity by registrar

10 (1) Where an indemnity under this Schedule is paid to a claimant in respect of any loss, the registrar is entitled (without prejudice to any other rights he may have)—

(a) to recover the amount paid from any person who caused or substantially contributed to the loss by his fraud, or
(b) for the purpose of recovering the amount paid, to enforce the rights of action referred to in sub-paragraph (2).

(2) Those rights of action are—

    (a) any right of action (of whatever nature and however arising) which the claimant would have been entitled to enforce had the indemnity not been paid, and

    (b) where the register has been rectified, any right of action (of whatever nature and however arising) which the person in whose favour the register has been rectified would have been entitled to enforce had it not been rectified.

(3) References in this paragraph to an indemnity include interest paid on an indemnity under rules under paragraph 9.

Commencement
Sch 8, para 10(1)–(3): 13 October 2003 (SI 2003/1725, art 2(1)).

Extent
Sch 8, para 10(1)–(3): England, Wales.

Interpretation

11   (1) For the purposes of this Schedule, references to a mistake in something include anything mistakenly omitted from it as well as anything mistakenly included in it.

(2) In this Schedule, references to rectification of the register are to alteration of the register which—

    (a) involves the correction of a mistake, and

    (b) prejudicially affects the title of a registered proprietor.

Commencement
Sch 8, para 11(1)–(2)(b): 13 October 2003 (SI 2003/1725, art 2(1)).

Extent
Sch 8, para 11(1)–(2)(b): England, Wales.

SCHEDULE 9
THE ADJUDICATOR

Section 107

Holding of office

1   (1) The adjudicator may at any time resign his office by written notice to the Lord Chancellor.

(2) The Lord Chancellor may [, with the concurrence of the Lord Chief Justice,][1] remove the adjudicator from office on the ground of incapacity or misbehaviour.

(3) Section 26 of the Judicial Pensions and Retirement Act 1993 (c. 8) (compulsory retirement at 70, subject to the possibility of annual extension up to 75) applies to the adjudicator.

(4) Subject to the above, a person appointed to be the adjudicator is to hold and vacate office in accordance with the terms of his appointment and, on ceasing to hold office, is eligible for reappointment.

Notes
1   Words inserted by Constitutional Reform Act 2005, Sch 4(1), para 303 (3 April 2006).

Commencement
Sch 9, para 1(1)–(4): April 28, 2003 (SI 2003/1028, art 2(a)).

Extent
Sch 9, para 1(1)–(4): England, Wales.

Remuneration

2 (1) The Lord Chancellor shall pay the adjudicator such remuneration, and such other allowances, as the Lord Chancellor may determine.

(2) The Lord Chancellor shall—

- (a) pay such pension, allowances or gratuities as he may determine to or in respect of a person who is or has been the adjudicator, or
- (b) make such payments as he may determine towards provision for the payment of a pension, allowances or gratuities to or in respect of such a person.

(3) Sub-paragraph (2) does not apply if the office of adjudicator is a qualifying judicial office within the meaning of the Judicial Pensions and Retirement Act 1993.

(4) If, when a person ceases to be the adjudicator, the Lord Chancellor determines that there are special circumstances which make it right that the person should receive compensation, the Lord Chancellor may pay to the person by way of compensation a sum of such amount as he may determine.

Commencement
Sch 9, para 2(1)–(4): 28 April 2003 (SI 2003/1028, art 2(a)).

Extent
Sch 9, para 2(1)–(4): England, Wales.

Staff

3 (1) The adjudicator may appoint such staff as he thinks fit.

(2) The terms and conditions of appointments under this paragraph shall be such as the adjudicator, with the approval of the Minister for the Civil Service, thinks fit.

Commencement
Sch 9, para 3(1)–(2): April 28, 2003 (SI 2003/1028, art 2(a)).

Extent
Sch 9, para 3(1)–(2): England, Wales.

Conduct of business

4 (1) Subject to sub-paragraph (2), any function of the adjudicator may be carried out by any member of his staff who is authorised by him for the purpose.

(2) In the case of functions which are not of an administrative character, sub-paragraph (1) only applies if the member of staff [satisfies the judicial-appointment eligibility condition on a 7-year basis][1]

Notes
1 Words substituted subject to transitional provisions specified in SI 2008/1653, art 3 by Tribunals, Courts and Enforcement Act 2007, Sch 10(1), para 35(3) (21 July 21: substitution has effect subject to transitional provisions specified in SI 2008/1653, art 3).

Commencement
Sch 9, para 4(1)–(2): 28 April 2003 (SI 2003/1028, art 2(a)).

Extent
Sch 9, para 4(1)–(2): England, Wales.

5   The Lord Chancellor may by regulations make provision about the carrying out of functions during any vacancy in the office of adjudicator.

Commencement
Sch 9, para 5: 28 April 2003 (SI 2003/1028, art 2(a)).

Extent
Sch 9, para 5: England, Wales.

Finances

6   The Lord Chancellor shall be liable to reimburse expenditure incurred by the adjudicator in the discharge of his functions.

Commencement
Sch 9, para 6: 28 April 2003 (SI 2003/1028, art 2(a)).

Extent
Sch 9, para 6: England, Wales.

7   The Lord Chancellor may require the registrar to make payments towards expenses of the Lord Chancellor under this Schedule.

Commencement
Sch 9, para 7: 28 April 2003 (SI 2003/1028, art 2(a)).

Extent
Sch 9, para 7: England, Wales.

Application of Tribunals and Inquiries Act 1992

8   In Schedule 1 to the Tribunal and Inquiries Act 1992 (c. 53) (tribunals under the supervision of the Council on Tribunals), after paragraph 27 there is inserted—

| "Land Registration | 27B. The Adjudicator to Her Majesty's Land Registry." |

Commencement
Sch 9, para 8: 28 April 2003 (SI 2003/1028, art 2(a)).

Extent
Sch 9, para 8: England, Wales.

Parliamentary disqualification

9   In Part 1 of Schedule 1 to the House of Commons Disqualification Act 1975 (c. 24) (judicial offices), there is inserted at the end—

"Adjudicator to Her Majesty's Land Registry.";

and a corresponding amendment is made in Part 1 of Schedule 1 to the Northern Ireland Assembly Disqualification Act 1975 (c. 25).

Commencement
Sch 9, para 9: 28 April 2003 (SI 2003/1028, art 2(a)).

Extent
Sch 9, para 9: England, Wales.

SCHEDULE 12
TRANSITION

Section 134

Existing entries in the register

1   Nothing in the repeals made by this Act affects the validity of any entry in the register.

Commencement
Sch 12, para 1: 13 October 2003 (SI 2003/1725, art 2(1)).

Extent
Sch 12, para 1: England, Wales.

2   (1) This Act applies to notices entered under the Land Registration Act 1925 (c. 21) as it applies to notices entered in pursuance of an application under section 34(2)(a).

(2) This Act applies to restrictions and inhibitions entered under the Land Registration Act 1925 as it applies to restrictions entered under this Act.

(3) Notwithstanding their repeal by this Act, sections 55 and 56 of the Land Registration Act 1925 shall continue to have effect so far as relating to cautions against dealings lodged under that Act.

(4) Rules may make provision about cautions against dealings entered under the Land Registration Act 1925.

(5) In this paragraph, references to the Land Registration Act 1925 include a reference to any enactment replaced (directly or indirectly) by that Act.

Commencement
Sch 12, para 2(1)–(5): 13 October 2003 (SI 2003/1725 art 2(1)).

Extent
Sch 12, para 2(1)–(5): England, Wales.

3   An entry in the register which, immediately before the repeal of section 144(1)(xi) of the Land Registration Act 1925, operated by virtue of rule 239 of the Land Registration Rules (SI 1925/1093) as a caution under section 54 of that Act shall continue to operate as such a caution.

Commencement
Sch 12, para 3: 13 October 2003 (SI 2003/1725, art 2(1)).

Extent
Sch 12, para 3: England, Wales.

Existing cautions against first registration

4   Notwithstanding the repeal of section 56(3) of the Land Registration Act 1925, that provision shall continue to have effect in relation to cautions against first registration lodged under that Act, or any enactment replaced (directly or indirectly) by that Act.

Commencement
Sch 12, para 4: 13 October 2003 (SI 2003/1725, art 2(1)).

Extent
Sch 12, para 4: England, Wales.

Pending applications

5   Notwithstanding the repeal of the Land Registration Act 1925, that Act shall continue to have effect in relation to an application for the entry in the register of a notice, restriction, inhibition or caution against dealings which is pending immediately before the repeal of the provision under which the application is made.

Commencement
Sch 12, para 5: 13 October 2003 (SI 2003/1725, art 2(1)).

Extent
Sch 12, para 5: England, Wales.

6   Notwithstanding the repeal of section 53 of the Land Registration Act 1925, subsections (1) and (2) of that section shall continue to have effect in relation to an application to lodge a caution against first registration which is pending immediately before the repeal of those provisions.

Commencement
Sch 12, para 6: 13 October 2003 (SI 2003/1725, art 2(1)).

Extent
Sch 12, para 6: England, Wales.

Former overriding interests

7   For the period of three years beginning with the day on which Schedule 1 comes into force, it has effect with the insertion after paragraph 14 of—

   "15.

   A right acquired under the Limitation Act 1980 before the coming into force of this Schedule."

Commencement
Sch 12, para 7: 13 October 2003 (SI 2003/1725, art 2(1)).

Extent
Sch 12, para 7: England, Wales.

8   Schedule 3 has effect with the insertion after paragraph 2 of—

   "2A

   (1) An interest which, immediately before the coming into force of this Schedule, was an overriding interest under section 70(1)(g) of the Land Registration Act 1925 by virtue of a person's receipt of rents and profits, except for an interest of a person of whom inquiry was made before the disposition and who failed to disclose the right when he could reasonably have been expected to do so.

   (2) Sub-paragraph (1) does not apply to an interest if at any time since the coming into force of this Schedule it has been an interest which, had the Land Registration Act 1925 (c. 21) continued in force, would not have been an overriding interest under section 70(1)(g) of that Act by virtue of a person's receipt of rents and profits"

Commencement
Sch 12, para 8: 13 October 2003 (SI 2003/1725, art 2(1)).

Extent
Sch 12, para 8: England, Wales.

9 (1) This paragraph applies to an easement or profit a prendre which was an overriding interest in relation to a registered estate immediately before the coming into force of Schedule 3, but which would not fall within paragraph 3 of that Schedule if created after the coming into force of that Schedule.

(2) In relation to an interest to which this paragraph applies, Schedule 3 has effect as if the interest were not excluded from paragraph 3.

Commencement
Sch 12, para 9(1)–(2): 13 October 2003 (SI 2003/1725, art 2(1)).

Extent
Sch 12, para 9(1)–(2): England, Wales.

10 For the period of three years beginning with the day on which Schedule 3 comes into force, paragraph 3 of the Schedule has effect with the omission of the exception.

Commencement
Sch 12, para 10: 13 October 2003 (SI 2003/1725, art 2(1)).

Extent
Sch 12, para 10: England, Wales

11 For the period of three years beginning with the day on which Schedule 3 comes into force, it has effect with the insertion after paragraph 14 of—

"15.

A right under paragraph 18(1) of Schedule 12."

Commencement
Sch 12, para 11: 13 October 2003 (SI 2003/1725, art 2(1)).

Extent
Sch 12, para 11: England, Wales.

12 Paragraph 1 of each of Schedules 1 and 3 shall be taken to include an interest which immediately before the coming into force of the Schedule was an overriding interest under section 70(1)(k) of the Land Registration Act 1925.

Commencement
Sch 12, para 12: 13 October 2003 (SI 2003/1725 art 2(1)).

Extent
Sch 12, para 12: England, Wales.

13 Paragraph 6 of each of Schedules 1 and 3 shall be taken to include an interest which immediately before the coming into force of the Schedule was an overriding interest under section 70(1)(i) of the Land Registration Act 1925 and whose status as such was preserved by section 19(3) of the Local Land Charges Act 1975 (c. 76) (transitional provision in relation to change in definition of "local land charge").

Commencement
Sch 12, para 13: 13 October 2003 (SI 2003/1725, art 2(1)).

Extent
Sch 12, para 13: England, Wales.

Cautions against first registration

14 (1) For the period of two years beginning with the day on which section 15 comes into force, it has effect with the following omissions—

(a)   in subsection (1), the words "Subject to subsection (3),", and
(b)   subsection (3).

(2) Any caution lodged by virtue of sub-paragraph (1) which is in force immediately before the end of the period mentioned in that sub-paragraph shall cease to have effect at the end of that period, except in relation to applications for registration made before the end of that period.

(3) This paragraph does not apply to section 15 as applied by section 81.

Commencement
Sch 12, para 14(1)–(3): 13 October 2003 (SI 2003/1725, art 2(1)).

Extent
Sch 12, para 14(1)–(3): England, Wales.

15 (1) As applied by section 81, section 15 has effect for the period of ten years beginning with the day on which it comes into force, or such longer period as rules may provide, with the omission of subsection (3)(a)(i).

(2) Any caution lodged by virtue of sub-paragraph (1) which is in force immediately before the end of the period mentioned in that sub-paragraph shall cease to have effect at the end of that period, except in relation to applications for registration made before the end of that period.

Commencement
Sch 12, para 15(1)–(2): 13 October 2003 (SI 2003/1725, art 2(1)).

Extent
Sch 12, para 15(1)–(2): England, Wales.

16 This Act shall apply as if the definition of "caution against first registration" in section 132 included cautions lodged under section 53 of the Land Registration Act 1925 (c. 21).

Commencement
Sch 12, para 16: 13 October 2003 (SI 2003/1725, art 2(1)).

Extent
Sch 12, para 16: England, Wales.

Applications under section 34 or 43 by cautioners

17 Where a caution under section 54 of the Land Registration Act 1925 is lodged in respect of a person's estate, right, interest or claim, he may only make an application under section 34 or 43 above in respect of that estate, right, interest or claim if he also applies to the registrar for the withdrawal of the caution.

Commencement
Sch 12, para 17: 13 October 2003 (SI 2003/1725, art 2(1)).

Extent
Sch 12, para 17: England, Wales.

Adverse possession

18 (1) Where a registered estate in land is held in trust for a person by virtue of section 75(1) of the Land Registration Act 1925 immediately before the coming into force of section 97, he is entitled to be registered as the proprietor of the estate.

(2) A person has a defence to any action for the possession of land (in addition to any other defence he may have) if he is entitled under this paragraph to be registered as the proprietor of an estate in the land.

(3) Where in an action for possession of land a court determines that a person is entitled to a defence under this paragraph, the court must order the registrar to register him as the proprietor of the estate in relation to which he is entitled under this paragraph to be registered.

(4) Entitlement under this paragraph shall be disregarded for the purposes of section 131(1).

(5) Rules may make transitional provision for cases where a rentcharge is held in trust under section 75(1) of the Land Registration Act 1925 immediately before the coming into force of section 97.

Commencement
Sch 12, para 18(1)–(5): 13 October 2003 (SI 2003/1725, art 2(1)).

Extent
Sch 12, para 18(1)–(5): England, Wales.

Indemnities

19 (1) Schedule 8 applies in relation to claims made before the commencement of that Schedule which have not been settled by agreement or finally determined by that time (as well as to claims for indemnity made after the commencement of that Schedule).

(2) But paragraph 3(1) of that Schedule does not apply in relation to costs and expenses incurred in respect of proceedings, negotiations or other matters begun before 27 April 1997.

Commencement
Sch 12, para 19(1)–(2): 13 October 2003 (SI 2003/1725 art 2(1)).

Extent
Sch 12, para 19(1)–(2): England, Wales.

Implied indemnity covenants on transfers of pre-1996 leases

20 (1) On a disposition of a registered leasehold estate by way of transfer, the following covenants are implied in the instrument effecting the disposition, unless the contrary intention is expressed—

(a) in the case of a transfer of the whole of the land comprised in the registered lease, the covenant in sub-paragraph (2), and
(b) in the case of a transfer of part of the land comprised in the lease—
  (i) the covenant in sub-paragraph (3), and
  (ii) where the transferor continues to hold land under the lease, the covenant in sub-paragraph (4).

(2) The transferee covenants with the transferor that during the residue of the term granted by the registered lease the transferee and the persons deriving title under him will—

  (a) pay the rent reserved by the lease,
  (b) comply with the covenants and conditions contained in the lease, and
  (c) keep the transferor and the persons deriving title under him indemnified against all actions, expenses and claims on account of any failure to comply with paragraphs (a) and (b).

(3) The transferee covenants with the transferor that during the residue of the term granted by the registered lease the transferee and the persons deriving title under him will—

  (a) where the rent reserved by the lease is apportioned, pay the rent apportioned to the part transferred,
  (b) comply with the covenants and conditions contained in the lease so far as affecting the part transferred, and
  (c) keep the transferor and the persons deriving title under him indemnified against all actions, expenses and claims on account of any failure to comply with paragraphs (a) and (b).

(4) The transferor covenants with the transferee that during the residue of the term granted by the registered lease the transferor and the persons deriving title under him will—

  (a) where the rent reserved by the lease is apportioned, pay the rent apportioned to the part retained,
  (b) comply with the covenants and conditions contained in the lease so far as affecting the part retained, and
  (c) keep the transferee and the persons deriving title under him indemnified against all actions, expenses and claims on account of any failure to comply with paragraphs (a) and (b).

(5) This paragraph does not apply to a lease which is a new tenancy for the purposes of section 1 of the Landlord and Tenant (Covenants) Act 1995 (c. 30).

Commencement
Sch 12, para 20(1)–(5): 13 October 2003 (SI 2003/1725, art 2(1)).

Extent
Sch 12, para 20(1)–(5): England, Wales.

Appendix 2

Land Registration Rules 2003
SI 2003/1417 (extracts)

PART 1
THE REGISTER OF TITLE

2.— Form and arrangement of the register of title

(1) The register of title may be kept in electronic or paper form, or partly in one form and partly in the other.

(2) Subject to rule 3, the register of title must include an individual register for each registered estate which is–

(a) an estate in land, or
(b) a rentcharge, franchise, manor or profit a prendre in gross, vested in a proprietor.

Commencement
Pt 1, r 2(1)–(2)(b): 13 October 2003 being the day on which Land Registration Act 2002, s 1 comes into force (LRA 2002, Pt 1, s 1; SI 2003/1417, Pt 100, r 1).

Extent
Pt 1, r 2(1)–(2)(b): England, Wales.

3.— Individual registers and more than one registered estate, division and amalgamation

(1) The registrar may include more than one registered estate in an individual register if the estates are of the same kind and are vested in the same proprietor.

(2) On first registration of a registered estate, the registrar may open an individual register for each separate area of land affected by the proprietor's registered estate as he designates.

(3) Subsequently, the registrar may open an individual register for part of the registered estate in a registered title and retain the existing individual register for the remainder–

(a) on the application of the proprietor of the registered estate and of any registered charge over it, or
(b) if he considers it desirable for the keeping of the register of title, or
(c) on the registration of a charge of part of the registered estate comprised in the registered title.

(4) The registrar may amalgamate two or more registered titles, or add an estate which is being registered for the first time to an existing registered title, if the estates are of the same kind and are vested in the same proprietor–

(a) on the application of the proprietor of the registered estate and of any registered charge over it, or
(b) if he considers it desirable for the keeping of the register of title.

(5) Where the registrar has divided a registered title under paragraph (3)(b) or amalgamated registered titles or an estate on first registration with a registered title under paragraph (4)(b) he–

    (a)   must notify the proprietor of the registered estate and any registered charge, unless they have agreed to such action, and

    (b)   may make a new edition of any individual register or make entries on any individual register to reflect the division or amalgamation.

Commencement

Pt 1, r 3(1)–(5)(b): 13 October 2003 being the day on which Land Registration Act 2002, s 1 comes into force (LRA 2002, Pt 1, s 1; SI 2003/1417,Pt 100, r 1).

Extent

Pt 1, r 3(1)–(5)(b): England, Wales.

4.— Arrangement of individual registers

(1) Each individual register must have a distinguishing number, or series of letters and numbers, known as the title number.

(2) Each individual register must consist of a property register, a proprietorship register and, where necessary, a charges register.

(3) An entry in an individual register may be made by reference to a plan or other document; in which case the registrar must keep the original or a copy of the document.

(4) Whenever the registrar considers it desirable, he may make a new edition of any individual register so that it contains only the subsisting entries, rearrange the entries in the register or alter its title number.

Commencement

Pt 1, r 4(1)–(4): 13 October 2003 being the day on which Land Registration Act 2002, s 1 comes into force (LRA 2002, Pt 1, s. 1; SI 2003/1417, Pt 100, r 1).

Extent

Pt 1, r 4(1)–(4): England, Wales.

5. Contents of the property register

[Except where otherwise permitted, the][1] property register of a registered estate must contain–

[Except where otherwise permitted, the][1] property register of a registered estate must contain–

    (a)   a description of the registered estate which in the case of a registered estate in land, rentcharge or registered franchise which is an affecting franchise must refer to a plan based on the Ordnance Survey map and known as the title plan;

    (b)   where appropriate, details of–

        (i)   the inclusion or exclusion of mines and minerals in or from the registration under rule 32,

        [(ii)   easements, rights and privileges benefiting the registered estate and other similar matters,][2]

        (iii)   all exceptions [or reservations][3] arising on enfranchisement of formerly copyhold land, and

(iv) any [...][4] matter [otherwise][5] required to be entered in any other part of the register which the registrar considers may more conveniently be entered in the property register, and

(c) such other matters as are required to be entered in the property register by these rules.

Notes
1   Word substituted by Land Registration (Amendment) Rules 2008, SI 2008/1919, Sch 1, para 1(a) (10 November 2008).
2   Substituted by Land Registration (Amendment) Rules 2008, SI 2008/1919, Sch 1, para 1(b) (10 November 2008).
3   Words inserted by Land Registration (Amendment) Rules 2008, SI 2008/1919, Sch 1, para 1(c) (10 November 2008).
4   Word repealed by Land Registration (Amendment) Rules 2008, SI 2008/1919, Sch 1, para 1(d) (10 November 2008).
5   Word inserted by Land Registration (Amendment) Rules 2008, SI 2008/1919, Sch 1, para 1(d) (10 November 2008).

Commencement
Pt 1, r 5(a)–(c): 13 October 2003 being the day on which Land Registration Act 2002, s 1 comes into force (LRA 2002, Pt 1, s 1; SI 2003/1417, Pt 100, r 1).

Extent
Pt 1, r 5(a)–(c): England, Wales.

6.— Property register of a registered leasehold estate

(1) The property register of a registered leasehold estate must also contain sufficient particulars of the registered lease to enable that lease to be identified.

(2) [Subject to rule 72A(3), if][1] the lease contains a provision that prohibits or restricts dispositions of the leasehold estate, the registrar must make an entry in the property register stating that [the lease prohibits or restricts dispositions of the estate][2].

Notes
1   Words inserted by Land Registration (Amendment) (No 2) Rules 2005, SI 2005/1982, Pt 2, r 4 (9 January 2006).
2   Words substituted by Land Registration (Amendment) Rules 2008, SI 2008/1919, Sch 1, para 2 (10 November 2008).

Commencement
Pt 1, r 6(1)–(2): 13 October 2003 being the day on which Land Registration Act 2002, s 1 comes into force (LRA 2002, Pt 1, s 1; SI 2003/1417, Pt 100, r 1).

Extent
Pt 1, r 6(1)–(2): England, Wales.

7. Property register of a registered estate in a rentcharge, a franchise or a profit a prendre in gross

[Where practicable, the][1] property register of a registered estate in a rentcharge, franchise or a profit a prendre in gross must, if the estate was created by an instrument, also contain sufficient particulars of the instrument to enable it to be identified.

Notes
1   Word substituted by Land Registration (Amendment) Rules 2008, SI 2008/1919, Sch 1, para 3 (10 November 2008).

Commencement
Pt 1, r 7: 13 October 2003 being the day on which Land Registration Act 2002, s 1 comes into force (LRA 2002, s 1; SI 2003/1417, Pt 100, r 1).

Extent
Pt 1, r 7: England, Wales.

8.— Contents of the proprietorship register

(1) The proprietorship register of a registered estate must contain, where appropriate–

- (a) the class of title,
- (b) the name of the proprietor of the registered estate including, where the proprietor is a company registered under the Companies Acts, or a limited liability partnership incorporated under the Limited Liability Partnerships Act 2000, its registered number,
- (c) an address for service of the proprietor of the registered estate in accordance with r 198,
- (d) restrictions under section 40 of the Act, including one entered under section 86(4) of the Act, in relation to the registered estate,
- (e) notices under section 86(2) of the Act in relation to the registered estate,
- (f) positive covenants by a transferor or transferee and indemnity convenants by a transferee entered under rules 64 or 65,
- (g) details of any modification of the covenants implied by paragraphs 20(2) and (3) of Schedule 12 to the Act entered under rule 66,
- (h) details of any modification of the covenants implied under the Law of Property (Miscellaneous Provisions) Act 1994 entered under rule 67(6), [and]¹
- (i) [...]¹
- (j) such other matters as are required to be entered in the proprietorship register by these rules.

[(2) Where practicable, the registrar must enter in the proprietorship register—
- (a) on first registration of a registered estate,
- (b) following completion by registration of a lease which is a registrable disposition, and
- (c) on a subsequent change of proprietor of a registered estate, the price paid or value declared for the registered estate.

(3) An entry made under paragraph (2) must remain until there is a change of proprietor, or some other change in the register of title which the registrar considers would result in the entry being misleading.]²

Notes
1   Revoked by Land Registration (Amendment) Rules 2008, SI 2008/1919, Sch 1, para 4(a) (10 November 2008).
2   Rules 8(2) and (3) substituted for r 8(2) by Land Registration (Amendment) Rules 2008, SI 2008/1919, Sch 1, para.4(b) (10 November 2008).

Commencement
Pt 1, r 8(1)–(2): 13 October 2003 being the day on which Land Registration Act 2002, s 1 comes into force (LRA 2002, Pt 1, s 1; SI 2003/1417, Pt 100, r 1).

Extent
Pt 1, r 8(1)–(3): England, Wales.

9. Contents of the charges register

[Except where otherwise permitted, the]¹ charges register of a registered estate must contain, where appropriate–

- (a) details of leases, charges, and any other interests which adversely affect the registered estate subsisting at the time of first registration of the estate or created thereafter,

(b) any dealings with the interests referred to in paragraph (a), or affecting their priority, which are capable of being noted on the register,

(c) sufficient details to enable any registered charge to be identified,

(d) the name of the proprietor of any registered charge including, where the proprietor is a company registered under the Companies Acts, or a limited liability partnership incorporated under the Limited Liability Partnerships Act 2000, its registered number,

(e) an address for service of the proprietor of any registered charge in accordance with rule 198,

(f) restrictions under section 40 of the Act, including one entered under section 86(4) of the Act, in relation to a registered charge,

(g) notices under section 86(2) of the Act in relation to a registered charge, [...]²

(h) such other matters affecting the registered estate or any registered charge as are required to be entered in the charges register by these rules [, and]³

[(i) any matter otherwise required to be entered in any other part of the register which the registrar considers may more conveniently be entered in the charges register.]⁴

Notes

1   Word substituted by Land Registration (Amendment) Rules 2008, SI 2008/1919, Sch 1, para 5(a) (10 November 2008).

2   Word repealed by Land Registration (Amendment) Rules 2008, SI 2008/1919, Sch 1, para 5(b) (10 November 2008).

3   Word substituted by Land Registration (Amendment) Rules 2008, SI 2008/1919, Sch 1, para 5(c) (10 November 2008).

4   Added by Land Registration (Amendment) Rules 2008, SI 2008/1919 Sch 1, para 5(d) (10 November 2008).

Commencement

Pt 1, r 9(a)–(h): 13 October 2003 being the day on which Land Registration Act 2002, s 1 comes into force (LRA 2002, Pt 1, s 1; SI 2003/1417, Pt 100, r 1).

Extent

Pt 1, r 9(a)–(i): England, Wales.

PART 3
APPLICATIONS: GENERAL PROVISIONS

13.— Form AP1

(1) Any application made under the Act or these rules for which no other application form is prescribed must be made in Form AP1.

(2) Paragraph (1) does not apply to–

(a) an application to remove from the register the name of a deceased joint registered proprietor,

(b) applications made under r 14, or

(c) outline applications as defined in r 54.

Commencement

Pt 3, r 13(1)–(2)(c): 13 October 2003 being the day on which Land Registration Act 2002, s 1 comes into force (LRA 2002, Pt 1, s 1; SI 2003/1417, Pt 100, r 1).

Extent

Pt 3, r 13(1)–(2)(c): England, Wales.

14. Electronic delivery of applications

Any application to which rule 15 applies (other than an outline application under rule 54) may during the currency of any notice given under Schedule 2, and subject to and in accordance with the limitations contained in that notice, be delivered by electronic means and the applicant shall provide, in such order as may be required by that notice, such of the particulars required for an application of that type as are appropriate in the circumstances and as are required by the notice.

Commencement
Pt 3, r 14: 13 October 2003 being the day on which Land Registration Act 2002, s 1 comes into force (LRA 2002, Pt 1, s 1; SI 2003/1417, Pt 100, r 1).

Extent
Pt 3, r 14: England, Wales.

15.— Time at which applications are taken to be made

(1) An application received on a business day is to be taken as made at the earlier of–

    (a) the time of the day that notice of it is entered in the day list, or
    (b) (i) midnight marking the end of the day it was received if the application was received before 12 noon, or
          (ii) midnight marking the end of the next business day after the day it was received if the application was received at or after 12 noon.

(2) An application received on a day which is not a business day is to be taken as made at the earlier of–

    (a) the time of [the]¹ day that notice of it is entered in the day list, or
    (b) midnight marking the end of the next business day after the day it was received.

(3) In this rule an application is received when it is delivered–

    (a) to the designated proper office in accordance with an order under section 100(3) of the Act, or
    (b) to the registrar in accordance with a written arrangement as to delivery made between the registrar and the applicant or between the registrar and the applicant's conveyancer, or
    (c) to the registrar under the provisions of any relevant notice given under Schedule 2.

(4) This rule does not apply to applications under Part 13, other than an application that the registrar designate a document an exempt information document under rule 136.

Notes
1   Words substituted by Land Registration (Electronic Conveyancing) Rules 2008, SI 2008/1750, Sch 2(1), para 2 (4 August 2008).

Commencement
Pt 3, r 15(1)–(4): 13 October 2003 being the day on which Land Registration Act 2002, s 1 comes into force (LRA 2002, Pt 1, s 1; SI 2003/1417, Pt 100, r 1).

Extent
Pt 3, r 15(1)–(4): England, Wales.

16.— Applications not in order

(1) If an application is not in order the registrar may raise such requisitions as he considers necessary, specifying a period (being not less than twenty business days) within which the applicant must comply with the requisitions.

(2) If the applicant fails to comply with the requisitions within that period, the registrar may cancel the application or may extend the period when this appears to him to be reasonable in the circumstances.

(3) If an application appears to the registrar to be substantially defective, he may reject it on delivery or he may cancel it at any time thereafter.

(4) Where a fee for an application is paid by means of a cheque and the registrar becomes aware, before that application has been completed, that the cheque has not been honoured, the application may be cancelled.

Commencement
Pt 3, r 16(1)–(4): 13 October 2003 being the day on which Land Registration Act 2002, s 1 comes into force (LRA 2002, Pt 1, s 1; SI 2003/1417, Pt 100, r 1).

Extent
Pt 3, r 16(1)–(4): England, Wales.

17. Additional evidence and enquiries

If the registrar at any time considers that the production of any further documents or evidence or the giving of any notice is necessary or desirable, he may refuse to complete or proceed with an application, or to do any act or make any entry, until such documents, evidence or notices have been supplied or given.

Commencement
Pt 3, r 17: 13 October 2003 being the day on which Land Registration Act 2002, s 1 comes into force (LRA 2002, Pt 1, s 1; SI 2003/1417, Pt 100, r 1).

Extent
Pt 3, r 17: England, Wales.

18. Continuation of application on a transfer by operation of law

If, before an application has been completed, the whole of the applicant's interest is transferred by operation of law, the application may be continued by the person entitled to that interest in consequence of that transfer.

Commencement
Pt 3, r 18: 13 October 2003 being the day on which Land Registration Act 2002, s 1 comes into force (LRA 2002, Pt 1, s 1; SI 2003/1417, Pt 100, r 1).

Extent
Pt 3, r 18: England, Wales.

19.— Objections

(1) Subject to paragraph (5), an objection under section 73 of the Act to an application must be made by delivering to the registrar at the appropriate office a written statement signed by the objector or his conveyancer.

(2) The statement must–

  (a) state that the objector objects to the application,

(b) state the grounds for the objection, and

(c) give the full name of the objector and an address [for service in accordance with rule 198][1].

(3) Subject to paragraph (5), the written statement referred to in paragraph (1) must be delivered–

(a) in paper form, or

(b) to the electronic address, or

(c) to the fax number.

(4) In paragraph (3) the reference to the electronic address and the fax number is to the electronic address or fax number for the appropriate office specified in a direction by the registrar under section 100(4) of the Act as that to be used for delivery of objections.

(5) Where a person is objecting to an application in response to a notice given by the registrar, he may alternatively do so in the manner and to the address stated in the notice as provided by rule 197(1)(c).

(6) In this rule the appropriate office is the same office as the proper office, designated under an order under section 100(3) of the Act, for the receipt of an application relating to the land in respect of which the objection is made, but on the assumption that if the order contains exceptions none of the exceptions apply to that application.

Notes
1   Words substituted by Land Registration (Amendment) Rules 2008, SI 2008/1919, Sch 1, para 7 (10 November 2008).

Commencement
Pt 3, r 19(1)–(6): 13 October 2003 being the day on which Land Registration Act 2002, s 1 comes into force (LRA 2002, Pt 1, s 1; SI 2003/1417, Pt 100, r 1).

Extent
Pt 3, r 19(1)–(6): England, Wales.

20.— Completion of applications

(1) Any entry in, removal of an entry from or alteration of the register pursuant to an application under the Act or these rules has effect from the time of the making of the application.

(2) This rule does not apply to the applications mentioned in section 74 of the Act.

Commencement
Pt 3, r 20(1)–(2): 13 October 2003 being the day on which Land Registration Act 2002, s 1 comes into force (LRA 2002, Pt 1, s. 1; SI 2003/1417, Pt 100, r 1).

Extent
Pt 3, r 20(1)–(2): England, Wales.

PART 12
ALTERATIONS AND CORRECTIONS

126.— Alteration under a court order — not rectification

(1) Subject to paragraphs (2) and (3), if in any proceedings the court decides that–

(a) there is a mistake in the register,

   (b)   the register is not up to date, or

   (c)   here is an estate, right or interest excepted from the effect of registration that should be given effect to,

it must make an order for alteration of the register under the power given by paragraph 2(1) of Schedule 4 to the Act.

(2) The court is not obliged to make an order if there are exceptional circumstances that justify not doing so.

(3) This rule does not apply to an alteration of the register that amounts to rectification.

Commencement
Pt 12, r 126(1)–(3): 13 October 2003 being the day on which Land Registration Act 2002, s 1 comes into force (LRA 2002, Pt 1, s 1; SI 2003/1417, Pt 100, r 1).

Extent
Pt 12, r 126(1)–(3): England, Wales.

127.— Court order for alteration of the register — form and service

(1) An order for alteration of the register must state the title number of the title affected and the alteration that is to be made, and must direct the registrar to make the alteration.

(2) Service on the registrar of an order for alteration of the register must be made by making an application for the registrar to give effect to the order, accompanied by the order.

Commencement
Pt 12, r 127(1)–(2): 13 October 2003 being the day on which Land Registration Act 2002, s 1 comes into force (LRA 2002, Pt 1, s 1; SI 2003/1417, Pt 100, r 1).

Extent
Pt 12, r 127(1)–(2): England, Wales.

128.— Alteration otherwise than pursuant to a court order — notice and enquiries

(1) Subject to paragraph (5), this rule applies where an application for alteration of the register has been made, or where the registrar is considering altering the register without an application having been made.

(2) The registrar must give notice of the proposed alteration to–

   (a)   the registered proprietor of any registered estate,

   (b)   the registered proprietor of any registered charge, and

   (c)   subject to paragraph (3), any person who appears to the registrar to be entitled to an interest protected by a notice,

where that estate, charge or interest would be affected by the proposed alteration, unless he is satisfied that such notice is unnecessary.

(3) The registrar is not obliged to give notice to a person referred to in paragraph (2)(c) if that person's name and his address for service under rule 198 are not set out in the individual register in which the notice is entered.

(4) The registrar may make such enquiries as he thinks fit.

(5) This rule does not apply to alteration of the register in the specific circumstances covered by any other rule.

Commencement
Pt 12, r 128(1)-(5): 13 October 2003 being the day on which Land Registration Act 2002, s 1 comes into force (LRA 2002, Pt 1, s 1; SI 2003/1417, Pt 100, r 1).

Extent
Pt 12, r 128(1)–(5): England, Wales.

129. Alteration otherwise than under a court order — evidence

Unless otherwise provided in these rules, an application for alteration of the register (otherwise than under a court order) must be supported by evidence to justify the alteration.

Commencement
Pt 12, r 129: 13 October 2003 being the day on which Land Registration Act 2002, s 1 comes into force (LRA 2002, Pt 1, s 1; SI 2003/1417, Pt 100, r 1).

Extent
Pt 12, r 129: England, Wales.

130.— Correction of mistakes in an application or accompanying document

(1) This rule applies to any alteration made by the registrar for the purpose of correcting a mistake in any application or accompanying document.

(2) The alteration will have effect as if made by the applicant or other interested party or parties–

(a)   in the case of a mistake of a clerical or like nature, in all circumstances,
(b)   in the case of any other mistake, only if the applicant and every other interested party has requested, or consented to, the alteration.

Commencement
Pt 12, r 130(1)–(2)(b): 13 October 2003 being the day on which Land Registration Act 2002, s 1 comes into force (LRA 2002, Pt 1, s 1; SI 2003/1417, Pt 100, r 1).

Extent
Pt 12, r 130(1)–(2)(b): England, Wales.

Appendix 3

Land Registration (Referral to the Adjudicator to HM Land Registry) Rules 2003 SI 2003/2114

1. Citation and commencement

These Rules may be cited as the Land Registration (Referral to the Adjudicator to HM Land Registry) Rules 2003 and shall come into force on 13 October 2003.

Commencement
Rule 1: 13 October 2003

Extent
Rule 1: England, Wales.

2. Interpretation

In these Rules–

> "the Act" means the Land Registration Act 2002;
> "business day" means a day when the land registry is open to the public under rule 216 of the Land Registration Rules 2003;
> "disputed application" means an application to the registrar under the Act to which an objection has been made;
> "objection" means an objection made under section 73 of the Act;
> "the parties" means the person who has made the disputed application and the person who has made an objection to that application.

Commencement
Rule 2 definition of "the Act"- definition of "the parties": 13 October 2003.

Extent
Rule 2 definition of "the Act"- definition of "the parties": England, Wales.

3.— Procedure for referral to the adjudicator

(1) When the registrar is obliged to refer a matter to the adjudicator under section 73(7) of the Act, he must as soon as practicable–

- (a) prepare a case summary containing the information set out in paragraph (2),
- (b) send a copy of the case summary to the parties,
- (c) give the parties an opportunity to make comments on the contents of the case summary in the manner, to the address, and within the time specified by him, and
- (d) inform the parties in writing that the case summary together with copies of the documents listed in it will be sent to the adjudicator with the notice referred to in rule 5(2).

(2) The case summary must contain the following information–

    (a)   the names of the parties,

    (b)   the addresses of the parties,

    (c)   details of their legal or other representatives (if any),

    (d)   a summary of the core facts,

    (e)   details of the disputed application,

    (f)   details of the objection to that application,

    (g)   a list of any documents that will be copied to the adjudicator, and

    (h)   anything else that the registrar may consider to be appropriate.

(3) The registrar may amend the case summary as he considers appropriate having considered any written comments made to him by the parties under paragraph (1)(c).

Commencement
Rule 3(1)–(3): 13 October 2003.

Extent
Rule 3(1)–(3): England, Wales.

4.— Parties' addresses

(1) If the address of a party set out in the case summary does not comply with paragraph (2), that party must provide the registrar with one that does.

(2) An address complies with this paragraph if it–

    (a)   is a postal address in England and Wales, and

    (b)   is either that of the party or of his representative.

Commencement
Rule 4(1)–(2)(b): 13 October 2003.

Extent
Rule 4(1)–(2)(b): England, Wales.

5.— Notice of referral to the adjudicator

(1) This rule applies–

    (a)   when the registrar has considered any written comments made by the parties under rule 3(1)(c), or

    (b)   if he has not received any comments from the parties within the time specified under rule 3(1)(c), on the expiry of that period, and

    (c)   when he has amended the case summary, if appropriate, under rule 3(3).

(2) The registrar must as soon as practicable–

    (a)   send to the adjudicator a written notice, accompanied by the documents set out in paragraph (3), informing him that the matter is referred to him under section 73(7) of the Act,

    (b)   inform the parties in writing that the matter has been referred to the adjudicator, and

    (c)   send the parties a copy of the case summary prepared under rule 3 in the form sent to the adjudicator.

(3) The notice sent to the adjudicator under paragraph (2)(a) must be accompanied by–

    (a)   the case summary prepared under rule 3 amended, if appropriate, by the registrar under rule 3(3), and

    (b)   copies of the documents listed in that case summary.

Commencement
Rule 5(1)–(3)(b): 13 October 2003.

Extent
Rule 5(1)–(3)(b): England, Wales.

6.— Specified time periods

(1) For the purposes of rule 3(1)(c), the time specified by the registrar must not end before 12 noon on the fifteenth business day after the date on which the registrar sends the copy of the case summary to the relevant party under rule 3(1)(b) or such earlier time as the parties may agree.

(2) On and after the date specified in any notice given pursuant to rule 216(2) of the Land Registration Rules 2003, paragraph (1) shall have effect with the substitution of the words "eighteenth business day" for the words "fifteenth business day".

Commencement
Rule 6(1)–(2): 13 October 2003.

Extent
Rule 6(1)–(2): England, Wales.

Appendix 4

Adjudicator to Her Majesty's Land Registry (Practice and Procedure) Rules 2003 SI 2003/2171 (as amended)

1. Citation and Commencement

These Rules may be cited as the Adjudicator to Her Majesty's Land Registry (Practice and Procedure) Rules 2003 and shall come into force on 13th October 2003.

Commencement
Rule 1: 13 October 2003.

Extent
Rule 1: England, Wales.

PART 1
INTRODUCTION

2.– Interpretation

(1) In these Rules–

"applicant" means the party whom the adjudicator designates as such under rule 5 or under rule 24, or the party who makes a rectification application;

["document" means anything in which information is recorded in any form, and an obligation in these Rules to provide or allow access to a document or a copy of a document for any purpose means, unless the adjudicator directs otherwise, an obligation to provide access to such document or copy in a legible form or in a form which can be readily made into a legible form;][1]

"hearing" means a sitting of the adjudicator for the purpose of enabling the adjudicator to reach or announce a substantive decision, but does not include a sitting of the adjudicator solely in the exercise of one or more of the following powers–

(a) to consider an application, representation or objection made in the interim part of the proceedings;

(b) to reach a substantive decision without an oral hearing; or

(c) to consider whether to grant permission to appeal a decision or to stay the implementation of a decision pending the outcome of an appeal;

"matter" means the subject of either a reference or a rectification application;

"office copy" means an official copy of a document held or issued by a public authority;

"original application" means the application originally made to the registrar that resulted in a reference;

161

"proceedings" means, except in the expression "court proceedings", the proceedings of the matter before the adjudicator but does not include any negotiations, communications or proceedings that occurred prior to the reference or rectification application;

"record of matters" means a record of references, rectification applications and certain other applications and decisions, kept in accordance with these Rules and in particular in accordance with rule 46;

"rectification application" means an application made to rectify or set aside a document under section 108(2) for determination of the matter by the adjudicator;

"reference" means a reference from the registrar to the adjudicator under section 73(7) for determination of the matter by the adjudicator;

"respondent" means the party or parties who the adjudicator designates as such under rule 5 or rule 24, or the party or parties making an objection to a rectification application;

["statement of truth" means–

(a) in the case of a witness statement, a statement signed by the maker of the statement that the maker of the statement believes that the facts stated in the witness statement are true; or

(b) in the case of other documents, a statement that the party by whom or on whose behalf the document is submitted believes the facts stated in the document are true, signed by either–

  (i) the party by whom or on whose behalf the document is submitted; or

  (ii) that party's authorised representative, in which case the statement of truth must state the name of the representative and the relationship of the representative to the party;][2]

"substantive decision" means a decision of the adjudicator on the matter or on any substantive issue that arises in it but does not include any direction in interim parts of the proceedings [, any order made under rule 8(4) or 9(4),][3] or any order as to costs or any order as to costs thrown away ;

"substantive order" means an order or direction that records and gives effect to a substantive decision;

"the Act" means the Land Registration Act 2002 and a reference to a section by number alone is a reference to a section of the Act;

"witness statement" means a written statement [...][4] containing the evidence that the witness intends to give [and verified by a statement of truth][5]; and

"working day" means any day other than a Saturday or Sunday, Christmas Day, Good Friday or any other bank holiday.

(2) [For the purposes of these][6] Rules a person has a document [...][7] in his possession or control if–

(a) it is in his physical possession;

(b) he has a right to possession of it; or

(c) he has a right to inspect or take copies of it.

Notes

1 Definition inserted by Adjudicator to Her Majesty's Land Registry (Practice and Procedure) (Amendment) Rules 2008, SI 2008/1731, r 5(a)(i) (25 July 2008).

2 Definition inserted by Adjudicator to Her Majesty's Land Registry (Practice and Procedure) (Amendment) Rules 2008, SI 2008/1731, r 5(a)(ii) (25 July 2008).

3   Words inserted by Adjudicator to Her Majesty's Land Registry (Practice and Procedure) (Amendment) Rules 2008, SI 2008/1731, r 5(a)(iii) (25 July 2008).
4   Words repealed by Adjudicator to Her Majesty's Land Registry (Practice and Procedure) (Amendment) Rules 2008, SI 2008/1731, r 5(a)(iv)(aa) (25 July 2008).
5   Words inserted by Adjudicator to Her Majesty's Land Registry (Practice and Procedure) (Amendment) Rules 2008, SI 2008/1731, r 5(a)(iv)(bb) (25 July 2008).
6   Words substituted by Adjudicator to Her Majesty's Land Registry (Practice and Procedure) (Amendment) Rules 2008, SI 2008/1731, r 5(b)(i) (25 July 2008).
7   Words repealed by Adjudicator to Her Majesty's Land Registry (Practice and Procedure) (Amendment) Rules 2008, SI 2008/1731, r 5(b)(ii) (25 July 2008).

Commencement
Pt 1, r 2(1)–(2)(c): 13 October 2003.

Extent
Pt 1, r 2(1)–(2)(c): England, Wales.

3.– The overriding objective

(1) The overriding objective of these Rules is to enable the adjudicator to deal with matters justly.

(2) Dealing with a matter justly includes, so far as is practicable–

    (a)   ensuring that the parties are on an equal footing;
    (b)   saving expense;
    (c)   dealing with the matter in ways that are proportionate–
        (i)   to the value of the land or other interests involved;
        (ii)   to the importance of the matter;
        (iii) to the complexity of the issues in the matter; and
        (iv)   to the financial position of each party; and
    (d)   ensuring that the matter is dealt with expeditiously and fairly.

(3) The adjudicator must seek to give effect to the overriding objective when he–

    (a)   exercises any power given to him by these Rules; or
    (b)   interprets these Rules.

(4) The parties are required to help the adjudicator to further the overriding objective.

Commencement
Pt 1, r 3(1)–(4): 13 October 2003.

Extent
Pt 1, r 3(1)–(4): England, Wales.

PART 2
REFERENCES TO THE ADJUDICATOR

4. Scope of this Part

The rules in this Part apply to references.

Commencement
Pt 2, r 4: 13 October 2003.

Extent
Pt 2, r 4: England, Wales.

5. Notice of receipt by the adjudicator of a reference

Following receipt by the adjudicator of a reference, the adjudicator must–

- (a) enter the particulars of the reference in the record of matters; and
- (b) serve on the parties notice in writing of–
  - (i) the fact that the reference has been received by the adjudicator;
  - (ii) the date when the adjudicator received the reference;
  - (iii) the matter number allocated to the reference;
  - (iv) the name and any known address and address for service of the parties to the proceedings; and
  - (v) which party will be the applicant for the purposes of the proceedings and which party or parties will be the respondent.

Commencement
Pt 2, r 5(a)–(b)(v): 13 October 2003.

Extent
Pt 2, r 5(a)–(b)(v): England, Wales.

6. Direction to commence court proceedings under section 110(1)

Where the adjudicator intends to direct a party to commence court proceedings under section 110(1), the parties may make representations or objections but any representations or objections must be concerned with one or more of the following–

- (a) whether the adjudicator should make such a direction;
- (b) which party should be directed to commence court proceedings;
- (c) the time within which court proceedings should commence; and
- (d) the questions the court should determine.

Commencement
Pt 2, r 6(a)–(d): 13 October 2003.

Extent
Pt 2, r 6(a)–(d): England, Wales.

7.– Notification to the adjudicator of court proceedings following a direction to commence court proceedings under section 110(1)

(1) In this Part–

> the date that the matter before the court is finally disposed of" means the earliest date by which the court proceedings relating to the matter or on the relevant part (including any court proceedings on or in consequence of an appeal) have been determined and any time for appealing or further appealing has expired; "the relevant part" means the part of the matter in relation to which the adjudicator has directed a party under section 110(1) to commence court proceedings; and
> "the final court order" means the order made by the court that records the court's final determination (on appeal or otherwise).

(2) A party who has been directed to commence court proceedings under section 110(1) must serve on the adjudicator–

- (a) within 14 days of the commencement of the court proceedings, a written notice stating–

    (i)   that court proceedings have been issued in accordance with directions given by the adjudicator;

    (ii) the date of issue of the court proceedings;

    (iii) the names and any known addresses of the parties to the court proceedings;

    (iv) the name of the court at which the court proceedings will be heard; and

    (v) the case number allocated to the court proceedings;

  (b) within 14 days of the date of the court's decision on any application for an extension of time, a copy of that decision; and

  (c) within 14 days of the date that the matter before the court is finally disposed of, a copy of the final court order.

Commencement
Pt 2, r 7(1)–(2)(c): 13 October 2003.

Extent
Pt 2, r 7(1)–(2)(c): England, Wales.

8.– Adjournment of proceedings before the adjudicator following a direction to commence court proceedings on the whole of the matter under section 110(1)

(1) This rule applies where the adjudicator has directed a party under section 110(1) to commence court proceedings for the court's decision on the whole of the matter.

(2) Once he has received notice under rule 7(2)(a) that court proceedings have been issued, the adjudicator must adjourn all of the proceedings before him pending the outcome of the court proceedings.

(3) [Subject to paragraph (4), once the adjudicator][1] has received a copy of the final court order [in accordance with rule 7(2)(c)][2] and unless the court directs otherwise, the adjudicator must close the proceedings before him without making a substantive decision.

[(4) Before closing the proceedings in accordance with paragraph (3) the adjudicator may make an order either with or without a hearing and either with or without giving prior notice to the parties if–

(a) such order is necessary, in addition to the final court order, to implement the decision of the court; and

(b) the adjudicator would have had the power to make such order if the adjudicator had made a substantive decision in relation to the proceedings.][3]

Notes
1   Words substituted by Adjudicator to Her Majesty's Land Registry (Practice and Procedure) (Amendment) Rules 2008, SI 2008/1731, r 6(a)(i) (25 July 2008).
2   Words inserted by Adjudicator to Her Majesty's Land Registry (Practice and Procedure) (Amendment) Rules 2008, SI 2008/1731, r 6(a)(ii) (25 July 2008).
3   Added by Adjudicator to Her Majesty's Land Registry (Practice and Procedure) (Amendment) Rules 2008, SI 2008/1731, r 6(b) (25 July 2008).

Commencement
Pt 2, r 8(1)–(3): 13 October 2003.

Extent
Pt 2, r 8(1)–(4)(b): England, Wales.

9.– Adjournment of proceedings before the adjudicator following a direction to commence court proceedings on part of the matter under section 110(1)

(1) This rule applies where the adjudicator has directed a party under section 110(1) to commence court proceedings for the court's decision on the relevant part.

[(2) Once the adjudicator has received notice under rule 7(2)(a) that court proceedings have been issued in relation to the relevant part, the adjudicator must adjourn the proceedings brought under these Rules in relation to that part, pending the outcome of the court proceedings.]¹

(3) [Subject to paragraph (4), once the adjudicator]² has received a copy of the final court order on the relevant part [in accordance with rule 7(2)(c)]³ and unless the court directs otherwise, the adjudicator must close the proceedings before him in relation to the relevant part without making a substantive decision on that relevant part.

[(3A) Before closing the proceedings in relation to the relevant part in accordance with paragraph (3) the adjudicator may make an order either with or without a hearing and either with or without giving prior notice to the parties if–

    (a)   such order is necessary, in addition to the final court order, to implement the decision of the court; and

    (b)   the adjudicator would have had the power to make such order if the adjudicator had made a substantive decision in relation to the relevant part.]⁴

(4) The adjudicator may adjourn the proceedings in relation to any other part of the matter before him pending the outcome of the court proceedings.

(5) While the court proceedings are still ongoing, the party directed to commence court proceedings must notify the court of any substantive decision made by the adjudicator within 14 days of service on that party of the substantive decision.

Notes
1   Substituted by 'Adjudicator to Her Majesty's Land Registry (Practice and Procedure) (Amendment) Rules 2008, SI 2008/1731, r 7(a) (25 July 2008).
2   Words substituted by Adjudicator to Her Majesty's Land Registry (Practice and Procedure) (Amendment) Rules 2008, SI 2008/1731, r 7(b)(i) (25 July 2008).
3   Words inserted by Adjudicator to Her Majesty's Land Registry (Practice and Procedure) (Amendment) Rules 2008, SI 2008/1731, r 7(b)(ii) (25 July 2008).
4   Added by Adjudicator to Her Majesty's Land Registry (Practice and Procedure) (Amendment) Rules 2008, SI 2008/1731, r 7(c) (25 July 2008).

Commencement
Pt 2, r 9(1)–(5): 13 October 2003.

Extent
Pt 2, r 9(1)–(5): England, Wales.

10. Notification where court proceedings are commenced otherwise than following a direction to commence court proceedings under section 110(1)

Where a party commences or has commenced court proceedings otherwise than following a direction under section 110(1) and those court proceedings concern or relate to the matter before the adjudicator, that party must serve–

(a) on the adjudicator within 14 days of the commencement of the court proceedings or, if later, within 7 days of service on that party of notification of the reference under rule 5(b), a written notice stating–
  (i) that court proceedings have been issued;
  (ii) the way and the extent to which the court proceedings concern or relate to the matter before the adjudicator;
  (iii) the date of issue of the court proceedings;
  (iv) the names and any known addresses of the parties to the court proceedings;
  (v) the name of the court at which the court proceedings will be heard; and
  (vi) the case number allocated to the court proceedings;
(b) on the adjudicator within 14 days of the date that the matter before the court is finally disposed of, a copy of the final court order; and
(c) on the court within 14 days of service on that party of such a decision, a copy of any substantive decision made by the adjudicator on the matter.

Commencement
Pt 2, r 10(a)–(c): 13 October 2003.

Extent
Pt 2, r 10(a)–(c): England, Wales.

11. Adjournment of proceedings before the adjudicator where court proceedings are commenced otherwise than following a direction to commence court proceedings under section 110(1)

Where court proceedings are commenced otherwise than following a direction to commence court proceedings under section 110(1), the adjudicator may adjourn the whole or part of the proceedings before him pending the outcome of the court proceedings.

Commencement
Pt 2, r 11: 13 October 2003.

Extent
Pt 2, r 11: England, Wales.

12. Applicant's statement of case and documents

Unless otherwise directed by the adjudicator, the applicant must serve on the adjudicator and each of the other parties within 28 days of service of the notification of the reference under rule 5(b)–

(a) his statement of case which must be in accordance with rule 14; and [(b) copies of any documents in the applicant's possession or control which–
  (i) are central to the applicant's case; or
  (ii) the adjudicator or any other party to the proceedings will require in order properly to understand the applicant's statement of case.][1]

Notes
1 Substituted by Adjudicator to Her Majesty's Land Registry (Practice and Procedure) (Amendment) Rules 2008, SI 2008/1731, r 8 (25 July 2008).

Commencement
Pt 2, r 12(a)–(b): 13 October 2003.

Extent
Pt 2, r 12(a)–(b)(ii): England, Wales.

13. Respondent's statement of case and documents

The respondent must serve on the adjudicator and each of the other parties within 28 days of service of the applicant's statement of case–

    (a) his statement of case which must be in accordance with rule 14; and
    [(b) copies of any documents in the respondent's possession or control which–
        (i)   are central to the respondent's case; or
        (ii) the adjudicator or any other party to the proceedings will require in order properly to understand the respondent's statement of case.]¹

Notes
1   Substituted by Adjudicator to Her Majesty's Land Registry (Practice and Procedure) (Amendment) Rules 2008, SI 2008/1731, r 9 (25 July 2008).

Commencement
Pt 2, r 13(a)–(b): 13 October 2003.

Extent
Pt 2, r 13(a)–(b)(ii): England, Wales.

14.– Statement of case

(1) Where under these Rules a party is required to provide a statement of case, that statement of case must be in writing [, be verified by a statement of truth and include]¹ –

    (a) the name of the party and confirmation of the party's address for service;
    (b) the party's reasons for supporting or objecting to the original application;
    (c) the facts on which the party intends to rely in the proceedings; [and]²
    (d) […]³
    (e) a list of witnesses that the party intends to call to give evidence in support of the party's case.

(2) If in relation to part only of the matter–

    (a) a party has been directed to commence or has commenced court proceedings; or
    (b) the adjudicator has adjourned proceedings before him, the adjudicator may direct that the statement of case should contain the information specified in paragraphs (1)(b) to (1)(e) inclusive only in relation to the part of the matter that is not before the court for the court's decision or has not been adjourned before the adjudicator.

Notes
1   Words substituted by Adjudicator to Her Majesty's Land Registry (Practice and Procedure) (Amendment) Rules 2008, SI 2008/1731, r 10(a) (25 July 2008).
2   Word inserted by Adjudicator to Her Majesty's Land Registry (Practice and Procedure) (Amendment) Rules 2008, SI 2008/1731, r 10(b) (25 July 2008).
3   Revoked by Adjudicator to Her Majesty's Land Registry (Practice and Procedure) (Amendment) Rules 2008, SI 2008/1731, r 10(c) (25 July 2008).

Commencement
Pt 2, r 14(1)–(2)(b): 13 October 2003.

Extent
Pt 2, r 14(1)–(2)(b): England, Wales.

PART 3
RECTIFICATION APPLICATION TO THE ADJUDICATOR TO RECTIFY OR SET ASIDE DOCUMENTS

15. Scope of this Part

The rules in this Part apply to rectification applications.

Commencement
Pt 3, r 15: 13 October 2003.

Extent
Pt 3, r 15: England, Wales.

16.– Form and contents of a rectification application

(1) A rectification application must–

- (a) be made in writing;
- (b) be dated and [verified by a statement of truth][1];
- (c) be addressed to the adjudicator;
- (d) include the following information–
    - (i) the name and address of the person or persons against whom the order is sought;
    - (ii) details of the remedy being sought;
    - (iii) the grounds on which the rectification application is based;
    - (iv) [...][2]
    - (v) a list of witnesses that the party intends to call to give evidence in support of the rectification application; and
    - (vi) the applicant's name and address for service;
- (e) include the following copies–
    - [(i) copies of any documents in the applicant's possession or control which–
        - (aa) are central to the applicant's case; or
        - (bb) the adjudicator or any other party to the proceedings will require in order properly to understand the rectification application; and][3]
    - (ii) a copy of the document to which the rectification application relates, or if a copy is not available, details of the document, which must include if available, its nature, its date, the parties to it and any version number or other similar identification number or code that it has; and
- (f) be served on the adjudicator.

(2) Following receipt by the adjudicator of a rectification application, the adjudicator must enter the particulars of the rectification application in the record of matters.

(3) If, having considered the rectification application and made any enquiries he thinks necessary, the adjudicator is satisfied that it is groundless, he must reject the rectification application.

Notes
1   Words substituted by Adjudicator to Her Majesty's Land Registry (Practice and Procedure) (Amendment) Rules 2008, SI 2008/1731, r 11(a) (25 July 2008).
2   Revoked by Adjudicator to Her Majesty's Land Registry (Practice and Procedure) (Amendment) Rules 2008, SI 2008/1731, r 11(b) (25 July 2008).
3   Substituted by Adjudicator to Her Majesty's Land Registry (Practice and Procedure) (Amendment) Rules 2008, SI 2008/1731, r 11(c) (25 July 2008).

Commencement
Pt 3, r 16(1)–(3): 13 October 2003.

Extent
Pt 3, r 16(1)–(3): England, Wales.

17.– Notice of a rectification application

(1) This rule does not apply where the adjudicator has rejected a rectification application under rule 16(3).

(2) Where a rectification application has been received by the adjudicator, he must [either serve, or direct the applicant to]¹ serve on the person against whom the order is sought and on any other person who, in the opinion of the adjudicator, should be a party to the proceedings–

    (a)   written notice of the rectification application; and
    (b)   a copy of the rectification application.

(3) The [...]² notice under paragraph (2)(a) [must specify]³ that if a party receiving the notice has any objection to the rectification application and that party wishes to lodge an objection, he must lodge his objection within 28 days of service of the notice under paragraph (2)(a).

Notes
1   Words inserted by Adjudicator to Her Majesty's Land Registry (Practice and Procedure) (Amendment) Rules 2008, SI 2008/1731, r 12(a) (25 July 2008).
2   Words repealed by Adjudicator to Her Majesty's Land Registry (Practice and Procedure) (Amendment) Rules 2008, SI 2008/1731, r 12(b)(i) (25 July 2008).
3   Words inserted by Adjudicator to Her Majesty's Land Registry (Practice and Procedure) (Amendment) Rules 2008, SI 2008/1731, r 12(b)(ii) (25 July 2008).

Commencement
Pt 3, r 17(1)–(3): 13 October 2003.

Extent
Pt 3, r 17(1)–(3): England, Wales.

18. Objection to a rectification application

A person lodges an objection under rule 17(3) if within 28 days of service of the notice under rule 17(2)(a) he serves–

    (a)   on the adjudicator–
        [(i)   a written statement addressed to the adjudicator, dated and verified by a statement of truth, setting out the grounds for the objection;]¹
        (ii) [...]²
        [(iii)copies of any documents in the party's possession or control which–
        (aa) are central to the party's case; or
        (bb) the adjudicator or any other party to the proceedings will require in order properly to understand the party's written statement;]³
        (iv) a written list of witnesses that the party intends to call to give evidence in support of the objection; and
        (v)   written confirmation of his name and address for service; and
    (b)   on the other parties a copy of all the information and documents served on the adjudicator under sub-paragraph (a).

Commencement
Pt 3, r 18(a)–(b): 13 October 2003.

Extent
Pt 3, r 18(a)–(b): England, Wales.

PART 4
PREPARATION FOR DETERMINATION OF REFERENCES AND RECTIFICATION APPLICATIONS

19. Scope of this Part

This Part sets out the procedure for the preparation for the determination of references and rectification applications.

Commencement
Pt 4, r 19: 13 October 2003.

Extent
Pt 4, r 19: England, Wales.

[20.– Directions

(1) The adjudicator may at any time, on the application of a party or otherwise, give directions to enable the parties to prepare for a hearing, or to assist the adjudicator to conduct the proceedings or determine any question in the proceedings with or without a hearing.

(2) Such directions may include, but are not limited to–

(a)   a direction that the parties attend a case management conference or a pre-hearing review; and
(b)   such other directions as are provided for in these Rules.][1]

Commencement
Pt 4, r 20: 13 October 2003.

Extent
Pt 4, r 20(1)–(2)(b): England, Wales.

21.– Form of directions

(1) Any direction made by the adjudicator must be–

(a)   in writing;
(b)   dated; and
(c)   except in the case of requirement notices under rule 28, served by him on–
    (i)   every party to the proceedings;

(ii) where the person who made the application, representation or objection that resulted in the direction was not a party, that person; and

(iii) where the direction requires the registrar to take action, the registrar.

(2) Directions containing a requirement must [, where appropriate,][1] include a statement of the possible consequences of failure to comply with the requirement within any time limit specified by these Rules, or imposed by the adjudicator.

(3) Directions requiring a party to provide or produce a document [...][2] may require the party to provide or produce it to the adjudicator or to another party or both.

Notes
1   Words inserted by Adjudicator to Her Majesty's Land Registry (Practice and Procedure) (Amendment) Rules 2008, SI 2008/1731, r 15(a) (25 July 2008).
2   Words repealed by Adjudicator to Her Majesty's Land Registry (Practice and Procedure) (Amendment) Rules 2008, SI 2008/1731, r 15(b) (25 July 2008).

Commencement
Pt 4, r 21(1)–(3): 13 October 2003.

Extent
Pt 4, r 21(1)–(3): England, Wales.

22. Consolidating proceedings

Where a reference or rectification application is related to another reference or rectification application and in the opinion of the adjudicator it is appropriate or practicable to do so, the adjudicator may direct that any or all of those related references or rectification applications be dealt with together.

Commencement
Pt 4, r 22: 13 October 2003.

Extent
Pt 4, r 22: England, Wales.

23. Intention to appear

The adjudicator may give directions requiring a party to state whether that party intends to–

(a) attend or be represented at the hearing; and
(b) call witnesses.

Commencement
Pt 4, r 23(a)–(b): 13 October 2003.

Extent
Pt 4, r 23(a)–(b): England, Wales.

24.– Addition and substitution of parties

(1) The adjudicator may give one or more of the following directions–

(a) that any person be added as a new party to the proceedings, if it appears to the adjudicator desirable for that person to be made a party;
(b) that any person cease to be a party to the proceedings, if it appears to the adjudicator that it is not desirable for that person to remain a party; and

    (c)   that a new party be substituted for an existing party, if–

        (i)   the existing party's interest or liability has passed to the new party; and

        (ii) it appears to the adjudicator desirable to do this to enable him to resolve the whole or part of the matter or any question of dispute in the proceedings.

(2) If the adjudicator directs that a new party is to be added to the proceedings, the adjudicator must specify–

    (a)   whether the new party is added as an applicant or a respondent; and

    (b)   how the new party is to be referred to.

(3) Each new party must be given a single identification that should be in accordance with the order in which they joined the proceedings, for example "second applicant" or "second respondent".

(4) If the adjudicator directs that a new party is to be substituted for an existing party, the adjudicator must specify which party the new party is to substitute, for example "respondent" or "second applicant".

(5) The adjudicator must [either serve, or direct one or more of the existing parties to][1] serve on each new party a copy of each of the following–

    (a)   the applicant's statement of case and copy documents served on the adjudicator under rule 12 or the applicant's rectification application served on the adjudicator under rule 16(1); and

    (b)   the respondent's statement of case and copy documents served on the adjudicator under rule 13 or the documents and information served by the respondent on the adjudicator under rule 18(a).

(6) If the new party is added to or substituted for parties to proceedings on a reference, the new party must serve on the adjudicator and each of the other parties within 28 days of service on him of the documents specified in paragraph (5)–

    (a)   his statement of case which must be in accordance with rule 14; and

    [(b) copies of any documents in the new party's possession or control which–

        (i)   are central to the new party's case; or

        (ii) the adjudicator or any other party to the proceedings will require in order properly to understand the new party's statement of case.][2]

(7) If the new party is added to or substituted for parties to proceedings on a rectification application, the new party must serve on the adjudicator and each of the other parties, within 28 days of service on him of the documents specified in paragraph (5)–

    (a)   if the new party is added or substituted as an applicant, his rectification application which must be in accordance with rule 16(1); or

    (b)   if the new party is added or substituted as a respondent, his objection to the rectification application which must be in accordance with rule 18(a).

(8) If a continuing party wishes to respond to the documents specified in paragraph (6) or (7), he may apply to the adjudicator for leave to do so.

(9) If the adjudicator grants the requested leave to respond, the adjudicator must require the party requesting leave to respond to serve a copy of his response on the adjudicator and all other parties.

(10) [When directing]³ the addition or substitution of parties [or at any time thereafter]⁴ and if it is necessary to do so, the adjudicator may give consequential directions, including for–

(a) the preparation and updating of a list of parties;
(b) the delivery and service of documents; and
(c) the waiver of the requirement to supply copies of documents [under paragraph (6)(b)]⁵ where copies have already been [served by or on the adjudicator and each of the other parties]⁶ in the course of the proceedings.

Notes
1 Words inserted by Adjudicator to Her Majesty's Land Registry (Practice and Procedure) (Amendment) Rules 2008, SI 2008/1731, r 16(a) (25 July 2008).
2 Added by Adjudicator to Her Majesty's Land Registry (Practice and Procedure) (Amendment) Rules 2008, SI 2008/1731, r 16(b) (25 July 2008).
3 Word substituted by Adjudicator to Her Majesty's Land Registry (Practice and Procedure) (Amendment) Rules 2008, SI 2008/1731, r 16(c)(i) (25 July 2008).
4 Words inserted by Adjudicator to Her Majesty's Land Registry (Practice and Procedure) (Amendment) Rules 2008, SI 2008/1731, r 16(c)(ii) (25 July 2008).
5 Words substituted by Adjudicator to Her Majesty's Land Registry (Practice and Procedure) (Amendment) Rules 2008, SI 2008/1731, r 16(c)(iii)(aa) (25 July 2008).
6 Words substituted by Adjudicator to Her Majesty's Land Registry (Practice and Procedure) (Amendment) Rules 2008, SI 2008/1731, r 16(c)(iii)(bb) (25 July 2008).

Commencement
Pt 4, r 24(1)–(10)(c): 13 October 2003.

Extent
Pt 4, r 24(1)–(10)(c): England, Wales.

25. Further information, supplementary statements and further responses to statements of case

The adjudicator may give directions requiring a party to provide one or more of the following–

(a) a statement of the facts in dispute or issues to be decided;
(b) a statement of the facts on which that party intends to rely and the allegations he intends to make;
(c) a summary of the arguments on which that party intends to rely; and
(d) such further information, responses to statements of case or supplementary statements as may reasonably be required for the determination of the whole or part of the matter or any question in dispute in the proceedings.

Commencement
Pt 4, r 25(a)–(d): 13 October 2003.

Extent
Pt 4, r 25(a)–(d): England, Wales.

26. Witness statements

The adjudicator may give directions requiring a party to provide a witness statement made by any witness on whose evidence that party intends to rely in the proceedings.

Commencement
Pt 4, r 26: 13 October 2003.

Extent
Pt 4, r 26: England, Wales.

27.– Disclosure and inspection of documents

(1) Any document [...][1] supplied to the adjudicator or to a party under this rule or under rule 28 may only be used for the purpose of the proceedings in which it was disclosed.

[(2) Within 28 days after service of the respondent's statement of case under rule 13 or the lodging of an objection under rule 18, each party must–

    (a) serve on the adjudicator and each of the other parties a list, which complies with rule 47, of all documents in that party's possession or control which–
        (i)   that party intends to rely upon in the proceedings;
        (ii) adversely affect that party's own case;
        (iii) adversely affect another party's case; or
        (iv) support another party's case; and
    (b) send to the adjudicator copies of all documents in the list served under sub-paragraph (a).

(3) Paragraph (4) applies to documents–

    (a) referred to in a party's–
        (i)   statement of case;
        (ii) rectification application under rule 16(1); or
        (iii) written statement under rule 18(a)(i); or
    (b) appearing on a list served by a party under paragraph (2).

(4) In addition to any other requirement in these rules to disclose or provide copies of documents, in relation to any document referred to in paragraph (3) each party must–

    (a) permit any other party to inspect and take copies on reasonable notice and at a reasonable time and place; and
    (b) provide a copy if requested by another party on payment by such other party of reasonable copying costs.

(5) Paragraphs (2), (3) and (4) are subject to any direction of the adjudicator to the contrary.

(6) The adjudicator may at any time give directions requiring a party to state whether that party has any particular document, or class of documents, in its possession or control and, if so, to comply with the requirements of paragraphs (2), (3) and (4) in relation to such documents as if one of the categories at paragraph (2)(a) applied to them.][2]

Notes
1   Words repealed by Adjudicator to Her Majesty's Land Registry (Practice and Procedure) (Amendment) Rules 2008, SI 2008/1731, r 17(a) (25 July 2008).
2   Rule 27(2)–(6) substituted for r 27(2) by Adjudicator to Her Majesty's Land Registry (Practice and Procedure) (Amendment) Rules 2008, SI 2008/1731, r 17(b) (25 July 2008).

Commencement
Pt 4, r 27(1)–(2)(b): 13 October 2003.

Extent
Pt 4, r 27(1)–(6): England, Wales.

28.– Requirement notices

(1) The adjudicator may, at any time, require the attendance of any person to give evidence or to produce any document […][1] specified by the adjudicator which is in that person's possession or control.

(2) The adjudicator must make any such requirement in a requirement notice.

(3) The requirement notice must be in the form specified by the adjudicator provided that the requirement notice–

   (a) is in writing;
   (b) identifies the person who must comply with the requirement;
   (c) identifies the matter to which the requirement relates;
   (d) states the nature of the requirement being imposed by the adjudicator;
   (e) specifies the time and place at which the adjudicator requires the person to attend and, if appropriate, produce any document […][1]; and
   (f) includes a statement of the possible consequences of failure to comply with the requirement notice.

(4) The party on whose behalf it is issued must serve the requirement notice.

(5) Subject to paragraph (6) a requirement notice will be binding only if, not less than 7 working days before the time that the person is required to attend–

   (a) the requirement notice is served on that person; and
   (b) except in the case where that person is a party to the proceedings, the necessary expenses of his attendance are offered and (unless he has refused the offer of payment of his expenses) paid to him.

(6) At any time before the time that the person is required to attend, that person and the party on whose behalf the requirement notice is issued may substitute a shorter period for the period of 7 working days specified in paragraph (5) by–

   (a) agreeing in writing such shorter period; and
   (b) before the time that the person is required to attend, serving a copy of that agreement on the adjudicator.

(7) Where a requirement has been imposed on a person under paragraph (1), that person may apply to the adjudicator for the requirement to be varied or set aside.

(8) Any application made under paragraph (7) must be made to the adjudicator before the time when the person is to comply with the requirement to which the application under paragraph (7) relates.

Notes
1   Words repealed by Adjudicator to Her Majesty's Land Registry (Practice and Procedure) (Amendment) Rules 2008, SI 2008/1731, r 18 (25 July 2008).

Commencement
Pt 4, r 28(1)–(8): 13 October 2003.

Extent
Pt 4, r 28(1)–(8): England, Wales.

29. Estimate of length of hearing

The adjudicator may require the parties to provide an estimate of the length of the hearing.

Commencement
Pt 4, r 29: 13 October 2003.

Extent
Pt 4, r 29: England, Wales.

30.– Site inspections

(1) In this rule–

> "the appropriate party" is the party who is in occupation or has ownership or control of the property;
>
> "the property" is the land or premises that the adjudicator wishes to inspect for the purposes of determining the whole or part of the matter; and
>
> "a request for entry" is a written request from the adjudicator to the appropriate party, requesting permission for the adjudicator to enter onto and inspect the property and such a request may include a request to be accompanied by one or more of–
>
> (a)   another party;
>
> (b)   such number of the adjudicator's officers or staff as he considers necessary; and
>
> (c)   if a member of the [Administrative Justice and Tribunals Council][1] informs the adjudicator that he wishes to attend the inspection, that member.

(2) The adjudicator, at any time for the purpose of determining the whole or part of the matter, may serve a request for entry on an appropriate party.

(3) The request for entry must specify a time for the entry that, unless otherwise agreed in writing by the appropriate party, must be not earlier than 7 days after the date of service of the request for entry.

(4) The adjudicator must serve a copy of the request for entry on any party (other than the appropriate party) and any member of the [Administrative Justice and Tribunals Council][1] named in the request for entry and, if reasonably practicable to do so in the circumstances, must notify them of any change in the time specified.

(5) If the adjudicator makes a request for entry and the appropriate party withholds or refuses his consent to the whole or part of the request without reasonable excuse, the adjudicator may take such refusal into account when making his substantive decision.

(6) If a request for entry includes a request for a member of the [Administrative Justice and Tribunals Council][1] to accompany the adjudicator and the appropriate party consents to the presence of that member, then that member shall be entitled to attend the site inspection but must not take an active part in the inspection.

Notes
1   Words substituted by Adjudicator to Her Majesty's Land Registry (Practice and Procedure) (Amendment) Rules 2008, SI 2008/1731, r 19 (25 July 2008).

Commencement
Pt 4, r 30(1)–(6): 13 October 2003.

Extent
Pt 4, r 30(1)–(6): England, Wales.

31.– Preliminary issues

(1) At any time and on the application of a party or of his own motion, the adjudicator may dispose of any matter or matters that are in dispute as a preliminary issue.

(2) If in the opinion of the adjudicator the decision on the preliminary issue will dispose of the whole of the matter then the decision on the preliminary issue must be–

    (a)   made in accordance with the provisions in these Rules on substantive decisions; and

    (b)   treated as a substantive decision.

Commencement
Pt 4, r 31(1)–(2)(b): 13 October 2003.

Extent
Pt 4, r 31(1)–(2)(b): England, Wales.

PART 5
HEARINGS AND SUBSTANTIVE DECISIONS

32. Scope of this Part

This Part sets out the procedure for determination of references and rectification applications, the format of substantive decisions and substantive orders and rules on costs.

Commencement
Pt 5, r 32: 13 October 2003.

Extent
Pt 5, r 32: England, Wales.

[32A.– Summary disposal

(1) The adjudicator may summarily dispose of the proceedings or any particular issue in the proceedings on an application by a party or of its own motion if–

    (a)   the adjudicator considers that the applicant or respondent has no real prospect of succeeding in the proceedings or on the issue; and

    (b)   there is no other compelling reason why the proceedings or issue should not be disposed of summarily.

(2) Except with the permission of the adjudicator, an applicant may not apply for summary disposal until the respondent has served a statement of case or lodged an objection (as appropriate), or the respondent's time to do so has expired.

(3) A respondent may apply for summary disposal at any time after the applicant has served a statement of case or rectification application (as appropriate), or (in the case of service of a statement of case) the applicant's time to do so has expired.

(4) Paragraph (5) applies where–

    (a)   a respondent applies for summary disposal before serving a statement of case or lodging an objection (as appropriate) and before the time to do so has expired; and

    (b)   that application does not result in the disposal of the entire proceedings.

(5) In the circumstances described in paragraph (4) the respondent's time for serving a statement of case or lodging an objection is extended to–

(a) 28 days after service on the respondent of the adjudicator's decision in relation to the application for summary disposal; or

(b) such other time as the adjudicator directs.

(6) An application for summary disposal must include a witness statement in support of the application. That witness statement must state that the party making the application–

(a) believes that the other party has no real prospect of succeeding on the proceedings or on the issue to which the application relates; and

(b) knows of no other reason why the disposal of the proceedings or issue should not be disposed of summarily.

(7) When serving a notice under rule 51(5) or (7), or directing the party making the application to serve a notice under rule 51(5), and such notice relates in whole or in part to summary disposal, the adjudicator must give directions for the service of evidence by the parties and for the determination of the issue of summary disposal.

(8) When the adjudicator determines the issue of summary disposal the adjudicator may make an order–

(a) disposing of the proceedings or of any issue; or

(b) dismissing the application for or intention to consider summary disposal.

(9) Where an order made under paragraph (8) does not dispose of the entire proceedings, the adjudicator must give case management directions as to the future conduct of the proceedings.][1]

Notes
1   Added by Adjudicator to Her Majesty's Land Registry (Practice and Procedure) (Amendment) Rules 2008, SI 2008/1731, r 20 (25 July 2008).

Extent
Pt 5, r 32A(1)–(9): England, Wales.

33.– Substantive decision without a hearing

(1) There is a presumption that a substantive decision is made following a hearing.

(2) Subject to paragraph (1), the adjudicator may make a substantive decision without a hearing if–

(a) he is satisfied that there is no important public interest consideration that requires a hearing in public; and

(b) unless paragraph (3) applies, he has served written notice on the parties in accordance with these Rules that he intends to make a substantive decision without a hearing or that he has received an application requesting that the substantive decision be made without a hearing and–

    (i) the parties agree to the substantive decision being made without a hearing; or

    (ii) the parties fail to object within the specified period for objection to the substantive decision being made without a hearing.

(3) The adjudicator is not required to serve notice under paragraph (2)(b) if all parties have requested the adjudicator to make the substantive decision without a hearing.

Commencement
Pt 5, r 33(1)–(3): 13 October 2003.

Extent
Pt 5, r 33(1)–(3): England, Wales.

34.– Notice of hearing

(1) Where the adjudicator is to hold a hearing, he must serve written notice of his intention to hear on such parties as he considers necessary.

(2) The adjudicator must specify in the notice under paragraph (1), the date, time and location of the hearing.

(3) The adjudicator must serve the notice under paragraph (1)–

- (a)   no later than 28 days before the hearing; or
- (b)   before the expiry of such shorter notice period as agreed by all the parties on whom he intends to serve notice under paragraph (1).

Commencement
Pt 5, r 34(1)–(3)(b): 13 October 2003.

Extent
Pt 5, r 34(1)–(3)(b): England, Wales.

35.– Representation at the hearing

(1) At the hearing a party may conduct his case himself or, subject to paragraph (2), be represented or assisted by any person, whether or not legally qualified.

(2) If, in any particular case, the adjudicator is satisfied that there is sufficient reason for doing so, he may refuse to permit a particular person to represent or assist a party at the hearing.

Commencement
Pt 5, r 35(1)–(2): 13 October 2003.

Extent
Pt 5, r 35(1)–(2): England, Wales.

36. Publication of hearings

The adjudicator must publish details of all listed hearings at the office of the adjudicator and, if different, the venue at which the hearing is to take place.

Commencement
Pt 5, r 36: 13 October 2003.

Extent
Pt 5, r 36: England, Wales.

37. [...][1]

Notes
1   Revoked by Adjudicator to Her Majesty's Land Registry (Practice and Procedure) (Amendment) Rules 2008, SI 2008/1731, r 21 (25 July 2008).

38.– Absence of parties

(1) If any party does not attend and is not represented at any hearing of which notice has been served on him in accordance with these Rules, the adjudicator–

(a) may proceed with the hearing and reach a substantive decision in that party's absence if–
    (i) the adjudicator is not satisfied that any reasons given for the absence are justified;
    (ii) the absent party consents; or
    (iii) it would be unjust to adjourn the hearing; or
(b) must otherwise adjourn the hearing.

(2) Following a decision by the adjudicator under paragraph (1) to proceed with or adjourn the hearing, the adjudicator may make such consequential directions as he sees fit.

Commencement
Pt 5, r 38(1)–(2): 13 October 2003.

Extent
Pt 5, r 38(1)–(2): England, Wales.

39.– Substantive decision of the adjudicator

(1) Where there is a hearing, the substantive decision of the adjudicator may be given orally at the end of the hearing or reserved.

(2) A substantive decision of the adjudicator, whether made at a hearing or without a hearing, must be recorded in a substantive order.

(3) The adjudicator may not vary or set aside a substantive decision.

Commencement
Pt 5, r 39(1)–(3): 13 October 2003.

Extent
Pt 5, r 39(1)–(3): England, Wales.

40.– Substantive orders and written reasons

(1) A substantive order must–

(a) be dated;
(b) be in writing;
[(c) be sealed and state the name of the person making the order;][1]
(d) state the substantive decision that has been reached;
(e) state any steps that must be taken to give effect to that substantive decision; and
(f) where appropriate,][2] state the possible consequences of a party's failure to comply with the substantive order within any specified time limits.

(2) The substantive order must be served by the adjudicator on–
(a) every party to the proceedings; and
(b) where the substantive order requires the registrar to take action, the registrar.

(3) A substantive order requiring a party to provide or produce a document [...][3] may require the party to provide or produce it to any or all of the adjudicator, the registrar or another party.

(4) Unless the adjudicator directs otherwise, the substantive order must be publicly available.

(5) Where the substantive order is publicly available, the adjudicator may provide copies of it to the public on request.

(6) The adjudicator must give in writing to all parties his reasons for–

> (a)   his substantive decision; and
> (b)   any steps that must be taken to give effect to that substantive decision.

(7) The adjudicator's reasons referred to in paragraph (6) need not be given in the substantive order.

Notes
1   Substituted by Adjudicator to Her Majesty's Land Registry (Practice and Procedure) (Amendment) Rules 2008, SI 2008/1731, r 22(a) (25 July 2008).
2   Words inserted by Adjudicator to Her Majesty's Land Registry (Practice and Procedure) (Amendment) Rules 2008, SI 2008/1731, r 22(b) (25 July 2008).
3   Words repealed by Adjudicator to Her Majesty's Land Registry (Practice and Procedure) (Amendment) Rules 2008, SI 2008/1731, r 22(c) (25 July 2008).

Commencement
Pt 5, r 40(1)–(7): 13 October 2003.

Extent
Pt 5, r 40(1)–(7): England, Wales.

41.– Substantive orders on a reference that include requirements on the registrar

(1) Where the adjudicator has made a substantive decision on a reference, the substantive order giving effect to that substantive decision may include a requirement on the registrar to–

> (a)   give effect to the original application in whole or in part as if the objection to that original application had not been made; or
> (b)   cancel the original application in whole or in part.

(2) A requirement on the registrar under this rule may include–

> (a)   a condition that a specified entry be made on the register of any title affected; or
> (b)   a requirement to reject any future application of a specified kind by a named party to the proceedings–
> > (i)   unconditionally; or
> > (ii) unless that party satisfies specified conditions.

Commencement
Pt 5, r 41(1)–(2)(b)(ii): 13 October 2003.

Extent
Pt 5, r 41(1)–(2)(b)(ii): England, Wales.

[41A. Orders under rule 8(4) or 9(4)

An order made under rule 8(4) or 9(4) must–

> (a)   comply with the requirements of rule 40(1)(a), (b), (c) and (f), (2), (3), (4) and (5) as if it were a substantive order;
> (b)   identify the decision of the court which the order implements; and
> (c)   state the reasons why the order complies with rule 8(4)(a) or 9(4)(a).][1]

Notes
1   Added by Adjudicator to Her Majesty's Land Registry (Practice and Procedure) (Amendment) Rules 2008, SI 2008/1731, r 23 (25 July 2008).

Extent
Pt 5, r 41A(a)–(c): England, Wales.

42.– Costs

(1) In this rule–

    (a)   all the circumstances" are all the circumstances of the proceedings and include–

        [(i)   the conduct of the parties–

            (aa) in respect of proceedings commenced by a reference, during (but not prior to) the proceedings; or

            (bb) in respect of proceedings commenced by a rectification application, before and during the proceedings;][1]

        (ii)   whether a party has succeeded on part of his case, even if he has not been wholly successful; and

        (iii) any representations made to the adjudicator by the parties; and

    (b)   the conduct of the parties [...][2] includes–

        (i)   whether it was reasonable for a party to raise, pursue or contest a particular allegation or issue;

        (ii)   the manner in which a party has pursued or defended his case or a particular allegation or issue; and

        (iii) whether a party who has succeeded in his case in whole or in part exaggerated his case.

(2) The adjudicator may, on the application of a party or of his own motion, make an order as to costs.

(3) In deciding what order as to costs (if any) to make, the adjudicator must have regard to all the circumstances.

[(4) An order as to costs may, without limitation–

    (a)   require a party to pay the whole or a part of the costs of another party and–

        (i)   specify a fixed sum or proportion to be paid; or

        (ii)   specify that costs from or until a certain date are to be paid;

    (b)   if the adjudicator considers it impracticable to make an order in respect of the relevant part of a party's costs under paragraph (a), specify that costs relating to a distinct part of the proceedings are to be paid;

    (c)   specify an amount to be paid on account before costs are agreed or assessed; or

    (d)   specify the time within which costs are to be paid.][3]

[(5) The adjudicator may–

    (a)   summarily assess the whole or a part of a party's costs; or

    (b)   specify that, if the parties are unable to reach agreement on an amount to be paid, the whole or a part of a party's costs be assessed in a specified manner.][4]

(6) [An order as to costs must be recorded in a costs order and][5] must–

    (a)   be in writing;

    (b)   be dated;

(c)   be [sealed and state the name of the person making the order]⁶;
(d)   state the order as to costs; and
(e)   be served by the adjudicator on the parties.

(7) Where the costs are to be assessed by the adjudicator, he may assess the costs–

(a)   on the standard basis; or
(b)   on the indemnity basis, but in either case the adjudicator will not allow costs that have been unreasonably incurred or are unreasonable in amount.

(8) The adjudicator must inform the parties of the basis on which he will be assessing the costs.

(9) Where the amount of the costs are to be assessed on the standard basis, the adjudicator must–

(a)   only allow costs which are proportionate to the matters in issue; and
(b)   resolve any doubt that he may have as to whether costs were reasonably incurred or reasonable and proportionate in favour of the paying party.

(10) In deciding whether costs assessed on the standard basis were either proportionately and reasonably incurred or proportionate and reasonable in amount, the adjudicator must have regard to all the circumstances.

[(11) Where costs are to be assessed on the indemnity basis, the adjudicator must resolve in favour of the receiving party any doubt as to the reasonableness of the incurring or the amount of the costs.]⁷

(12) In deciding whether costs assessed on the indemnity basis were either reasonably incurred or reasonable in amount, the adjudicator must have regard to all the circumstances.

(13) Once the adjudicator has assessed the costs, he must serve on the parties written notice–

(a)   of the amount which must be paid;
(b)   by whom and to whom the amount must be paid; and
(c)   if appropriate, the time by when the amount must be paid.

Notes
1   Substituted by Adjudicator to Her Majesty's Land Registry (Practice and Procedure) (Amendment) Rules 2008, SI 2008/1731, r 24(a) (25 July 2008).
2   Words repealed by Adjudicator to Her Majesty's Land Registry (Practice and Procedure) (Amendment) Rules 2008, SI 2008/1731, r 24(b) (25 July 2008).
3   Substituted by Adjudicator to Her Majesty's Land Registry (Practice and Procedure) (Amendment) Rules 2008, SI 2008/1731, r 24(c) (25 July 2008).
4   Substituted by Adjudicator to Her Majesty's Land Registry (Practice and Procedure) (Amendment) Rules 2008, SI 2008/1731, r 24(d) (25 July 2008).
5   Words substituted by Adjudicator to Her Majesty's Land Registry (Practice and Procedure) (Amendment) Rules 2008, SI 2008/1731, r 24(e)(i) (25 July 2008).
6   Words substituted by Adjudicator to Her Majesty's Land Registry (Practice and Procedure) (Amendment) Rules 2008, SI 2008/1731, r 24(e)(ii) (25 July 2008).
7   Substituted by Adjudicator to Her Majesty's Land Registry (Practice and Procedure) (Amendment) Rules 2008, SI 2008/1731, r 24(f) (25 July 2008).

Commencement
Pt 5, r 42(1)–(13)(c): 13 October 2003.

Extent
Pt 5, r 42(1)–(13)(c): England, Wales.

43.– Costs thrown away

(1) In this rule–

> "costs thrown away" means costs of the proceedings resulting from any neglect or delay of the legal representative during (but not prior to) the proceedings and which–
> (a)   have been incurred by a party; or
> (b)   have been–
>> (i)   paid by a party to another party; or
>> (ii)   awarded to a party,
>
> under an order made under rule 42;
> "an order as to costs thrown away" means an order requiring the legal representative concerned to meet the whole or part of the costs thrown away; and
> "the legal representative" means the legally qualified representative of a party.

(2) The adjudicator may, on the application of a party or otherwise, make an order as to costs thrown away provided the adjudicator is satisfied that–

(a)   a party has incurred costs of the proceedings unnecessarily as a result of the neglect or delay of the legal representative; and

(b)   it is just in all the circumstances for the legal representative to compensate the party who has incurred or paid the costs thrown away, for the whole or part of those costs.

(3) If the adjudicator has received an application for or proposes to make an order as to costs thrown away, he may give directions to the parties and the legal representative about the procedure to be followed to ensure that the issues are dealt with in a way that is fair and as simple and summary as the circumstances permit.

(4) An order as to costs thrown away may–

(a)   specify the amount of costs to be paid by the legal representative; and

(b)   if the adjudicator considers it appropriate, specify the time within which the costs are to be paid.

(5) An order as to costs thrown away must be recorded in a costs thrown away order.

(6) A costs thrown away order must–

(a)   be in writing;
(b)   be dated;
(c)   be [sealed and state the name of the person making the order][1];
(d)   state the order as to costs thrown away; and
(e)   be served by the adjudicator on the parties and the legal representative.

Notes
1   Words substituted by Adjudicator to Her Majesty's Land Registry (Practice and Procedure) (Amendment) Rules 2008, SI 2008/1731, r 25 (25 July 2008).

Commencement
Pt 5, r 43(1)–(6)(e): 13 October 2003.

Extent
Pt 5, r 43(1)–(6)(e): England, Wales.

PART 6
APPEALS FROM ADJUDICATOR

44. Scope of this Part

This Part contains provisions in relation to appeals to the High Court of decisions by the adjudicator and includes provisions about the adjudicator staying implementation of his decision pending the outcome of an appeal.

Commencement
Pt 6, r 44: 13 October 2003.

Extent
Pt 6 r 44: England, Wales.

45.– Appeals to the High Court

(1) Where a party is granted permission to appeal, the adjudicator may, of his own motion or on the application of a party, stay the implementation of the whole or part of his decision pending the outcome of the appeal.

(2) A party who wishes to apply to the adjudicator to stay the implementation of the whole or part of a decision pending the outcome of the appeal must make such an application to the adjudicator at the same time that he applies to the adjudicator for permission to appeal.

(3) Where a party applies under paragraph (2) to the adjudicator to stay implementation of the whole or part of a decision, that party must at the same time provide reasons for the application.

(4) Before reaching a decision as to whether to grant permission to appeal a decision or to stay implementation of a decision, the adjudicator must allow the parties the opportunity to make representations or objections.

(5) The adjudicator must serve written notice on the parties of any decision that he makes as to whether to grant permission to appeal or to stay the implementation of the whole or part of his decision pending the outcome of the appeal.

(6) Where the adjudicator's decision to grant permission to appeal or to stay implementation of a decision relates to a decision contained in a substantive order, the adjudicator must serve on the registrar a copy of the notice under paragraph (5).

(7) The notice under paragraph (5) must–

  (a) be in writing;
  (b) be dated;
  (c) specify the decision made by the adjudicator;
  (d) include the adjudicator's reasons for his decision; and
  (e) be [sealed and state the name of the person making the order][1].

Notes
1   Words substituted by Adjudicator to Her Majesty's Land Registry (Practice and Procedure) (Amendment) Rules 2008, SI 2008/1731, r 26 (25 July 2008).

Commencement
Pt 6, r 45(1)–(7)(e): 13 October 2003.

Extent
Pt 6, r 45(1)–(7)(e): England, Wales.

PART 7
GENERAL

46.– Record of matters

(1) The adjudicator must keep at his principal office a record of matters that records the particulars of all–

(a) references;
(b) rectification applications;
(c) substantive decisions; and
(d) all applications and decisions made under rule 45.

(2) Subject to paragraph (3), the record of matters must be open to the inspection of any person without charge at all reasonable hours on working days.

(3) Where the adjudicator is satisfied that it is just and reasonable to do so, the adjudicator may exclude from inspection any information contained in the record of matters.

(4) Depending on all the circumstances, it may be just and reasonable for the adjudicator to exclude from inspection any information contained in the record of matters if it is in the interest of morals, public order, national security, juveniles or the protection of the private lives of the parties to the proceedings, or where the adjudicator considers that publicity would prejudice the interests of justice.

Commencement
Pt 7, r 46(1)–(4): 13 October 2003.

Extent
Pt 7, r 46(1)–(4): England, Wales.

47.– List of documents and documents

(1) For the purposes of these Rules, a list of documents must be in writing and [, subject to paragraph (1A),]¹ must contain the following information where available in relation to each document–

(a) a brief description of the nature of the document;
(b) [...]²
(c) whether the document is an original, a copy certified to be a true copy of the original, an office copy or another type of copy;
(d) the date of the document;
(e) the document parties or the original author and recipient of the document; and
(f) the version number or similar identification number or code of the document.

[(1A) If a large number of documents fall into a particular class, that class of documents may be listed in accordance with paragraph (1) as if it were an individual document.

(1B) If a class of documents is listed in accordance with paragraph (1A), the description of the class of documents must be sufficiently clear and precise to enable any party receiving the list to identify–

187

    (a) the nature of the contents of each document included within that class of documents; and

    (b) whether any particular document which exists is included within that class of documents.][3]

(2) Unless the adjudicator otherwise permits, where a document provided for the purposes of the proceedings is or contains a coloured map, plan or drawing, any copy provided of that map, plan or drawing must be in the same colours as the map, plan or drawing of which it is a copy (so for example, where a plan shows the boundary of a property in red, a copy of the plan must also show the boundary in red).

Notes
1   Words inserted by Adjudicator to Her Majesty's Land Registry (Practice and Procedure) (Amendment) Rules 2008, SI 2008/1731, r 27(a)(i) (25 July 2008).
2   Revoked by Adjudicator to Her Majesty's Land Registry (Practice and Procedure) (Amendment) Rules 2008, SI 2008/1731, r 27(a)(ii) (25 July 2008).
3   Added by Adjudicator to Her Majesty's Land Registry (Practice and Procedure) (Amendment) Rules 2008, SI 2008/1731, r 27(b) (25 July 2008).

Commencement
Pt 7, r 47(1)–(2): 13 October 2003.

Extent
Pt 7, r 47(1)–(2): England, Wales.

48.– Evidence

(1) The adjudicator may require any witness to give evidence on oath or affirmation and for that purpose there may be administered an oath or affirmation in due form.

(2) No person may be compelled to give any evidence or produce any document […][1] that that person could not be compelled to give or produce on a trial of an action in a court of law in England and Wales.

Notes
1   Words repealed by Adjudicator to Her Majesty's Land Registry (Practice and Procedure) (Amendment) Rules 2008, SI 2008/1731, r 28 (25 July 2008).

Commencement
Pt 7, r 48(1)–(2): 13 October 2003.

Extent
Pt 7, r 48(1)–(2): England, Wales.

49. Expert evidence

No party may call an expert, or submit an expert's report as evidence, without the adjudicator's permission.

Commencement
Pt 7, r 49: 13 October 2003.

Extent
Pt 7, r 49: England, Wales.

50.– Service of documents

(1) A party's address for service must be a postal address in England and Wales.

(2) The address for service in paragraph (1) must be either that of the party or of the party's representative who has been appointed as his representative for the purposes of the proceedings.

(3) A party's address for service remains that party's address for service for the purposes of these Rules unless and until he serves on the adjudicator and the other parties notice of a different address for service.

(4) Any document to be served on or delivered to any person (other than the adjudicator) under these Rules may only be served–

    (a) by first class post to his postal address given as his address for service;
    (b) by leaving it at his address for service;
    (c) [...]¹ by document exchange;
    (d) subject to paragraph (6), by fax;
    (e) subject to paragraph (7), by email; or
    (f) where no address for service has been given, by post to or leaving it at his registered office, principal place of business, head or main office or last known address, as appropriate.

(5) [...]²

(6) A document may be served by fax on any person other than the adjudicator, to a fax number at the address for service for that person if, in advance, the recipient has informed the adjudicator and all parties in writing–

    (a) that the recipient is willing to accept service by fax; and
    (b) of the fax number to which the documents should be sent.

(7) A document may be served by email on any person other than the adjudicator, if, in advance, the recipient has informed the adjudicator and all parties in writing–

    (a) that the recipient is willing to accept service by email;
    (b) of the email address to which documents should be sent, which shall be deemed to be at the recipient's address for service; and
    (c) if the recipient wishes to so specify, the format in which documents must be sent.

(8) Any document addressed to the adjudicator must be sent–

    (a) by first class post to an address specified by the adjudicator; or
    (b) by such other method as the adjudicator may specify, including document exchange, fax or email.

(9) Where under paragraph (8)(b) the adjudicator specifies another method of service, the adjudicator may–

    (a) specify that that method may be used generally or only in relation to a certain document or documents;
    (b) specify that the specified method is no longer available or substitute that specified method with another specified method; and
    (c) make such directions in relation to the use of the specified method as he deems appropriate.

(10) Any document served on an unincorporated body may be sent to its secretary, manager or similar officer duly authorised to accept such service.

(11) Any document which is served in accordance with this rule shall be regarded as having been served on the day shown in the table below–

(12) The adjudicator may direct that service under these Rules of any document may be dispensed with and in those circumstances may make such consequential directions as he deems appropriate.

Method of service	Day of Service
First class post to a postal address within England and Wales	The second working day after it was posted.
Leaving it at a postal address within England and Wales	The working day after it was left.
Document exchange within England and Wales	The second working day after it was left at the document exchange.
Fax	The working day after it was transmitted.
Email	The working day after it was transmitted

Notes
1   Words repealed by Adjudicator to Her Majesty's Land Registry (Practice and Procedure) (Amendment) Rules 2008, SI 2008/1731, r 29(a) (25 July 2008).
2   Revoked by Adjudicator to Her Majesty's Land Registry (Practice and Procedure) (Amendment) Rules 2008, SI 2008/1731, r 29(b) (25 July 2008).

Commencement
Pt 7, r 50(1)–(12): 13 October 2003.

Extent
Pt 7, r 50(1)–(12): England, Wales.

51.– Applications, actions by the adjudicator of his own motion, notification, representations and objections

(1) This rule does not apply to Part 3 and rule 45.

(2) An application to the adjudicator must–

  (a)   be in writing;
  (b)   state the name of the person applying or on whose behalf the application is made;
  (c)   be addressed to the adjudicator;
  (d)   state the nature of the application;
  (e)   state the reason or reasons for the application; and
  (f)   if any of the parties or persons who would be affected by the application consent to it, either–
    (i)   be signed by all the parties or persons who consent or their duly authorised representatives; or
    (ii)   have attached to it a copy of their written consent.

(3) The adjudicator may dispense with any or all of the requirements under paragraph (2)–

  (a)   in relation to an application made to the adjudicator at a time when all persons who would be affected by the application are present before the adjudicator; or
  (b)   if the adjudicator otherwise considers it appropriate or practicable to do so.

(4) For the purposes of paragraph (2)(f), the written consent referred to in that paragraph may be in the form of a letter, fax or email.

(5) If an application is not consented to by all persons who will be affected by the application then, subject to paragraph (10), the adjudicator must [either serve, or direct the party making the application to][1] serve written notice on

persons who have not consented to the application but who would be affected by it [, and any such direction to the party making the application must include the information to be included in the notice under paragraph (6)(d)]².

(6) [The]³ notice under paragraph (5) [...]⁴ must state–

(a)   that the application has been made;
(b)   details of the application;
(c)   that the person has a right to make written objections to or representations about the application; and
(d)   the period within which such objections or representations must be lodged with the adjudicator.

(7) If the adjudicator intends to act of his own motion under these Rules then, subject to paragraph (10), he must serve written notice of his intention on all persons who will be affected by the action.

(8) In the notice under paragraph (7) the adjudicator must state–

(a)   that the adjudicator intends to take action of his own motion;
(b)   the action the adjudicator intends to take;
(c)   that a person has a right to make written objections or representations to the action that the adjudicator intends to take; and
(d)   the period within which such objections or representations must be lodged with the adjudicator.

(9) A person lodges an objection or representation if within the specified period he serves–

(a)   on the adjudicator a written statement setting out the grounds for his objection or representation; and
(b)   on all the other persons who will be affected by the action a copy of the written statement served on the adjudicator under sub-paragraph (a).

(10) The adjudicator shall not be required to [serve, or direct the applicant to]⁵ serve notice under paragraphs (5) and (7) if, in the circumstances, he does not consider it appropriate or practicable to do so.

[(11) Paragraph (10) does not apply to notices–

(a)   under paragraphs (5) or (7) which relate to a proposal that the adjudicator exercise the power under rule 32A(1); or
(b)   required to be served by rule 33.]⁶

Notes
1   Words inserted by Adjudicator to Her Majesty's Land Registry (Practice and Procedure) (Amendment) Rules 2008, SI 2008/1731, r 30(a)(i) (25 July 2008).
2   Words inserted by Adjudicator to Her Majesty's Land Registry (Practice and Procedure) (Amendment) Rules 2008, SI 2008/1731, r 30(a)(ii) (25 July 2008).
3   Words substituted by Adjudicator to Her Majesty's Land Registry (Practice and Procedure) (Amendment) Rules 2008, SI 2008/1731, r 30(b)(i) (25 July 2008).
4   Words repealed by Adjudicator to Her Majesty's Land Registry (Practice and Procedure) (Amendment) Rules 2008, SI 2008/1731, r 30(b)(ii) (25 July 2008).
5   Words inserted by Adjudicator to Her Majesty's Land Registry (Practice and Procedure) (Amendment) Rules 2008, SI 2008/1731, r 30(c) (25 July 2008).
6   Substituted by Adjudicator to Her Majesty's Land Registry (Practice and Procedure) (Amendment) Rules 2008, SI 2008/1731, r 30(d) (25 July 2008).

Commencement
Pt 7, r 51(1)–(11): 13 October 2003.

Extent
Pt 7, r 51(1)–(11)(b): England, Wales.

52.– Consideration by the adjudicator of applications (including applications for directions), representations and objections

(1) In relation to any application, representation or objection made to the adjudicator, unless–

(a) the adjudicator is satisfied that it is frivolous or vexatious; or

(b) it is received by the adjudicator after the expiry of any time limit specified for making that application, representation or objection,

the adjudicator must consider all applications, representations or objections made to him.

(2) If an application, representation or objection is received by the adjudicator after the expiry of any time limit specified for making it, the adjudicator may consider the application, representation or objection, but he is not bound to do so.

(3) In considering any application, representation or objection, the adjudicator must make all enquiries he thinks necessary and must, if required by these Rules or if he considers it necessary, give the person making the application, representation or objection and the parties or other persons who will be affected by it the opportunity to appear before him or to submit written representations.

(4) The adjudicator may decide to accept or reject an application, representation or objection in whole or in part.

(5) Following his consideration of any applications, representations or objections that are made to him, the adjudicator must notify the person who made the application, representation or objection and the parties and any other persons who will be affected by it, of his decision in accordance with these Rules.

Commencement
Pt 7, r 52(1)–(5): 13 October 2003.

Extent
Pt 7, r 52(1)–(5): England, Wales.

53. Adjournment

In addition to the powers and obligations to adjourn proceedings contained in Part 2 and rule 38, the adjudicator may adjourn the whole or part of the proceedings when and to the extent that he feels it reasonable to do so.

Commencement
Pt 7, r 53: 13 October 2003.

Extent
Pt 7, r 53: England, Wales.

54. Power to vary or set aside directions

Subject to these Rules, the adjudicator may at any time, on the application of a party or otherwise, vary or set aside directions made under these Rules.

Commencement
Pt 7, r 54: 13 October 2003.

Extent
Pt 7, r 54: England, Wales.

55.– Failure to comply with a direction

(1) Where a party has failed to comply with a direction given by the adjudicator (including a direction to commence court proceedings under section 110(1)) the adjudicator may impose a sanction on the defaulting party–

(a) on the application of any other party; or
(b) of his own motion.

(2) Where the defaulting party was the person who made (or has been substituted for or added to the party who made) the original application, the sanction may include requiring the registrar to cancel the original application in whole or in part.

(3) Where the defaulting party was a person who objected to (or has been substituted for or added to the party who objected to) the original application, the sanction may include requiring the registrar to give effect to the original application in whole or in part as if the objection had not been made.

(4) A sanction that includes either of the requirements on the registrar under paragraph (2) or (3) shall be treated as the substantive decision on that matter.

(5) If the sanction does not include either of the requirements on the registrar under paragraph (2) or (3), the adjudicator must serve written notice on the parties of his decision as to what if any sanctions are imposed, and he may make consequential directions.

Commencement
Pt 7, r 55(1)–(5): 13 October 2003.

Extent
Pt 7, r 55(1)–(5): England, Wales.

56. Errors of procedure

Where, before the adjudicator has made his final substantive order in relation to a matter, there has been an error of procedure such as a failure to comply with a rule–

(a) the error does not invalidate any step taken in the proceedings, unless the adjudicator so orders; and
(b) the adjudicator may make an order or take any other step that he considers appropriate to remedy the error.

Commencement
Pt 7, r 56(a)–(b): 13 October 2003.

Extent
Pt 7, r 56(a)–(b): England, Wales.

57. Accidental slips or omissions

The adjudicator may at any time amend an order or direction to correct a clerical error or other accidental slip or omission.

Commencement
Pt 7, r 57: 13 October 2003.

Extent
Pt 7, r 57: England, Wales.

58. Time and place

If the adjudicator deems it appropriate to do so, he may alter–

(a) any time limit specified in these Rules;

(b) any time limit set by the adjudicator; or

(c) the date, time or location appointed for a hearing or for any other appearance of the parties before him.

Commencement
Pt 7, r 58(a)–(c): 13 October 2003.

Extent
Pt 7, r 58(a)–(c): England, Wales.

59.– Calculation of time

(1) Where a period of time for doing an act is specified by these Rules or by a direction of the adjudicator, that period is to be calculated–

(a) excluding the day on which the period begins; and

(b) unless otherwise specified, by reference to calendar days.

(2) Where the time specified by these Rules or by a direction of the adjudicator for doing an act ends on a day which is not a working day, that act is done in time if it is done on the next working day.

Commencement
Pt 7, r 59(1)–(2): 13 October 2003.

Extent
Pt 7, r 59(1)–(2): England, Wales.

60.– Representation of parties

(1) If a party who was previously unrepresented appoints a representative or, having been represented, appoints a replacement representative, that party must, as soon as reasonably practicable following the appointment, notify the adjudicator and the other parties in writing–

(a) of the fact that he has appointed a representative or replacement representative;

(b) the name and contact details of the representative or replacement representative;

(c) whether the representative or replacement representative has been authorised by the party to accept service of documents; and

(d) if the representative or replacement representative has been authorised to accept service, the address for service.

(2) If a party who was previously represented ceases to be represented, that party must, as soon as reasonably practicable following the ending of his representation, notify the adjudicator and the other parties in writing–

(a) of the fact that he is no longer represented; and

(b) where the party's address for service had previously been the address of the representative, the party's new address for service.

Commencement
Pt 7, r 60(1)–(2)(b): 13 October 2003.

Extent
Pt 7, r 60(1)–(2)(b): England, Wales.

61. Independence of adjudicator's staff

When undertaking a non-administrative function of the adjudicator on the adjudicator's authorisation, a member of the adjudicator's staff is not subject to the direction of the Lord Chancellor or any other person or body.

Commencement
Pt 7, r 61: 13 October 2003.

Extent
Pt 7, r 61: England, Wales.

Appendix 5

Network Access Appeal Rules 2008
SI 2008/1730

PART 1
INTRODUCTION

1. Citation and commencement

These Rules may be cited as the Network Access Appeal Rules 2008 and come into force on 25th July 2008.

Commencement
Pt 1, rule 1: 25 July 2008.

Extent
Pt 1, r 1: England, Wales.

2.— Interpretation

(1) In these Rules—

"the 2002 Act" means the Land Registration Act 2002;

"appeal" means an appeal to the adjudicator under paragraph 4(1) of Schedule 5 to the 2002 Act or, if appropriate, an appeal from a decision of the adjudicator to the High Court under section 111(1) and (2) of the 2002 Act;

"appeal notice" means a notice filed under rule 20;

"appellant" means a person who makes an appeal to the adjudicator;

"document" means anything in which information is recorded in any form, and an obligation under these Rules to provide or allow access to a document or a copy of a document for any purpose means, unless the adjudicator directs otherwise, an obligation to provide or allow access to such a document or copy in a legible form or in a form which can be readily made into a legible form;

"file" means send to the adjudicator so that the document is received by the adjudicator within any time limit specified by a direction or under these Rules;

"final decision" means the decision of the adjudicator that determines the appeal;

"party" means the appellant or registrar or any other person who is made a party and references to "other party" shall be construed accordingly;

"register" means the register kept by the adjudicator to record the particulars of appeals to the adjudicator and final decisions of the adjudicator under these Rules;

"registrar's decision" means the final decision of the registrar that is the subject matter of the appeal;

"response" means the document filed by the registrar under rule 21;

"serve" means send a document to a party so that the document is received by that party within any time limit specified by a direction or under these Rules;

"statement of truth" means a statement signed by the maker of the statement that the maker of the statement believes that the facts stated in the witness statement are true;

"working day" means any day except for Saturday, Sunday, Christmas Day, Good Friday or a bank holiday under the Banking and Financial Dealings Act 1971.

(2) Except where rule 28(1)(a) applies, anything permitted or required by these Rules to be done by a party may be done by the representative of that party.

Commencement
Pt 1, r 2(1)–(2): 25 July 2008.

Extent
Pt 1, r 2(1)–(2): England, Wales.

PART 2
GENERAL POWERS OF THE ADJUDICATOR

3. Power of adjudicator to regulate proceedings

Subject to the provisions of the 2002 Act and these Rules, the adjudicator may regulate the procedure to be followed when an appeal is made.

Commencement
Pt 2, r 3: 25 July 2008.

Extent
Pt 2, r 3: England, Wales.

4.— Case management conferences

(1) The adjudicator may, for the purpose of managing the proceedings, direct the parties to attend a case management conference.

(2) The adjudicator must give the parties not less than 14 days notice of the time and place of a case management conference under paragraph (1) unless—

    (a)   the parties agree to shorter notice; or
    (b)   the adjudicator considers that it is necessary in the interests of justice to expedite the matter.

Commencement
Pt 2, r 4(1)–(2)(b): 25 July 2008.

Extent
Pt 2, r 4(1)–(2)(b): England, Wales.

5.— Directions

(1) The adjudicator may at any time give directions including (but not limited to) directions provided for in these Rules to—

    (a)   enable the parties to prepare for the hearing of the appeal;
    (b)   assist the adjudicator to determine the issues; and
    (c)   ensure the just, expeditious and economical determination of the appeal.

(2) The adjudicator may give directions—

    (a)   at the request of any party; or
    (b)   on the adjudicator's own initiative.

(3) Where the adjudicator gives a direction on the adjudicator's own initiative under paragraph (2)(b) the adjudicator may (but need not) give prior notice to the parties of his intention to do so.

(4) Any request for directions must—

    (a)   include the reasons for making that request; and

    (b)   be filed, except where it is made during the course of a hearing.

(5) The party making the request for directions must at the same time notify each other party of the request except where the request—

    (a)   is accompanied by the written consent of each other party;

    (b)   is made during a hearing; or

    (c)   concerns an application to withhold the disclosure of documents under rule 18(3).

(6) Where the adjudicator directs that a hearing is to be held to consider a request under this rule, the adjudicator must give the parties not less than 14 days notice of the hearing—

    (a)   unless the parties consent to shorter notice; or

    (b)   the adjudicator considers it is necessary in the interests of justice to expedite the matter.

(7) Directions may be given in writing or orally at a hearing.

(8) Where a direction is given under these Rules, that direction—

    (a)   may include a statement of the possible consequences of a party's failure to comply with the direction; and

    (b)   may specify a time limit for complying with the direction.

(9) The adjudicator may make a direction varying or setting aside a direction given under these Rules—

    (a)   at the adjudicator's own initiative;

    (b)   at the request of a party; or

    (c)   at the request of a witness affected by that direction.

(10) The adjudicator must not give a direction to vary or set aside a direction under paragraph (9) without first giving any party who requested the direction an opportunity to oppose such a direction.

Commencement
Pt 2, r 5(1)–(10): 25 July 2008.

Extent
Pt 2, r 5(1)–(10): England, Wales.

6. Related appeals

The adjudicator may direct that two or more appeals, or any particular issue raised in the appeals, be heard together.

Commencement
Pt 2, r 6: 25 July 2008.

Extent
Pt 2, r 6: England, Wales.

7.— Preliminary questions

(1) The adjudicator may direct that any preliminary question of fact or law, which appears to be in issue in relation to the appeal, be determined at a preliminary hearing.

(2) As soon as is practicable after a determination is made under paragraph (1), the adjudicator must notify the parties of that determination and the reasons for it in writing.

(3) If, in the opinion of the adjudicator, the determination of that preliminary question substantially determines the appeal, the adjudicator may—

    (a)   treat the preliminary hearing as the hearing of the appeal; and
    (b)   make such order by way of disposing of the appeal as the adjudicator thinks fit.

(4) If the parties agree in writing, the adjudicator may determine the preliminary question without a hearing.

(5) Where the adjudicator determines the preliminary question in accordance with paragraph (4), the adjudicator must not at the same time determine the appeal unless the parties have agreed in writing that the adjudicator may do so.

Commencement
Pt 2, r 7(1)–(5): 25 July 2008.

Extent
Pt 2, r 7(1)–(5): England, Wales.

8.— Representation at hearings

(1) Subject to paragraph (2), the parties may appear at a hearing and may be assisted or represented by any person, whether or not that person is a legally qualified representative.

(2) If the adjudicator is satisfied that there are good reasons for doing so, the adjudicator may refuse to permit a person to assist or represent a party at a hearing.

Commencement
Pt 2, r 8(1)–(2): 25 July 2008.

Extent
Pt 2, r 8(1)–(2): England, Wales.

9.— Adjournment of hearing

(1) Where a party requests an adjournment of a hearing that party must—

    (a)   notify all other parties of the request for an adjournment;
    (b)   show good reason why an adjournment is necessary; and
    (c)   where appropriate produce evidence of any fact or matter relied upon in support of the request for an adjournment.

(2) The adjudicator may adjourn a hearing on such terms (if any) as the adjudicator thinks fit.

(3) Where the hearing is adjourned, the adjudicator must fix a new hearing date to take place as soon as is reasonably practicable after the original hearing date.

Commencement
Pt 2, r 9(1)–(3): 25 July 2008.

Extent
Pt 2, r 9(1)–(3): England, Wales.

10.— Powers of adjudicator to strike out

(1) The adjudicator may direct that the whole or part of any appeal notice or response be struck out at any stage of the proceedings on the ground that it—

    (a) discloses no reasonable grounds for bringing or defending an appeal;

    (b) is an abuse of the appeal process; or

    (c) is likely to obstruct the just determination of the proceedings.

(2) Before making an order under paragraph (1), the adjudicator must provide an opportunity for the party against whom it is proposed that the order should be made, to make representations against the making of the order.

Commencement
Pt 2, r 10(1)–(2): 25 July 2008.

Extent
Pt 2, r 10(1)–(2): England, Wales.

11.— Failure to comply

(1) The adjudicator may take such steps as the adjudicator considers appropriate in the circumstances in respect of a party where that party has, without reasonable excuse, failed to comply—

    (a) with a direction given under these Rules; or

    (b) with a provision of these Rules.

(2) The adjudicator must not take any steps under this rule in respect of a party unless the adjudicator has given that party an opportunity to make representations.

Commencement
Pt 2, r 11(1)–(2): 25 July 2008.

Extent
Pt 2, r 11(1)–(2): England, Wales.

12.— Remedying irregularities

(1) An irregularity that arises before the adjudicator has reached a decision resulting from a failure to comply with any provision of these Rules or with a direction of the adjudicator, does not of itself render the proceedings void.

(2) When any such failure comes to the attention of the adjudicator, the adjudicator may give such directions to remedy or waive the irregularity as the adjudicator thinks necessary.

(3) The adjudicator may at any time amend an order or amend a direction to correct a clerical error or other accidental slip or omission.

Commencement
Pt 2, r 12(1)–(3): 25 July 2008.

Extent
Pt 2, r 12(1)–(3): England, Wales.

13.— Proof of documents

(1) Any document purporting to be a document duly executed or issued by or on behalf of the adjudicator must, unless proved to the contrary, be deemed to be a document so executed or issued.

(2) A document purporting to be certified by or on behalf of the adjudicator to be a true copy of any entry of a decision in the register will, unless proved to the contrary, be sufficient evidence of the entry and of the matters referred to in it.

Commencement
Pt 2, r 13(1)–(2): 25 July 2008.

Extent
Pt 2, r 13(1)–(2): England, Wales.

14. Signature of documents

Any requirement in these Rules or in a direction of the adjudicator for a document to be signed by a person is satisfied, in the case of a document which is sent electronically in accordance with these Rules or in accordance with a direction of the adjudicator, by the individual who is required to sign the document typing their name or producing their name using a computer or other electronic means.

Commencement
Pt 2, r 14: 25 July 2008.

Extent
Pt 2, r 14: England, Wales.

15. Calculation of time

Where the time prescribed for doing any act under these Rules expires on a day which is not a working day, the act is done in time if done on the next working day.

Commencement
Pt 2, r 15: 25 July 2008.

Extent
Pt 2, r 15: England, Wales.

16.— Change of representative

(1) A party must as soon as is reasonably practicable notify the adjudicator and each other party in writing of the information in paragraph (2) if a party who was previously—

  (a) unrepresented appoints a representative; or
  (b) represented appoints a replacement representative.

(2) The information referred to in paragraph (1) consists of—

  (a) the fact that the party has appointed a representative or a replacement representative;
  (b) the name and contact details of the representative or replacement representative; and
  (c) whether the representative or replacement representative has been authorised to accept service of documents, and if so, the address at which service may be effected.

(3) A notification under paragraph (1) must be signed by the party making the appointment.

(4) If a party who was previously represented ceases to be represented that party must, as soon as reasonably practicable, notify the adjudicator and each other party in writing of—

    (a)   the fact that they are no longer represented; and

    (b)   any new address for service.

Commencement
Pt 2, r 16(1)–(4)(b): 25 July 2008.

Extent
Pt 2, r 16(1)–(4)(b): England, Wales.

17.— Sending and receipt of notices

(1) Any documents to be served under these Rules must be served—

    (a)   by first class post (or an alternative service which provides for delivery on the next working day) or by personal delivery to the postal address given as the address for service;

    (b)   where no address for service has been provided, by first class post (or an alternative service which provides for delivery on the next working day) or by personal delivery to the party's registered office, principal place of business, head or main office or last known address; or

    (c)   subject to paragraph (2), by an alternative method of service.

(2) Documents may be served by an alternative method of service if the intended recipient has informed the adjudicator and each other party in writing—

    (a)   that the intended recipient is willing to accept service by an alternative method; and

    (b)   of the relevant information to allow documents to be served by that alternative method.

(3) Any document which is to be served on an unincorporated body may be served on the secretary, manager or similar officer of that body.

(4) Any documents to be filed with the adjudicator must be filed—

    (a)   by first class post (or an alternative service which provides for delivery on the next working day) or by personal delivery to an address specified by the adjudicator; or

    (b)   by such alternative method as the adjudicator may specify.

(5) Where the adjudicator specifies that documents may be filed using an alternative method of service under paragraph (4)(b), the adjudicator may make such directions in relation to the use of that alternative method as the adjudicator deems appropriate.

(6) Except where rule 20(4) applies, any document which is served or filed in accordance with these Rules shall, unless the contrary is proved, be regarded as having been received—

    (a)   where it is sent by first class post (or an alternative service which provides for delivery on the next working day), the second working day after it is posted;

    (b)   where it is delivered to the specified address for service, the working day after it is delivered;

    (c)   where it is sent by email or by fax, the working day after it is sent; and

    (d)   where it is sent by document exchange, the second working day after it is left at the document exchange.

(7) Any document that is served or filed under these Rules must specify the date on which it is served or filed.

(8) The adjudicator may direct that service or filing under these Rules of any documents may be dispensed with and, in those circumstances, may make such consequential directions as the adjudicator deems appropriate.

(9) A party's address for service remains the address specified under rules 20 and 21 until a party serves on the adjudicator and each other party notice of a different address for service.

Commencement
Pt 2, r 17(1)–(9): 25 July 2008.

Extent
Pt 2, r 17(1)–(9): England, Wales.

18.— Disclosure of documents by list and inspection of listed documents

(1) In this rule "relevant document" means a document which is or has been in a party's possession or control and—

    (a)   that party relies on in the proceedings;

    (b)   adversely affects that party's own case;

    (c)   adversely affects another party's case; or

    (d)   supports another party's case.

(2) The adjudicator may give a direction that one or more parties must file, and serve on each other party, a list of—

    (a)   all relevant documents; or

    (b)   relevant documents which relate to specified issues.

(3) A party may make a request for a direction under rule 5 (directions) without giving notice to each other party, authorising that party not to include any relevant document on a list required under these Rules.

(4) A party on whom a list has been served may take or inspect a copy of any document on that list at a reasonable time and place, on giving reasonable notice, except where—

    (a)   the document is no longer in the possession or control of the party who served the list; or

    (b)   the party who served the list has a right or duty to withhold inspection of the document.

(5) Unless otherwise permitted by a direction, any document provided to the adjudicator or to a party under these Rules may only be used for the purpose of the proceedings in which it was disclosed.

(6) No person may be compelled to produce any document that they could not be compelled to give or produce on a trial of an action in a court of law.

Commencement
Pt 2, r 18(1)–(6): 25 July 2008.

Extent
Pt 2, r 18(1)–(6): England, Wales.

19.— Form of list of documents

(1) A list of documents must be in writing and, subject to paragraph (2), must contain the following information, where available, in relation to each document listed—

    (a) a brief description of the nature of the document;

    (b) whether the document is in the possession or under the control of the party and if it is not, its current location;

    (c) whether it is a document in respect of which the party claims a right or duty to withhold inspection;

    (d) whether the document is an original, a copy certified to be a true copy of the original, an office copy or another type of copy;

    (e) the date of the document;

    (f) the parties to the document or the original author and recipient of the document; and

    (g) the version number or similar identification number or code of the document.

(2) If a large number of documents fall into a particular class, that class of documents may be listed in accordance with paragraph (1) as if it were an individual document.

(3) If a class of documents is listed in accordance with paragraph (2), the description of the class of documents must be sufficiently clear and precise to enable any party receiving the list to identify—

    (a) the nature of the contents of each document included within that class of documents; and

    (b) whether any particular document which exists is included within that class of documents.

Commencement
Pt 2, r 19(1)–(3)(b): 25 July 2008.

Extent
Pt 2, r 19(1)–(3)(b): England, Wales.

PART 3
STARTING PROCEEDINGS BEFORE THE ADJUDICATOR

20.— Appeal notice

(1) An appeal must be made by way of a written notice ('the appeal notice') signed, dated and filed by the appellant.

(2) An appeal notice under paragraph (1) must be filed no later than 28 days after the date on which the appellant received notification of the registrar's decision.

(3) Without prejudice to the generality of paragraph (10), an appellant may request a direction under rule 5 (directions) to allow the appeal to be made later than the time limit under paragraph (2).

(4) For the purpose of paragraph (2), the registrar's decision is deemed to have been notified to the appellant, unless the contrary is proved—

    (a) if sent by post to an address in the United Kingdom, the second working day after posting;

    (b) if sent by post to an address outside the United Kingdom, the seventh working day after posting;

    (c) if sent by electronic transmission, the second working day after transmission;

    (d) if sent by document exchange, the second working day after it was left at the document exchange; or

    (e) if communicated by telephone, the day of the telephone conversation.

(5) The appeal notice must state—

    (a) the name and address of the appellant;

    (b) the name and address of the appellant's representative (if any);

    (c) the address for service;

    (d) that the appeal notice concerns an appeal against the registrar's decision;

    (e) the grounds upon which the appeal should be granted in the appellant's favour; and

    (f) the remedy sought by the appellant.

(6) In paragraph (5)(a), "address" in respect of a corporation means the address of the registered or principal office.

(7) Where a representative, other than a legally qualified representative, is named in paragraph (5)(b) and the appeal notice is signed by that representative on behalf of the appellant, a statement that the representative is authorised to act on the appellant's behalf must be—

    (a) filed with the appeal notice; and

    (b) signed by the appellant.

(8) Except when there is a good reason why it is not possible, the appellant must, at the same time as filing an appeal notice under paragraph (2), file a copy of—

    (a) the registrar's decision forming the subject matter of the appeal; and

    (b) any statement of reasons for the registrar's decision.

(9) The appeal notice must be accompanied by a list of the documents that the appellant relies on in support of the appeal.

(10) The appellant may make a request for directions under rule 5 (directions) when filing the appeal notice.

(11) At the same time as filing the appeal notice, the appellant must serve a copy of that notice and a copy of any other document filed with the appeal notice including any request for a direction (unless rule 5(5)(c) applies) on each other party.

(12) Except where the appeal notice has been struck out in accordance with rule 10 (strike out), as soon as is reasonably practicable the adjudicator must—

    (a) enter particulars of the appeal in the register;

    (b) inform the parties in writing of the date when the adjudicator received the appeal notice; and

    (c) except where rule 5(5)(c) applies, inform the parties in writing of the adjudicator's determination relating to a request for a direction.

Commencement
Pt 3, r 20(1)–(12)(c): 25 July 2008.

Extent
Pt 3, r 20(1)–(12)(c): England, Wales.

21.— Registrar's response

(1) The registrar must file a response to the appeal notice.

(2) A response under paragraph (1) must be received by the adjudicator no later than 28 days after the date on which the registrar received the documents served by the appellant in accordance with rule 20(11).

(3) Without prejudice to the generality of paragraph (8), the registrar may request a direction under rule 5 (directions) to allow the response to be made later than the time limit under paragraph (2).

(4) The response must include—

    (a) a statement of whether the registrar intends to take an active part in the appeal proceedings;

    (b) if the registrar intends to take an active part in the proceedings, a statement of the grounds on which the registrar disagrees with the appeal notice;

    (c) the name and address of the registrar's representative (if any);

    (d) an address for service; and

    (e) a signature made by or on behalf of the registrar.

(5) The response must be accompanied by a list of any documents that the registrar relies upon in the response.

(6) If they were not attached to the appeal notice, the registrar must attach to the response a copy of the decision forming the subject matter of the appeal and the reasons for that decision.

(7) At the same time as the registrar files the response, the registrar must serve a copy of that response and any other document filed with the response (including a request for a direction unless rule 5(5)(c) applies) on the appellant.

(8) The registrar may make a request for directions in accordance with rule 5 (directions) when filing the response.

(9) Except where rule 5(5)(c) applies, when a request under paragraph (3) or (8) has been determined, the adjudicator must serve a copy of the adjudicator's decision relating to that determination on the parties.

Commencement
Pt 3, r 21(1)–(9): 25 July 2008.

Extent
Pt 3, r 21(1)–(9): England, Wales.

PART 4
HEARING OF APPEALS

22.— Withdrawal of appeal and unopposed appeals

(1) The appellant may withdraw the appeal at any time by filing a notice in writing to that effect and the adjudicator must dismiss the appeal.

(2) The registrar may withdraw the registrar's opposition to the appeal at any time by filing a notice in writing to that effect and the adjudicator must allow the appeal.

Commencement
Pt 4, r 22(1)–(2): 25 July 2008.

Extent
Pt 4, r 22(1)–(2): England, Wales.

23.— Requirement notice

(1) The adjudicator may, at any stage of the proceedings, require the attendance of any person to give evidence or to produce any relevant documents.

(2) A requirement by the adjudicator under paragraph (1) may be made on the adjudicator's own initiative or at the request of a party.

(3) A requirement notice must—

    (a)   be in writing;

    (b)   identify the person who is intended to comply with the requirement;

    (c)   identify the matter to which the requirement notice relates;

    (d)   state the nature of the requirement being imposed by the adjudicator;

    (e)   specify the time and place at which the adjudicator requires the person to attend (if appropriate); and

    (f)   specify whether the adjudicator requires the person to produce any documents and if so, how and when those documents are to be produced.

(4) The party on whose behalf the adjudicator states that it is being issued must serve the requirement notice.

(5) Unless the person on whom the requirement notice is served agrees to shorter notice, a requirement notice must be served not less than 7 working days before that person is required to appear before the adjudicator.

(6) At the time of service of a requirement notice, any person that it is served on who is not a party to the proceedings, must be offered a sum by the party on whose behalf the requirement notice is being served, to cover any expenses necessarily incurred by travelling to and from the place specified in that requirement notice.

(7) Where a requirement notice has been served on a person, that person may apply to the adjudicator for the requirement notice to be varied or set aside.

(8) The adjudicator must not vary or set aside a requirement notice without first giving any person who requested the requirement notice an opportunity to oppose the application under paragraph (7).

Commencement
Pt 4, r 23(1)–(8): 25 July 2008.

Extent
Pt 4, r 23(1)–(8): England, Wales.

24.— Notification of witnesses

(1) If a party intends to call a witness, including an expert witness that the adjudicator has allowed a party to call in accordance with rule 28(1)(b), that

party must, not less than 14 days before the day fixed for the hearing of the appeal (unless the adjudicator directs otherwise) file—

    (a)   a written notice stating the name of the witness; and

    (b)   a statement of the evidence the witness will give, verified by a statement of truth.

(2) At the same time as filing the documents under this rule, each party must serve a copy on each other party.

Commencement
Pt 4, r 24(1)–(2): 25 July 2008.

Extent
Pt 4, r 24(1)–(2): England, Wales.

25. Fixing the time and place of the hearing of the appeal

Unless the parties agree to shorter notice or the adjudicator considers that it is necessary in the interests of justice to expedite the matter, the adjudicator must give the parties not less than 28 days notice of the time and place of the hearing of the appeal.

Commencement
Pt 4, r 25: 25 July 2008.

Extent
Pt 4, r 25: England, Wales.

26. Determination without hearing

The adjudicator may determine an appeal, or any particular issue, without a hearing if—

    (a)   the parties agree in writing; or

    (b)   the issue concerns only a request for directions.

Commencement
Pt 4, r 26(a)–(b): 25 July 2008.

Extent
Pt 4, r 26(a)–(b): England, Wales.

27.— Public hearings and directions for private hearings

(1) In this rule, "hearing" means any hearing under these Rules except for a directions hearing that takes place without notice to any other party to consider a request under rule 18(3).

(2) In accordance with section 109 of the 2002 Act, the adjudicator may direct that all or part of a hearing is to be in private.

(3) Before giving a direction under paragraph (2) that all of a hearing is to be in private, the adjudicator must consider whether it is only necessary that part of the hearing be in private.

(4) The adjudicator may permit any individual to attend a hearing which is to be held in private.

(5) The adjudicator may exclude from the whole or part of any hearing any individual whose conduct, in the opinion of the adjudicator, has disrupted or is likely to disrupt the hearing.

(6) Subject to any direction under paragraph (7), the adjudicator must allow for the public inspection of—

    (a)   a daily list of all hearings; and

    (b)   information about the time and place fixed for the hearings.

(7) Where it is decided that all or part of a hearing is to be held in private, the adjudicator may direct that information about the whole or the relevant part of the proceedings before the adjudicator (including information that might help to identify any person) must not be made public.

Commencement
Pt 4, r 27(1)–(7): 25 July 2008.

Extent
Pt 4, r 27(1)–(7): England, Wales.

28.— Evidence

(1) Subject to rule 24 (notification of witnesses) and to any directions by the adjudicator, a party may—

    (a)   give evidence;

    (b)   with the permission of the adjudicator under rule 5 (directions), bring expert evidence;

    (c)   call witnesses;

    (d)   question any witnesses; and

    (e)   address the adjudicator on the evidence, and generally on the subject matter of the appeal.

(2) No person may be compelled to give any evidence or produce any document that the person could not be compelled to give or produce at the trial of an action in a court of law in England and Wales.

(3) The adjudicator may require any person to give evidence on oath or affirmation.

(4) Evidence may be admitted by the adjudicator whether or not it—

    (a)   would be admissible in a civil trial in England and Wales; or

    (b)   was available to the registrar when the registrar's decision was made.

Commencement
Pt 4, r 28(1)–(4)(b): 25 July 2008.

Extent
Pt 4, r 28(1)–(4)(b): England, Wales.

29.— Failure to attend a hearing

(1) If a party who is due to attend any hearing fails to attend or be represented, the adjudicator may, if satisfied that there is no sufficient reason for the absence—

    (a)   hear and determine the appeal in the party's absence; or

    (b)   (i)   adjourn the hearing; and

        (ii) give such directions as the adjudicator considers necessary.

(2) Where a party can subsequently show sufficient reason for not attending or being represented at a hearing at which the adjudicator proceeded in the party's absence, that party may request the adjudicator's permission to have the hearing re-opened.

Commencement
Pt 4, r 29(1)–(2): 25 July 2008.

Extent
Pt 4, r 29(1)–(2): England, Wales.

30.— Publication of adjudicator's decision

(1) Except to the extent that paragraph (2) applies, the adjudicator—

(a)   must make arrangements to publish the adjudicator's final decision; and
(b)   may make arrangements to publish any other decision made by the adjudicator.

(2) If the adjudicator decides that a restriction on publication is necessary, the adjudicator may take any steps, including any one or more of the steps specified in paragraph (3) with a view to ensuring the minimum restriction on publication that is consistent with the need for the restriction.

(3) The steps referred to in paragraph (2) are—

(a)   anonymising the decision;
(b)   editing the text of the decision; and
(c)   declining to publish the whole or part of the decision.

(4) Before reaching a decision under paragraph (1) on whether to impose restrictions on publication the adjudicator must invite the parties to make representations.

Commencement
Pt 4, r 30(1)–(4): 25 July 2008.

Extent
Pt 4, r 30(1)–(4): England, Wales.

31.— Notification of adjudicator's decision

(1) The adjudicator must as soon as practicable—

(a)   whether there has been a hearing or not, serve on each party a notification of the final decision and the reasons for it;
(b)   subject to any steps taken under these Rules to restrict publication, enter the final decision and the reasons for reaching it in the register; and
(c)   except where the parties are present or represented at a hearing when the decision is given, serve on each party a notification of any other decision made by the adjudicator in the appeal and, where appropriate, the reasons for it.

(2) Every notification under paragraph (1) must be accompanied by a notification of—

(a)   the right of appeal from a decision of the adjudicator to the High Court under section 111 of the 2002 Act; and
(b)   the time within which, and the place at which, an application for permission to appeal may be made.

Commencement
Pt 4, r 31(1)–(2)(b): 25 July 2008.

Extent
Pt 4, r 31(1)–(2)(b): England, Wales.

32.— Costs

(1) The adjudicator may on the application of a party or on the adjudicator's own initiative make an order as to costs.

(2) In deciding what order (if any) as to costs to make the adjudicator must have regard to all of the circumstances including—

    (a)   the conduct of the parties during the proceedings;

    (b)   whether a party has succeeded on the whole or part of their case; and

    (c)   specifically in relation to the registrar, whether the registrar's decision which is the subject matter of the appeal is irrational.

(3) The adjudicator may make a costs order against a legally qualified representative of a party if the adjudicator considers that a party has incurred costs of the proceedings unnecessarily as a result of negligence or delay by the legally qualified representative.

(4) The adjudicator may only make a costs order under paragraph (3) if the adjudicator considers that it is just in all of the circumstances for the legally qualified representative to compensate a party who has incurred the whole or part of those costs.

(5) No costs order may be made under this rule without first giving the paying party (including a legally qualified representative who is ordered to pay costs under this rule) an opportunity to make representations against the making of an order.

(6) Rule 42(4) to (13) of the Adjudicator to Her Majesty's Land Registry (Practice and Procedure) Rules 2003 apply when an order as to costs is made under paragraph (1).

Commencement
Pt 4, r 32(1)–(6): 25 July 2008.

Extent
Pt 4, r 32(1)–(6): England, Wales.

PART 5
APPEALS FROM THE ADJUDICATOR

33.— Permission to appeal to the High Court

(1) A request to the adjudicator for permission to appeal to the High Court may be made by a party—

    (a)   orally at the hearing immediately following the announcement of a decision by the adjudicator; or

    (b)   by way of a request filed not later than 14 days after the date on which the notification of a decision is received by the party making the application whether or not the decision was announced orally at a hearing.

(2) When a request is made under paragraph (1)(b), it must be signed by the party seeking permission and must—

(a) state the name and address of the party seeking permission and of any representative of that party;

(b) identify the decision of the adjudicator to which the request relates; and

(c) state the grounds on which the party seeking permission intends to rely before the High Court.

Commencement
Pt 5, r 33(1)–(2)(c): 25 July 2008.

Extent
Pt 5, r 33(1)–(2)(c): England, Wales.

34.— Decision as to permission to appeal to the High Court

(1) A request to the adjudicator for permission to appeal to the High Court must be decided without a hearing unless—

(a) the decision is made immediately following an oral request under rule 33(1)(a); or

(b) the adjudicator considers that special circumstances make it appropriate to hold a hearing.

(2) The decision of the adjudicator following a request for permission to appeal to the High Court, together with the reasons for the adjudicator's decision, must be recorded in writing and sent to the parties.

(3) If the adjudicator refuses the request, the notification under paragraph (2) must include notification of the time within which a request may be made to the High Court for permission to appeal to that court.

Commencement
Pt 5, r 34(1)–(3): 25 July 2008.

Extent
Pt 5, r 34(1)–(3): England, Wales.

35.— Stay of decision pending appeal

(1) A party who wishes to make a request under paragraph (2) must make such a request, and set out the grounds for making it, at the same time as making an application to the adjudicator for permission to appeal.

(2) Where the adjudicator grants a party permission to appeal to the High Court, the adjudicator may, on the adjudicator's own initiative or at the request of the party granted permission, stay the implementation of the whole or part of the adjudicator's decision pending the outcome of the appeal to the High Court.

(3) Before reaching a decision under paragraph (2), the adjudicator must invite and consider representations from each other party against the staying of a decision under that paragraph.

(4) The adjudicator must serve notification of any decision made under this rule, and the reasons for that decision, on the parties.

Commencement
Pt 5, r 35(1)–(4): 25 July 2008.

Extent
Pt 5, r 35(1)–(4): England, Wales.

36. Appeal remitted by the High Court for rehearing

Where the High Court remits a case to the adjudicator—

    (a)   these Rules, so far as relevant, apply to the case as they did to the original appeal; and

    (b)   the adjudicator must, as soon as is reasonably practicable after the remittal, give directions in relation to the case.

Commencement
Pt 5, r 36(a)–(b): 25 July 2008.

Extent
Pt 5, r 36(a)–(b): England, Wales.

Index

[References are to paragraph numbers]

A

Adjournment
court proceedings 3.18
Adjudicator to Her Majesty's Land Registry (AHMLR)
jurisdiction, *see* Jurisdiction
post of, creation and background to 1.01–1.03
procedure 1.10
reference to, *see* Reference
roles 1.09, 1.12
statutory powers 2.01–2.11
statutory office holder 1.10
Adverse possession 7.01 *et seq*
boundary dispute case 7.01, 7.24, 7.29–7.31
estoppel 7.25–7.27
'factual' 7.05, 7.06–7.08
'intention to possess' 7.05, 7.09–7.10
legal regime
interruption of possession 7.34
limitation period 7.18
new 7.17 *et seq*, 7.34, 7.35
possession proximate to application 7.19
previous 7.02, 7.12–7.14, 7.34, 7.35
transitional provisions 7.15, 7.16
meaning 7.03–7.10
standard for determination 7.11
period of 7.18, 7.35
registration application by squatter 7.17, 7.21
no objections 7.23
not possible, circumstances 7.20
notice of 7.21
objection to 7.24–7.31
re-application 7.32, 7.33
'some other reason' applications 7.28
successive squatters 7.35
Appeal
adjudicator's decision, from 3.104, 3.105
network access agreement jurisdiction 2.08, 2.09
website information 6.05, 6.13

B

Beneficial interest in property, *see* Co-ownership, beneficial interests on

C

Boundary dispute 8.01 *et seq*
adjudicator, decision by 8.02, 8.09
adverse possession case 7.01, 7.24, 7.29–7.31
application to Registrar for determination 8.07–8.09
objections, reference to adjudicator 8.09
court proceedings 8.02
identification of boundary 8.03–8.06
preparation and evidence 8.10, 8.11

Case summary 3.07–3.13, 5.05
contents 3.10–3.13
Land Registry prepares 3.07
specimen 3.09
Charge, legal
rectification power 2.11
Charges Register 9.59
Cohabitants 10.01, *see also* Co-ownership, beneficial interests on
Constructive trust 10.13–10.16
common intention 10.13, 10.15
detrimental reliance, demonstration of 10.16
Co-ownership, beneficial interests on 10.01, 10.03 *et seq*
adjudicator's involvement 10.17, 10.18
factual determination 10.21
assertion of 10.05
evidence to adjudicator 10.19, 10.20
restriction on register, and objection to 10.17
joint tenancy 10.04, 10.05
tenants in common 10.05–10.07
calculation of size of interests 10.06, 10.21
trust of land 10.03, 10.04
constructive 10.13–10.16
express 10.08–10.10
resulting 10.11, 10.12
Costs 3.25, 3.99–3.103
Court proceedings 3.16–3.19, 5.09
adjournment 3.18
boundary dispute 8.02

215